THE HISTORY OF THE
NATIONAL *ENCUENTROS*

D1521449

THE
HISTORY
OF THE
NATIONAL
ENCUENTROS

Hispanic Americans in the One Catholic Church

MARIO J. PAREDES

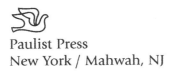

Paulist Press
New York / Mahwah, NJ

Library of Congress Cataloging-in-Publication Data

Paredes, Mario J., author.
    The history of the national encuentros : Hispanic Americans in the one Catholic Church / Mario J. Paredes.
        pages cm
    Includes bibliographical references.
    ISBN 978-0-8091-4905-6 (pbk. : alk. paper) — ISBN 978-1-58768-433-3 (ebook)
    1. Church work with Hispanic Americans—Catholic Church—Congresses—History. I. Title.
    BX1407.H55P37 2014
    282`7308968—dc23
                                                                            2014020342

ISBN 978-0-8091-4905-6 (paperback)
ISBN 978-1-58768-433-3 (e-book)

Published by Paulist Press
997 Macarthur Boulevard
Mahwah, New Jersey 07430

www.paulistpress.com

Printed and bound in the
United States of America

Dedicated to
Reverend Monsignor Robert Stern
Archdiocese New York
Pioneer in the movement to organize and integrate
Hispanic American Catholics in the life of the one
Catholic Church in the United States.

And to all North American priests around the country who have consecrated their lives to Hispanic ministry by learning our language and culture, and for serving our communities oftentimes in very challenging situations.

CONTENTS

Contents

FOREWORD BY CARDINAL SEÁN O'MALLEY, OFM CAP.

Washington, DC, was quite an interesting place in the early 1970s. The ascent of the civil rights movement in the prior decade had created great hope for the possibility of meaningful progress for the minority communities in the United States. In marked contrast, the turbulence following the tragic death of Dr. Martin Luther King, Jr. brought about much fear and anxiety. The United States found itself at the intersection of hopeful enthusiasm that was the engine of community organizing—in which the Catholic Church and other faith-based communities played an important role—and the turmoil of social unrest. It was a time when people of good will who were trying to help others move ahead in life realized that the task ahead of them was very great indeed. Some began to wonder whether the efforts to improve the circumstances of marginalized and oppressed communities would be successful.

In the midst of this environment of the early 1970s, thousands of Hispanic immigrants began to arrive in Washington, fleeing the danger of the wars in Central America, often taking only their family members and the most basic provisions as they fled in haste. Their arrival called to mind the Exodus experience of the Jewish community, oppressed by Pharaoh, and was reminiscent of Mary and Joseph's flight into Egypt, shielding the infant Jesus from the threats of Herod. People in desperate need were coming to the United States with the prayer that they would find safe harbor and the compassionate love of God.

It was in that setting that I first met Mario Paredes. Some forty years later, I count that meeting and the deep friendship that has grown since then among my greatest blessings. As we began a journey of outreach and ministry to the Hispanic Catholic community, it seemed that the possibilities were endless, but very often so too were the challenges. It was a time when more than anything else we relied on our faith in God and were strengthened by the confidence that if we gave our best effort to follow the call of the Lord, we would be able to help our Hispanic brothers and sisters who found themselves wandering in the desert of life as undocumented, unprotected refugees. It was a time of *encuentro*.

The first *Encuentro Nacional Hispano de Pastoral* took place in Washington, DC, in the summer of 1972. With the help of Cardinal O'Boyle and many clergy, religious, and laity, we had recently established the Archdiocese of Washington's *Centro Catolico Hispano*, a multi-service pastoral and social service agency for immigrants. It is a testament to the dedication and commitment of all involved with the founding of the *Centro* that to this day it continues the mission of outreach and support, though now in facilities that are appropriately quite improved from our humble beginnings. All who were associated with the *Centro* were encouraged by the first *Encuentro* and the prospect of the Hispanic Catholic community achieving greater recognition in the life of the Church and being lifted up to leadership positions. The themes of unity, responsibility, and the importance of integrating the social Gospel in the development of a plan for Hispanic ministry were a source of great hope. Just over ten years later, the third *Encuentro Nacional* drew almost ten times the attendees of the inaugural gathering and produced the framework for a National Pastoral Plan for Hispanic Ministry. The presence and importance of the Hispanic Catholic community in the United States had been clearly established.

Much has accomplished been since the early years of the *Encuentro*, as the community began to move forward. Mario Paredes documents those experiences in this book, ensuring that we will remember the hopes of the founders and their confidence that Hispanic Catholics could accomplish much for building up the kingdom of God. Informed by the history of those who initiated the movement, we now look to the future. The statistics concerning the Hispanic Catholic community in the United States are compelling, particularly with regard to youth and young adults. These men and women will be leaders in government, business, and society at large in the coming decades. They will be leaders in the Church, and we must provide them the best possible spiritual pastoral and formation. *Encuentro* is not something only of the past, to be sentimentally recalled and admired. It is an ongoing encounter with the Lord, an experience of faith alive in our midst. There is great potential for growth and vitality in the Church when we all understand the call to discipleship to include the work of evangelization. *The History of the National Encuentros* helpfully brings to light both the achievements and the shortfalls of outreach to the Hispanic Catholic community and reminds us that there is much work yet to be done. May this book be a prompting for the Church in the United States to renew the commitment to our brothers and sisters in the Lord.

Cardinal Seán O'Malley, OFM Cap.
Archbishop of Boston

FOREWORD BY
TIMOTHY MATOVINA

The national Hispanic Pastoral *Encuentros* (1972, 1977, and 1985) were at the center of a wide-ranging Hispanic ministry movement that is one of the most significant developments in U.S. Catholicism during the Vatican II era. Several studies have begun to assess the historical legacy and ongoing significance of the *Encuentros* for the life of the Church, such as the forthcoming Catholic University of America doctoral dissertation of Luis Tampe, SJ, "*Encuentro Nacional Hispano de Pastoral* (1972–1985): An Historical and Ecclesiological Analysis." It is an honor to introduce readers to Mario Paredes's contribution to this growing body of scholarship and pastoral reflection. He presents us the first book-length analysis of the *Encuentros* from the perspective of a leader who has participated in the development of Hispanic ministry from the very first *Encuentro* down to the present.

But the volume you hold in your hands is not merely a memoir about events of several decades past. Mario certainly provides a valuable summary of the committee meetings, procedures, keynote addresses, workshops, conclusions, and follow-up plans for each of the three *Encuentros*. His timeline and attention to detail provide a valuable chronicle, as I can personally attest in gratitude to Mario for providing me with his previously unpublished manuscript to guide my own research. At the same time, however, Mario offers his own critical reflections on the failures and successes of the *Encuentros* from the vantage point of our current ecclesial and social context. He interweaves into his analysis the three documents of the U.S. bishops most closely associated with the *Encuentros*: the bishops' 1983 pastoral letter on Hispanic ministry, *The Hispanic Presence: Challenge and Commitment*; their 1987 National Pastoral Plan for Hispanic Ministry; and their most recent official statement on Hispanic ministry, *Encuentro and Mission: A Renewed Pastoral Framework for Hispanic Ministry*, released in 2002 on the occasion of the fifteenth anniversary of the National Pastoral Plan. Mario examines the *Encuentros* in light of the one Catholic faith, providing a particular focus on the ecclesial integration of Latinos in the Catholic Church in the United States. Like the ongoing debates about the meaning and implementation of Vatican II, an ecclesial event that Mario rightly notes was foundational for the *Encuentros*, not everyone will agree with his assessments about the *Encuentro* conclusions and their subsequent execution. This is, in fact, one of the book's contributions. I welcome Mario's publication as an invitation to deepen and expand our collective Catholic conversation—even debate—about the *Encuentros*. Too often and among too many, the *Encuentros* are forgotten, if, in fact, they were ever even known at all. Mario's passion beckons us to reengage these remarkable ecclesial events and their ongoing implications for our Church.

Mario reminds us that, like Vatican II, first and foremost the *Encuentros* were, indeed, ecclesial events. Of course, the concluding documents of each *Encuentro* are important. But no concluding document can fully capture the sense of solidarity among Hispanic leaders coming together nationally for the first time, the power of such an ambiance to enhance creativity of pastoral and theological vision, and the courage these gatherings gave participants to break silence and form a united front to confront their experiences of injustice. Arguably, the most significant legacy of the *Encuentros* is their part in the formation of several thousand leaders who dedicated their energies and even their life's work to the advancement of Hispanic ministry. Many leaders attest that the *Encuentros* are a primary focal point for the sense of common purpose based on a shared history that has linked various Catholics from Mexican, Puerto Rican, Cuban, and other backgrounds in Hispanic Catholic initiatives and organizations.

The advances in Hispanic ministry have not been all that *Encuentro* participants hoped for and desired, but I think it undeniable that the *Encuentros* and the wider movement to promote

Hispanic ministry have had a major impact on the Catholic Church in the United States. In tandem with the *Encuentros* and in their aftermath, Latino Catholics established national organizations to support and advocate for Hispanics in virtually every category of Church leadership: liturgical ministers, pastoral musicians, youth and young adult ministers, catechists, seminarians, deacons, priests, lay and religious women, Church historians, theologians, pastoral formation institute personnel, and diocesan directors of Hispanic ministry.

With the support of leaders from these groups, a number of the *Encuentro* conclusions won acceptance and gradual though uneven implementation, expanding developments in Hispanic ministry down to the present day. These developments include more diocesan offices for Hispanic ministry, Spanish-speaking personnel in Church agencies, training in Hispanic cultures and the Spanish language for seminarians and priests, an increase in the number of married Hispanic deacons as a means to address the lack of Hispanic priests, religious education programs that engage Hispanics in their faith, Spanish sections of diocesan newspapers, Hispanic bishops, and funding for Hispanic ministry initiatives. More broadly, Hispanic ministry leaders joined with U.S. bishops to enact the *Encuentros'* call for heightened recognition and respect of the Hispanic presence in the Catholic Church, greater apostolic zeal for Hispanic ministry, and the expansion of resources and personnel dedicated to that work.

Most importantly, the *Encuentros* and the bishops' statements on Hispanic ministry comprise the most conspicuous means Hispanics have engaged in conversations and efforts to renew Catholicism in the United States since Vatican II. Drawing on the teachings of Vatican II, the Latin American bishops in their conferences at Medellín and Puebla, and the popes during the *Encuentro* era, Popes Paul VI and John Paul II, Hispanic Catholic leaders proposed core pastoral and theological precepts for the enhancement both of Hispanic ministry and of Catholic ecclesial life. Prominent among these precepts are respect for diverse languages, cultures, and faith traditions as part of the beauty of God's creation; the commitment to evangelization and justice as constitutive of the Church's mission to proclaim Jesus Christ; the urgency to serve and foster leadership among marginal groups such as farm workers, women, young people, and the wider Hispanic population; and the call to transform personal lives as well as cultures, society, and the internal dynamics of the Church itself. Underlying these convictions is a core ecclesiology. The concluding document of the Third *Encuentro* deemed the Church the body of Christ that "incarnates itself and wishes to journey together with the people in all their cultural, political, and religious reality." This perspective echoes the Vatican II statement that "the Church…must implant itself among all these groups in the same way that Christ by his incarnation committed himself to the particular social and cultural circumstances of the women and men among who he lived" (*Ad Gentes*, no. 10). Underscoring the Church as a community charged to embody Christ's presence in the concrete circumstances of human life, the *Encuentro* vision encapsulates the theological foundation that animated Hispanic ministry leaders in their collective efforts to revitalize their faith and Church through pastoral planning and action.

Yet Mario is right on target when he reminds us how much farther we still have to go. Father Virgilio Elizondo succinctly summarized the advancements in Hispanic ministry made in light of the *Encuentros*: "When I look at all that has been accomplished since that First *Encuentro*, it is nothing short of a miracle. But when I look at all that remains to be done, it is scary." Today, numerous Catholics in the United States remain uninformed about the *Encuentros* and their impact. Even many recently arrived priests, religious, and lay leaders from Latin America know little about the *Encuentros* and the rise of Hispanic ministry organizations that accompanied them. For these reasons and more, Mario's book on the inner workings and the continuing significance of the *Encuentros* is an important contribution to the life of the Church. Welcome, reader, to this opportunity to journey with Mario down the pathway of the *Encuentros*. May the Holy Spirit rekindle within us the fire of those blessed events and enable us to more faithfully serve our Lord, our Church, and our Hispanic sisters and brothers.

Timothy Matovina
University of Notre Dame

INTRODUCTION

Helping prepare for and putting on the three National Hispanic Pastoral *Encuentros* was a fascinating task—one considerably more difficult than I imagined at the outset, but full of gratifying intellectual challenges, remarkable spiritual growth, and a rich experience of fellowship. Memories of those heady days produce a deep satisfaction with all that happened. Yet, there is also serious concern about unfinished business—which includes putting the events in the context of the U.S. Church in the early twenty-first century.

But, before setting off on this exciting venture, a basic question needs answering: What exactly are *Encuentros*? Their genesis goes back to the mid-sixties, when, in the wake of Vatican II, CELAM (the Council of Latin American Bishops), began to develop and articulate a process of consultation and participation of *all the faithful*—action taken in direct response to the conciliar calls for reform, including the insistence on a closer, more concrete engagement of the laity in the life of the Church.

The Latin American Church leaders committed to develop a very particular praxis in pastoral work, which took the form of designing major meetings—indeed, *Encuentros*—that would allow the Church as a whole to study, analyze, and reflect upon the major issues facing the Catholic community of the day. The unique and crucial aspect of this process was that the hierarchy granted participation to all the members of the Church, from the grassroots all the way up to the top ranks in the institution.

In order to achieve this comprehensive consultation, the *Encuentros* developed tools that would—beginning with the rigorous and lengthy preparation for the *Encuentros* through their execution and concluding documents—allow for the consultation, participation, and consensus of all levels of the Church with regard to the most important issues facing the Church. This way, the entire Church community would wield a methodology that would "see, judge, and act," with regard to burning issues in the Church. For example, the *Encuentro* process would "see" the situation of the liturgy, "judge" the state of the liturgy, and, subsequently, "act" to make any necessary changes or course corrections; or, to use another example, "see" the Church's dealings with the poor, "judge" those dealings, and "act" accordingly.

The three *Encuentros* chronicled in this book took their cue from the Latin American model. Each of the *Encuentros* featured a consultation process that involved literally hundreds of thousands of Hispanic Catholics in the United States—at all levels of the Church, from the base communities, the parishes, the regions, the dioceses, and so on. This history is unique in the annals of the Church in North America—such a comprehensive consultation strategy has never been executed before. Yet, this mechanism was a direct response to Vatican II's call for various innovative, creative consultative bodies, many of which have sprung into life, such as the Synod of Bishops, Presbyteral Councils, diocesan advisory bodies, and so on—but none quite so comprehensive and consistent as the *Encuentro* process.

The spur to writing this history of the *Encuentros* was the fiftieth anniversary of Vatican II and, precisely, the groundbreaking call of its documents and deliberations for the laity to take on more responsibility in the Church; for the Catholic community as a whole to assertively, fearlessly, and creatively engage modern secular culture; and for evangelization to creatively and dynamically take into account peoples' and nations' cultural characteristics, not in the least vital forms of popular religiosity. The *Encuentros* were a direct response to these promptings of the Council. Their legacy endures, just as the Council's calls to action continue to resound and call for a response on the part of all believers.

The Council first initiated the integration of Hispanic American Catholics in the U.S. Church. The work was begun by a generation of priests directly shaped by Vatican II, most of them Americans driven by great enthusiasm for the task at hand with a firm commitment to reach out to the very poorest. They were the prime motor for the convocation of the First National *Encuentro*.

They were the ones who created Spanish-language pastoral programs to serve Hispanics in the United States, programs that took their cue from the Council in terms of inculturation—of being sensitive and welcoming to Hispanic forms of worship and this still utterly powerless community of believers' potential gifts to the Church at large.

Most of these priests—courageous advocates for the needs and rights of Hispanic Catholics, and on fire with love of the Gospel—were based in the inner city, ministering to the country's poorest neighborhoods in the sixties' and seventies' most distressed areas in urban centers. They began go give voice to the voiceless. The United States was spared the violence that racked Latin America in the sixties, which gave birth to liberation theology. Nonetheless, this country suffered its own social and political upheavals, which prompted these priests and religious toward their own authentic preferential option for the poor.

Hundreds of priests learned Spanish and spent considerable time in Mexico, Puerto Rico, and other Latin countries to immerse themselves in the culture of the new arrivals. Founded in 1966, the U.S. Catholic Conference did its share in sponsoring numerous dialogues between representatives of the U.S. Church and their counterparts in Latin America, where the Bishops' Council of Latin America (CELAM) would play a major role. This is how the journey toward the convocation of the First National *Encuentro* first began.

My objective in these pages—and readers will help me assess to what extent I have succeeded—is fourfold: 1) an attempt at a reconstruction of all that happened in a systematic and ordered way, 2) a historical portrait, 3) a reading of the events from the perspective of faith, and 4) an effort to capture a unique experience in the life of the Church when the faithful truly came *together*.

1. I have made an attempt at reconstructing all that happened and set all the materials in order; I have drawn up a chronological sequence of events, which allows for a convenient and clear overview of each of the three *Encuentros*. At the same

time, the reader is invited to consider them together as a whole, which makes for a powerful panorama of this exceptional and atypical phenomenon in the life of the U.S. Catholic Church.

This reconstruction seeks to present all that is essential in great detail and may serve as a starting point for further research of greater academic caliber and ambition. This process has great limitations, due to the absence of a formal bibliography. Instead, I have relied on a search for materials in the archives of the various participants—also tapping their personal memories—and through correspondence with the Secretariat for Hispanic Affairs. It is my hope that—despite all the limitations of method—the reader will find a consistent and coherent picture, one not without a certain elegance and élan that does justice to the *Encuentros*.

2. I have also sought to create a historical portrait, abiding by a philosophy of history in which the "protagonist" of each of the *Encuentros* is not a person, but rather the Hispanic people with their leaders and organizations. This sketch includes the protagonists' oft-forgotten past and their efforts to reconnect with their roots; it also features their present, which is still burdened by discrimination and scorn; and their future marked with the sign of hope and the faith that every genuine effort for the good carries with it the reward and certainty of ultimate triumph.

Historical remembrance by definition means only an approximation of doing justice to the events in the spotlight. Quite a few years have passed. The first *Encuentro Nacional Hispano de Pastoral* took place in 1972; the second, in 1977; and the third, in 1985. In any case, this book does not want to merely create a portrait of the past. It seeks to be a spur for the urgently needed evaluation of the three *Encuentros* in light of today's circumstances, as we have embarked on the second decade of the twenty-first century and are observing the fiftieth anniversary of Vatican II. Indeed, it bears repeating often, the Council's clarion call for the laity, clergy, and Church leadership to come and work together in brand new ways—each bringing their particular charism and expertise to the table—inspired the convocations of the *Encuentros*.

Rediscovering the *Encuentros* is not an exercise in mere recollection. On the contrary, it is a process that is vital for laying the foundation for a better future for Hispanic Catholics in the United States. The U.S. Catholic Hispanic leadership is called to avail itself of the riches of the three *Encuentros* because their history is essential to the identity of U.S. Hispanic Catholics. The *Encuentros'* call to action holds the key to Hispanics' full integration into the U.S. Catholic Church at a very critical time. Just as the conciliar calls to action endure after five decades and have yet to produce fully mature results, so the seeds sown by the three *Encuentros* have yet to come to full fruition.

Hispanic Catholics in the United States form part of what Pope Benedict XVI has called "the vastness of human experience" and the "vastness of the Word of God." Their voices deserve to be heard; indeed, they must be heard and not forgotten. The *Encuentros* first set the stage for U.S. Hispanic Catholics to come into their own and to begin slowly but surely making their contribution to the U.S. Catholic Church at large. This is a history that must be cherished. The task at hand is huge and it has barely begun.

The numbers tell the story. Hispanics have accounted for 70 percent of the growth of the U.S. Church in recent years. At present, Hispanics represent almost 40 percent of all Catholics; among the faithful under age twenty-five, they are already the majority. But the Church is still struggling mightily to welcome and empower Hispanic Catholics as full members of the Catholic community.

Research amply shows that despite the enormous growth in Hispanic populations in Catholic dioceses across the United States, resources for Hispanic pastoral outreach and leadership training remain scarce. Hispanic Catholics represent less than 4 percent of students enrolled in U.S. Catholic schools. There are few, if any, congregations of Latina women religious to serve the young or the old.

The Hispanic influx into its ranks is a great opportunity for the Catholic Church, but the pace of growth poses a formidable pastoral challenge—especially, if not exclusively, in those eighty-six U.S. dioceses that are considered "mission dioceses" in light of their already underserved Catholic populations and stretched human and material resources. Something has to change! The

U.S. Catholic hierarchy—its efforts spearheaded by the Hispanic leadership—must find ways to respond. The lessons of the *Encuentros* are a vital resource in this regard.

3. Beyond that, I have not limited myself to the horizontal plane when it comes to the significance of the three *Encuentros*. These pages also present a reading from the perspective of faith, an effort to trace the mysterious action of the Holy Spirit in the midst of the vicissitudes of each of the three *Encuentros*. It could not be otherwise. It is amazing—a true *Mirabilia Dei*—to discover that despite the ultimate poverty of all human undertakings, and the fact that the *Encuentros'* deliberations were conditioned by the theological and pastoral trends of the day, there are clear signs of the Lord's presence during it all.

God's wisdom was then, all those years ago, and is still today, guiding the path of Hispanic Catholics and their relationship with the Church that is on its pilgrimage in the United States. That means that today, in following the promptings of the Holy Spirit, we must be able to deepen our understanding of the *Encuentros* and recommit to the historic pathway for which they laid the foundation, a pathway that is profoundly changing the face of the Church in this country.

The Hispanic presence in the United States could have produced a national Church, a parallel model of the established Church. This is, of course, what occurred, according to a venerable tradition, with Catholics who are members of the various oriental rites. Hispanic Catholics in the United States could have lobbied for the creation of a Spanish-speaking, Hispanic-rite Catholic Church, one designed especially to welcome those who were far from their country of origin.

Yet none of this occurred. The Spirit has called Hispanic Catholics in the United States to a far more difficult path: that of the Hispanic faithful's integration, *without assimilation*, in the U.S. Church. Inspired by God—his ways often incomprehensible—the three *Encuentros* set this challenging process in motion. What will the future of the U.S. Church look like? We do not know in detail, but the reading in faith of the three *Encuentros* makes crystal clear that the U.S. Church will have the face of an Anglo-Hispanic hybrid. The Lord's providential actions are often slow, sometimes seemingly convoluted, and yet, they are always on target.

Latino Catholics bring the gift of the multicultural congregation, gradually sowing the seeds of change, offering alternatives to the dominant spirit of individualism and its insidious effect on the life of faith. In time, the spirit of Hispanic Catholicism may help overcome the U.S. Church's internal wrangling over sexual ethics, liturgical reform, the role of the laity, and the exercise of authority in the Church. These issues, crucial as some of them are and will remain, reflect one-sidedly Euro-American preoccupations. Grounded in his or her faith, the Hispanic Catholic brings to his/her adopted land a deep sense of beauty and sanctity, authentic Catholic culture in the form of art and devotion to the saints. Hispanics will continue to change the face of the U.S. Church. The *Encuentros* first sowed the seeds for this urgent process of renewal.

4. Finally, this book aims to capture an exceptional experience of togetherness in the life of the U.S. Church. No other group has traveled the way of the U.S. Hispanic Catholic people, which is characterized by the seal and guarantee of ecclesial propriety and authenticity. The three *Encuentros* were truly the work of the hierarchy of the United States; the *Encuentros* were convoked, presided over, and approved by the National Conference of Catholic Bishops/United States Catholic Conference.

Hence, this book aims to chronicle a unique and remarkable process and document the enormous impact the three *Encuentros* have had—not only on the Hispanic rank-and-file of the Church and on the Hispanic ministry apparatus, so to speak, but also the U.S. Church hierarchy itself. The U.S. bishops' 1983 letter, "The Hispanic Presence: Hope and Commitment"—marking an absolute milestone—is lasting testimony to this amazing achievement.

This is the story of crucial chapters in the ongoing process of the integration of Hispanic Catholics in both the U.S. Church and society. The First *Encuentro*, led valiantly by courageous Hispanic leadership—lay, clergy, religious—created the blueprint to help reshape the way of being a Church in accordance with the dictates of Vatican II—a Church that truly welcomes the poor, the stranger, and the outcast.

This enormous blessing from the Lord makes the three *Encuentros* into an experience that the U.S. Church can proudly and gratefully claim as its own—for in its name, the three extraordinary gatherings came into being. This dimension alone should give these pages a flavor and color that is distinct from those of a sociological treatise, an academic exercise, or a mere historical record.

Mario J. Paredes
New York, December 2014

I

THE HISTORY OF THE FIRST NATIONAL HISPANIC PASTORAL *ENCUENTRO*

Trinity College, Washington, DC (June 19–22, 1972)

1

CHRONICLE OF THE FIRST NATIONAL HISPANIC PASTORAL *ENCUENTRO*

1.1 EMERGENCE OF THE IDEA FOR AN *ENCUENTRO*

In 1971, the idea emerged in three different localities: New York, Miami, and Washington, DC. The chronology traces four consecutive steps.

1. The *first* meeting occurs in September in New York. It is called by Father Robert Stern, director of the Hispanic Apostolate of the Archdiocese of New York, to plan Hispanic pastoral activities. During the deliberations, an official of the Secretariat General of the Latin American Episcopal Conference (CELAM), Father Edgar Beltran, proposes the idea of organizing a national *Encuentro* of Hispanic leaders of the United States; the proposal is accepted and enthusiastically embraced.
2. The *second* meeting takes place in Miami in October: the National Congress of Catholic Educators, during which a group of more than one hundred Hispanic delegates drafts a Declaration due to be presented to the National Conference of Catholic Bishops' plenary session the following November. The Declaration calls for a convocation of a National Congress of Hispanic Catholic leaders; the document also insists on greater Hispanic representation in the parish and

an adequate formation for Church personnel serving in the Hispanic apostolate.

3. The *third* occurs in November in New York at a meeting of the Interdiocesan Coordinating Committee for Hispanics in the New York metropolitan region, which reconsiders and reaffirms the proposal made at the September meeting. Father Stern and Father John O'Brien, director of the Hispanic Apostolate of the Brooklyn Diocese, are given the task of presenting the idea to Pablo Sedillo, national director of the Spanish-speaking Division of the Social Justice Department of the National Conference of Catholic Bishops/United States Catholic Conference (NCCB/USCC).

4. A *fourth* crucial meeting happens in December in Washington, DC, at which Pablo Sedillo endorses the proposal presented to him by Frs. Stern and O'Brien, beginning the process of submitting the plan to the hierarchy, along with the call for a national Hispanic congress made in the Declaration drawn up by the Hispanic educators at the Miami Congress. The plan for the first *Encuentro* is formally presented in January 1972 to the Secretary General of the bishops' conference, Bishop Joseph L. Bernardin, at that time serving as auxiliary bishop of Atlanta. The prelate promptly backs the proposal, and with the assistance of the Spanish-speaking division of the NCCB/USCC, initiates the organization of the first *Encuentro* by mandating a Planning Committee.

1.2 PREPARATION FOR THE *ENCUENTRO*

Preparations take place in the first semester of 1972, with the work largely done at the three meetings of the Planning Committee:

1. The first is held in the Center for Continuing Education at the University of Chicago on February 9 and 10. An initial date and place are selected (spring, in Chicago), which end up not working out. But participants agree on a name: "The

First Hispanic Pastoral *Encuentro*," to which was later added the adjective *National*. Subcommissions are named and critical tasks are assigned.

2. The second planning meeting is held at the Asuncion Seminary of the Archdiocese of San Antonio, Texas, on April 17 and 18. Mrs. Encarnacion P. Armas, president of the Planning Committee, confirms the setting and date of the first *Encuentro*: Trinity College in Washington, DC, June 19–22. In addition, planners review the program and the list of participants; they also draft a Declaration of Purpose, establish guidelines for the presentation of study tasks, and settle on the format for presenting the conclusions from all the *Encuentro*'s deliberations. It is decided that the minutes of the *Encuentro* will be published in both Spanish and English. Without a doubt, this second meeting of the Planning Committee is decisive for the organization and launch of the first *Encuentro*.

3. The third and final meeting of the committee is held in Washington, DC, on June 18, prior to the kickoff of the First *Encuentro*, to take care of final details, assign last-minute tasks, and determine the key players' responsibilities during the proceedings.

2

THE FIRST NATIONAL HISPANIC PASTORAL *ENCUENTRO*

2.1 PURPOSES OF THE *ENCUENTRO*

In accordance with the Declaration of Purpose, approved in the second meeting of the Planning Committee, the four key objectives of the First *Encuentro* are as follows:

1. To begin to develop a pastoral plan for Hispanic-Americans, who at the time made up 25 percent of the U.S. Catholic faithful. The procedure to follow is set forth in five steps:
    a. An analysis of the pastoral situation in the Hispanic community.
    b. Discussion of possible solutions for obvious problems.
    c. Correlating newly obtained information with existing knowledge.
    d. The placing of all material coming out of the proceedings at the disposition of the National Conference of Catholic Bishops (NCCB) and the dioceses.
    e. The Conference and the dioceses will make all decisions concerning the execution of the *Encuentro*'s recommendations.

2. The *Encuentro* is considered an official function of the NCCB, as administered by the Conference's division for Spanish-speaking Catholics that is part of the NCCB's Social Justice Department. This implies that the participants of the First

Encuentro are diocesan bishops and their official delegates, as well as staff and experts who have special responsibilities for the Hispanic apostolate.

3. The *Encuentro* is not designed as a congress, but rather as a workshop, with strong emphasis on hands-on participation by the delegates in seven areas of pastoral work. These areas of focus are set forth in a working document. The First *Encuentro* features only two general presentations to provide the theological and practical foundations for an overall pastoral plan.

4. Fourth and final objective: To provide specific guidelines for the *Encuentro*, so that, coming out of each of the seven areas of discussion, declarations and conclusions might be formulated in harmonious fashion, allowing them to be subsequently combined in a single, overarching concluding document.

2.2 GENERAL ASSEMBLY PRESENTATIONS AT THE FIRST *ENCUENTRO*

Five documents, reports, and presentations from the First *Encuentro* provide the central structure. They are as follows:

1. The words of welcome given by Bishop Joseph L. Bernardin, Secretary General of the NCCB. In addition to giving thanks to the organizers, he emphasizes the importance of leadership in the Hispanic community, while calling for a proper balance between being responsive to pastoral needs and remaining faithful to the Church. This, he argues, will preserve the unity of American Catholicism.

2. The report "The Theology of Pastoral Ministry" is presented by Bishop Raul Zambrano Camader of Facatativa, Colombia, a CELAM official. The bishop lays out ten points:

   a. Pastoral responsibility hinges on two poles: proclaiming the universal plan of salvation manifested in the Word of God, on the one hand, and on the other, responding to the specific pastoral needs of specific human beings in a particular time and space, in this case, the Hispanic people in the United States. These faithful form a subculture in both the U.S. Church and society, one transplanted from the Hispano-American world to predominantly Anglo North America.

b. The ultimate goal of pastoral activity is evangelization: triggering the people of God's conversion and prompting their positive response to God's invitation.

c. The Church is the bearer of salvation—it is, in fact, a universal sacrament of salvation that embraces the entire human family.

d. According to Vatican II's *Gaudium et Spes*, the Church must pay careful attention to changing human cultural conditions, reading the signs of the times. This implies the assumption of a critical prophetic function on the part of the Church in confronting problems such as discrimination, arms buildup, lagging development of nations and peoples, pollution, and so on.

e. The Church's sense of community is a reflection of the life of the Trinity, which is manifested, in particular, in specific ecclesial communities, and which is celebrated in the Eucharist. It rouses the laity to faith and action through what in Spanish is referred to as the "integral promotion" of the human person, which involves a holistic approach to assisting the flourishing of the human being in mind, body, and spirit.

f. In recognition of human dignity, the Church must respect human conscience and liberty. Hence, authoritarian dogmatism is inadmissible, along with casuistic moralism and a passive submission to the Church's hierarchy.

g. The Chruch is on a pilgrimage. So is the individual Christian, whose ultimate citizenship is in heaven. The Hispanic people are dispersed, but they are not a remnant lost in a pagan world. Rather, they are on the move from one particular Church, in their homelands, to another, in their adopted country, the United States. The latter has different external characteristics, but it is part of the universal

Church, just like the Church they left behind. The Hispanic faithful must recognize this continuity and wholeheartedly participate in their "adopted" Church.

h. There is a pedagogy found in the entire history of salvation. Medellín warned about the potential danger of popular religiosity and the inherent risk of a certain inappropriate devotion to Mary. There is a great need for a watchful, "progressive pastoral" approach that will ensure the Virgin's proper place in the history of salvation as well as the integration of Hispanic popular religiosity and liturgical traditions.

i. The report calls for a review of the nature of ministry in the Church, warning against a strictly juridical understanding of Church structures. At the same time, it calls attention to the advantages of the institution, understood as a fruit of the incarnation of the Church in the world and whose goal it is to ensure and protect ultimate human liberty.

j. There is a need for a coordinated pastoral effort on the part of the Church and all its parts and all its members. In Spanish, this is called the *pastoral de conjunto*.

3. The report "Pastoral Planning for the Spanish-speaking people of the United States" is presented by Father Virgilio Elizondo, who, referring back to the National Catechetical Congress meeting in Miami (see 1.1, second), divides the task at hand into three parts:

a. First, he argues that Spanish-speaking persons in the United States are characterized by three factors: a higher birthrate compared to the general population, a growing sense of Latin and Hispanic identity, and an increased value placed on having substantial aspects of their culture and language in common. Father Elizondo notes that 85 percent of Hispanics in the United States are Catholic, constituting 25 percent of the Catholic population of the United States. These figures prompt four questions: Is there a specific Hispanic pastoral responsibility, as urged by the document *Pastoralis Migratorum* (August 15, 1969)? What would be the guidelines of ministering to Hispanics as a migrant and immigrant people? Do they really prompt a specific pastoral responsibility? And would such a specific pastoral plan be practical and doable?

b. Second, Father Elizondo examines the phenomenon from both a theological and sociological perspective. Concerning theology, he reminds his hearers that the Church's mission is concerned with concrete, flesh-and-blood people, a sign of the salvation that Christ offers to all—including those who are hurt by economic and social systems. The question then becomes: To whom should Hispanic ministry direct its primary energies? Tackling the sociological dimension, Father Elizondo notes that Hispanics exhibit a great number of similarities as well as differences, as is evident in the three largest groups of the moment: those of Mexican, Puerto Rican, and Cuban heritage. The expert notes the great value put on the *fiesta* and the sense of family that characterizes all the groups.

c. Third, Father Elizondo reflects on the orientation of the hoped-for pastoral plan, laying out a number of major concerns: the need for more apostolic personnel who speak Spanish; more Spanish-language resources, written and otherwise; more public celebrations centering on Hispanic Catholics; more assistance to defend the rights of Hispanic Catholics; and more economic support for all these initiatives. He makes the following recommendations: the establishment of national and regional research centers; the creation of specialized training centers that prepare clergy and laity for the Hispanic apostolate; dedicated programs of catechism, liturgy, and social development; leadership formation; training of Hispanic deacons; raising awareness that developing adequate Hispanic pastoral care is a challenge for—and the responsibility of—the entire North American Church; a push for cooperation among those dioceses most affected; the creation of a Commission for Hispanic Issues at the level of the U.S.

bishops' conference; and the development and launch of effective fundraising campaigns.

4. The fourth plenary presentation comes under the banner of "The Diocesan and National Church," in the words of Bishop Patrick Flores, [then] serving as Auxiliary Bishop of San Antonio, Texas, and president of the Association PADRES, the association of Hispanic clergy (see Appendix D). Monsignor Flores expresses his love for the Church and stresses the need for integral human development. He questions and critiques the American Church for not defending Hispanic Catholics in the preservation of their customs, their history, and their popular forms of religious expression. He also levels the charge of indifference shown toward Hispanics as found in attitudes that apparently aim to "Americanize" Hispanic believers, yet without providing them with the necessary structures. Monsignor Flores specifically proposes to install more Hispanic bishops to oversee Hispanic communities, establish national parishes for Hispanics, create regional alliances for Hispanics, and set up seminaries for Hispanics, in addition to other key measures.

The bishop revisits the resolution that PADRES presented at its National Convention in Los Angeles in 1971, when the group called for a National Hispanic Church within the overall structure of Catholicism, but separate from the North American episcopate. Monsignor Flores concedes that such a plan is not workable, and that Hispanic Catholics and their leadership must work within the structure of the American Church. Yet the problem is that, as he puts it, Hispanics do not yet consider themselves really part of the structure of the U.S. Church; they all too often still feel like second-class citizens in the U.S. Catholic community. This clearly points to the need for more Hispanic bishops and a national Hispanic seminary, according to the bishop.

5. The fifth plenary intervention comes from Cardinal John Krol, Archbishop of Philadelphia and president of the NCCB. He opens with a quote from Ephesians: "You are no

longer strangers and pilgrims" (2:19). The cardinal's talk centers on two indispensable values in the life of the Church: diversity and unity. The Cardinal insists that there is an urgent need for specialized programs to meet the particular needs of Hispanics.

The Cardinal offers his full support to the undertaking, promising to bring the full weight to bear of his office as president of the Conference of Bishops. In following Saint Peter, he says, it is clear that all people are one in Christ and that there should be no distinctions. Then he speaks of the principle of solidarity that's operative between the Bishops' Conference and the individual dioceses, a relationship that advocates for decentralization of the Spanish-speaking department into various regions, thus freeing energy and resources for a host of initiatives. Holding up examples of creative approaches to the challenges at hand, he refers to a research project at the University of California, Los Angeles, which is titled "The Mexican-American people, the second largest minority group in the nation." The cardinal also praises, among other initiatives, the work of the Committee for Agricultural Work at the Conference of Bishops.

2.3 THE WORKSHOPS OF THE *ENCUENTRO*

Although, at first, there is talk of seven workshops, only six appear in the program. But the first workshop features four presentations, which makes for nine different subjects. This nine-point scheme is adopted here.

1. The first workshop subject focuses on the diaconate and is presented by Father Thomas Bissonette, director of the diaconate program for Spanish-speaking persons of the Archdiocese of Detroit. He begins with three theological premises: that the mission of the Church has many ministries, and among them the ordained offices or "orders"; that the orders, adhering to a unity maintained under the

authority of the bishop, are a mandate for public leadership; and that such leadership implies proclaiming the Word, building community, serving (*diakonia*) all materially and socially, and being in charge of liturgical celebration. From these premises Father Bissonette draws five conclusions with regard to the office of deacon: 1) Candidates for the office must have leadership qualities, an ability to bring people together. 2) The deacon should be a servant—one who is able to reconcile members of the community. 3) The deacon has specific functions, even when they are not well defined. 4) Age is not a determining factor. 5) In his preparation, the candidate must clearly come to understand the mission of the Church, grasp postconciliar theology, be intimate with Christ, even as he is familiar with modern psychology, communication techniques, and more. The deacon, in fact, should be both prophet and teacher, insists Bissonette. In conclusion, the speaker poses several questions: Is it necessary to ordain deacons? What should constitute the special preparation for Latino deacons? Are any changes in Church law needed?

Ordination: He acknowledges that to be a leader, one does not need to be a deacon, but he touches on the possibility that a deaconate of married persons could pave the way for married priests. However, he notes, when it comes to liturgy, laypersons can do almost everything that deacons do. He does not recommend deacons who are very clerical in style, urging that symbols of clericalism be avoided.

Special preparation: Father Bissonette argues that deacons serving Hispanic Catholics should be bilingual and bicultural, putting particular emphasis on the cultural dimension. Care should be exercised with regard to the involvement of the wives and the planning of the liturgy.

Changes in Church Law: Participants are told that U.S. Church leaders have petitioned Rome to lower the age for ordination to the diaconate to age thirty; if that will become the norm and given the faculty of dispensation that the U.S. bishops can wield, the process of training could begin at age twenty-six-and-a-half. Father Bissonette believes that the imminence of widowerhood should not be required and that the process should be more flexible with regard to both incardination and excardination. Finally, the speaker expects that, in time, the ordination of deaconesses will also become possible.

2. The second workshop subject concerns ecclesiastical personnel of non-Hispanic origin who are serving Hispanic faithful, a topic tackled by Father Robert L. Stern, director of the Hispanic Apostolate of the Archdiocese of New York and coordinator of the conclusions of the *Encuentro*. It is a very brief report in which he highlights the following key issues:

   a. It is optimal for those studying to become clergy and religious in a particular community to be prepared in such a way that they will be able to establish intimate relationships in those communities.
   b. Ideally, these clergy and religious hail from the community in which they will be serving.
   c. The reality of the Hispanic apostolate in the United States is a challenging one; there is a shortage of Hispanic-born personnel, and as a result, non-Hispanics must render services to Hispanics.
   d. In the long run, priority must be given to the formation of Hispanic clergy and religious to eventually take the place of non-Hispanic clergy and religious, who, for their part, must be willing to cede their positions when the time comes.
   e. An adequate preparation is essential for everyone. This includes, on the part of Hispanics, mastering the English language and discovering—indeed, embracing—American culture; for their part, non-Hispanics must learn the Spanish language and immerse themselves in Hispanic culture.
   f. It will be necessary to establish—in four or five different regions of the United States—well-equipped training centers to provide preparation for Church workers committed to working with Hispanics.

g. Father Stern stressed two points in particular: it is essential to improve the registration and training of foreign personnel and of non-Hispanics, and the Church must do everything in its power to encourage the development of an authentic indigenous leadership within the Spanish-speaking community.

3. The third workshop subject concerns the formation and ongoing education of Hispanic priests in the United States, a topic spoken on by Father Raul Baca, parish priest at Nuestra Señora la Reina del Cielo in Albuquerque, New Mexico. The principal points of his presentation are as follows:

a. The account of the election of Matthias found in the Acts of the Apostles is the first example of an individual's incorporation into apostolic ministry.
b. According to tradition, the apostles began choosing and putting in place successors, who were later called bishops.
c. The decree of Vatican II concerning the ministry and life of the presbyters considers them collaborators of the bishops, celebrators of the Eucharist, and charged with a pastoral ministry to lead God's people.
d. Saint Paul sets forth certain qualities looked for in prospective priests-apostles in Titus 1:5–9. These qualities, of course, transcend race and nationality.
e. Father Baca poses a hypothetical problem: How should a young man who is poor and has a vocation relate to a rich bishop? This situation, says Father Baca, is not unusual among the so-called "Chicano" vocations.
f. What happens to Chicanos in the culture at large—where they are often denied the use of their language, and barred from their cultural heritage and the support of their community—also happens to Chicanos who have a vocation and must find their way in the U.S. Church structure.
g. The speaker urges a return to the liturgy of Holy Thursday: to the institution of the Eucharist, to the priesthood, and to the mandate of service—the very foundation of a

Church that transcends ethnic and cultural barriers and distinctions.

h. He also recalls the triple ministry of the Word, the sacraments, and pastoral service.

i. Taking a cue from the stress on being sensitive to culture called for in *Gaudium et Spes*, Father Baca argues for the convenience and necessity of smaller seminaries for Chicanos and of Hispanic cultural centers like those found in San Antonio, Texas.

4. The fourth workshop subject deals with the Church's handling of those religious for whom Spanish is the mother tongue. This workshop is presented by Sister Clarita Trujillo, OLVM, who is based in Los Angeles. She proclaims:

a. Women who participate in religious vocations do so to serve; and the apostolate of their congregation responds to the desires of the local bishop.

b. However, many religious are dissenting, considering excessive the number of women dedicated to education and health. Many believe it is imperative that religious be in the vanguard of social change. The Church recognizes that there is much social injustice; hence, priests, religious, and all Church workers must struggle in favor of justice.

c. As Hispanics, these religious believe that they should help their Hispanic brothers and sisters. At times, this puts them in the minority within their own congregation, which can create tensions. For this reason, an organization has been formed: *Las Hermanas* (The Sisters).

d. The new organization has three purposes: leadership training; the promotion of positive social change; and working with Hispanic faithful so that they might become more familiar with, and take greater advantage of, their cultural heritage.

e. Urging a greater sensitivity on the part of those who work in the Hispanic apostolate, Sister Trujillo calls for the creation of a national training center for Hispanic vocations. (At this time, three Sisters are being trained at the Latin

American Pastoral Institute [IPLA] in Quito, Ecuador. They are focusing on three areas: social awareness, theological analysis, and pastoral action.)

f. Once back in the United States, the three Sisters will concentrate on getting the national center off the ground, bearing three goals in mind in particular: the training of new teams, the establishment of an ever-wider network of contacts, and the implementation of various measures.

g. The main priorities are vocations and personnel.

h. Sister Trujillo offers six recommendations: 1) that the bishops agree that these religious be freed to devote themselves to the Hispanic apostolate; 2) that resources are made available to support the new pastoral teams; 3) that the Major Superiors support this new ministry and 4) assist in organizing the teams; 5) that the Sisters in question be relieved of traditional work; and 6) Church that authorities make available appropriate facilities.

i. The Family Movement, Cursillos, the First *Encuentro*, and others have encouraged these initiatives.

j. This effort on behalf of Hispanic Catholics overall is based on a key principle: That the potential of a person increases as he or she exercises free will.

k. If Hispanic Catholic pastoral teams do not function as they should, the development of the Church will suffer, more (Hispanic) youth will abandon their faith communities, and there will be a drop in vocations.

5. The fifth workshop subject studies the lay apostolate. It is presented by Luis Fontanez, vice-president of the Secretariat of the Cursillo Movement, who, relying on the group's own particular methodological order, lays out the movement's approach to the issues at hand:

a. Fontanez stresses the Cursillo premise that a Christian vocation is, by its own nature, a vocation to the apostolate, whether ordained or not. The world needs God's presence and those who are baptized are the ones who have the mission to preach to every man, woman, and child. He refers,

in particular, to the mandates found in Vatican II documents *Lumen Gentium* and *Apostolicam Actuositatem.*

b. There are two objectives of the secular apostolate: 1) to
evangelize and sanctify people, and 2) to make the temporal order more Christian; this second objective hinges
on three strategies: arranging temporal issues according to
God's will, transforming society in a Christian manner,
and making the Church more of a presence in the home.

c. The apostolate should have six qualities: authenticity in its
motivation; authenticity in its objective, reflections, and
programming; constancy; balance; prayer; and sacrifice.

d. The execution of the lay apostolate should keep in mind
three dimensions: the person, the community, and the
world as a whole.

e. The person places an obligation on every Christian; his or
her liberty must be respected by all. In the other two
realms, action is optional.

f. There are several fields of action: family, resources, the
workplace, as well as every other setting and environment.

g. Through the individual apostolate, the Cursillos make possible a personal *encuentro* with Christ; in the apostolate for
groups, they serve the *ultreyas*—those who have made their
Cursillo retreat—and the basic communities. The organized
apostolate also engages traditional parish organizations,
such as the catechumenate, religious education, programs
for adults (Light and Life, and so on.), the Youth Movement,
the Family Movement, as well as the Saint Vincent de Paul
Society, among other parish-based groups and initiatives.

h. With regard to a comprehensive diocesan pastoral program, there are four organizations that have a national
and international presence: Cursillos, Youth Movement,
Family Movement, and the Saint Vincent de Paul Society.
(The common denominator is friendship.)

6. The sixth workshop subject tackles the liturgy. It is presented
by Father Edgar Beltran, executive secretary of the Department
of Pastoral Planning of CELAM. He delivers a compact
overview of his findings and recommendations:

a. The liturgy should be more broadly studied, particularly with regard to the sacraments and popular religiosity.

b. Vatican II recognizes the liturgy as the culmination of the Christian life. It is here presented as an expression of the faith of the Hispanic people in the United States. It should be centered on Christ and be incarnated [in people's lives] so as to reveal their commitment to their fellow men and women.

c. The two poles in "unity in diversity" are of equal importance. The liturgy should express them clearly, ensuring that their distinction is not lost. One difficulty is the ignorance that many faithful have about their culture—but that is precisely where the liturgy should be incarnated. Lack of experience on this front, however, causes doubt and uncertainty; there also have been abuses, notes Father Beltran.

d. The situation calls for dialogue with Church authorities in accord with *Sacrosanctum Concilium* 40; Father Beltran calls for more study, not only about liturgical issues, but also involving the social sciences. Church personnel should be better trained across the board.

e. Two levels of work are a priority: service to the parish services and service to the basic ecclesial communities.

f. Some topics deserving special attention are the Eucharist, the sacraments of Christian initiation, marriage, funeral rites, and popular religiosity.

7. The seventh workshop subject is devoted to the so-called basic ecclesial communities. It is also presented by Father Edgar Beltran. This is a summary of his comments:

a. He begins with the experience of an "ecclesial" conversion. Vatican II gave the formation of these communities an impulse, but there are two pitfalls: a false satisfaction that assumes that everything is all right; and sometimes a certain superficiality. "Ecclesial" conversion confers the presence of the Holy Spirit, which is a validation of this form of ecclesial community.

b. The essential elements of the basic ecclesial community are: the Church in its basic form, as an authentic and small community with three key functions: prophetic, priestly, and dealing with ordinary life. The fulfillment of these functions requires a proclamation (*kerigma*) and a catechesis. Each function nourishes the other two, so that together they bring about the "ferment" of the world.

c. There are various important tasks: above all, the promotion of an atmosphere of ecclesiastic conversion, a path that must be adhered to from the outset and which involves an ongoing review and reorientation of the needs and demands of the community of the faithful.

8. The eighth workshop theme is the education of Hispanic children, presented by Sister Maria Ramona Perez of the department of education of the Diocese of Brooklyn. Her brief presentation underscores the following key points:

a. In the Catholic primary schools of the great cities, there are a large number of Hispanic children, and in some cases, they practically compose the entire student body. There are also schools where another specific ethnic group predominates.

b. Few schools offer bilingual programs and this becomes more of a problem when there are no Hispanic teachers. Few schools offer classes in Hispanic heritage, for lack of teachers, time, and the difficulty in selecting a specific Hispanic heritage.

c. Less than 10 percent of Hispanic students who attend Catholic primary schools continue in Church-run secondary schools, fundamentally due to the high cost, but also because of an inferior grade average. The progress of those who do go to Catholic High Schools is good.

d. At the university level, there are a large number of scholarships available to Hispanics, and there are attractive two-year programs. The policy of free access to universities, as in New York—and depending on a state's economic health—makes this possible.

   e. There are three urgent needs: bilingual teachers, cultural studies, and greater economic opportunities.

9. The ninth and final workshop subject is Hispanic Pastoral Catechism in North America, presented by Francisco Diana, coordinator for Hispanics of the Confraternity of Christian Doctrine (CCD) of the Diocese of Brooklyn. His is a wide-ranging presentation, whose main points are as follows:

   a. He begins by speaking about the development of theological thought.
   b. Then he seeks to establish a relationship between the signs of the times and the catechism.
   c. Next, he speaks of the relationship between catechism and liberation theology, insisting that catechism should move in two directions: prophetic warning about current evils and prophetic proclamation of liberation.
   d. He also establishes the relationship between catechism and creation, and between catechism and Revelation. He affirms that the Church is seeking to capture and express the "total language of God."
   e. Then he outlines the challenge of catechism as a double process of communicating to people the content of Revelation, while, at the same time, helping them to be disposed to accept the message.
   f. Then he speaks at length about God's manifestation through specific persons, the signs of the times, the community—describing the nature of the Lord's liberating action as progressive and dynamic.
   g. Finally, in a lengthy exposition, he speaks of the methodology and of "special" catechetical material, which is especially designed for use with Hispanics in the United States. Among many affirmations, he underscores the formulation: "God is our Mother."

2.4 CONCLUSIONS OF THE FIRST *ENCUENTRO*

Father Robert L. Stern is the coordinator of the Conclusions Committee; he is joined by Father Edgar Beltran, William Espinoza, Gloria Gallardo, Father John O'Brien, and Father Bryan O. Walsh. The final text consists of a preface, an introduction, and seventy-eight conclusions. These are grouped into nine sections, two of which are subdivided—the first section featuring three subsections and the third section consisting of five subsections. The entire document is published in a bilingual edition by the Division for Spanish-speaking faithful of the Catholic Conference of the United States.

1. The preface recapitulates the conclusions, while reaffirming the two priorities of the *Encuentro* as ratified and supported by the general assembly. They are as follows:

    a. Spanish-speaking persons should have greater representation in the leadership and the decision-making process at every level of the Church in the United States.

    b. Regional pastoral centers should be established—their activities coordinated on a national scale—for the study and development of the training of [Hispanic] Christian leaders at all levels of the U.S. Church.

       These two priorities are based on a principle set forth at the end of the preface, which holds: "We, the American Catholics of Hispanic origin, convinced of the unity of the United States Church and of the values of our own heritage, feel the impulse of the Spirit prompting us to share the responsibility of the development of the Kingdom of God among our people and all the people of our country."

2. The introduction opens by citing the two mottos defining the culture of the United States: *E Pluribus Unum* and "In God We Trust," both of which are also endorsed by the Church. Then follows a reflection on the number of Hispanic Catholics in the country and their insertion in the U.S. Church; their

importance is reaffirmed, along with an acknowledgment of their wish to preserve their own culture, language, and tradition and their demand for proportional recognition and representation in the hierarchy—all of which makes evident the need for a specific pastoral plan.

3. The first of the sections presenting the conclusions is titled "The Church: National and Diocesan." It contains conclusions Nos. 1 to 18 and is divided into three subsections: pertaining to the national level (Nos. 1 to 8), the regional level (Nos. 9 to 11) and the diocesan level (Nos. 12 to 18).

   a. At the national level, the First *Encuentro* proposes: to transform the Spanish-speaking department at the bishops' conference into a special office that reports directly to the Secretary General of the Catholic Conference of the United States (No. 1); to enlist bilingual Hispano-American personnel (No. 2); to create a national episcopal committee, preferably chaired by a Hispano-American bishop (No. 3); that the remaining committees of the NCCB/USCC all incorporate bilingual and/or bicultural bishops (No. 4); to ordain new Hispanic bishops according to the number of Hispanic faithful (No. 5); to allocate a greater portion of funds [to pastoral activity aimed at Hispanics] (No. 6); to establish a national Hispanic pastoral institute (No. 7); and to establish a national seminary (No. 8).
   b. At the regional level, the First *Encuentro* proposes: to create regional directors (No. 9); that these directors organize regional *Encuentros* (No. 10); that the Mexican American Cultural Center (in San Antonio, Texas) become the Pastoral Institute of the Southwest and help establish others of its kind (No. 11).
   c. At the diocesan level, the First *Encuentro* proposes: the appointment in each diocese of a director of the Hispanic apostolate, who reports directly to the bishop and has a bilingual and bicultural background (No. 12); that this position be that of an episcopal vicar with real authority

(No. 13); that, in those dioceses in which more than a third of the faithful are Hispanic, this official be an auxiliary bishop (No. 14); that in each diocese, there be an open process for the submission of candidates for the post (No. 15); that in each diocese, there be an advisory group that collaborates with the deputy (No. 16); that in each diocese where there is a notable proportion of Hispanics, there be Hispanics in position of responsibility, or at least bilingual persons who are sympathetic to Hispanic concerns (No. 17); that wherever there are publications in a diocese with a significant number of Hispanic Catholics, these feature Spanish-language content (No. 18).

4. The second section includes Conclusions 19 to 22 and is dedicated to the basic ecclesial communities. These conclusions are based on this principle: "Each member of the Church, if he or she is truly committed, should become part of a local community dedicated to renewal and development, both human and Christian." There is a call for the formation of basic Hispanic communities (No. 19); their leaders should be chosen from within the same community (No. 20); such "personal" parishes should be included as forms of legitimate pastoral infrastructure, along with the traditional national and territorial parishes (No. 21); and in each parish, the linguistic and cultural expression of the Hispanic people should be respected (No. 22).

5. The third section notes that:

   a. Concerning the bishops, the principle of proportionality is affirmed in relation to the size of the local Hispanic Catholic population (No. 23).
   b. With regard to priests, there is a proposal to develop alternative programs for the formation of candidates (No. 24); these should be bilingual and bicultural (No. 25); "mature married men should be considered as possible candidates to the priesthood" (No. 26); the apostolic work should be more oriented to serving the community

at large and less to the parish institution as such (No. 27); in some areas and dioceses, mixed Anglo-Hispanic pastoral teams should be formed to support local priests (No. 28); and more responsibility should be given to Spanish-speaking priests (No. 29).

c. With reference to deacons, whose roles are considered to be a special opportunity for leadership, it is proposed: to name a national coordinator for Hispanics, and that this person must be a member of the Committee for the Permanent Diaconate (No. 30); that training programs for Hispanic deacons should be bilingual and bicultural (No. 31); that these programs should be executed under the direction of Hispanics, at least in part (No. 32); that local communities must have say regarding the duties and responsibilities of the deacons assigned to them (No. 33); that the qualities of a candidate to become deacon should include a strong spirit of faith, openness, adaptability, understanding of the Christian mission, and a strong ability to communicate (No. 34); that canon law should be changed in key respects: lowering the minimum age of a deacon to thirty, giving widowers the right to marry again, allowing single persons who have become deacons to marry, making it easier for a deacon to move from one diocese to another, allowing deacons to "serve as ministers of the sacraments of penitence and for the anointing of the sick," and allowing women to be ordained to the diaconate (No. 35); deacons be encouraged to work in mixed teams (No. 36); and that, in those areas where there aren't enough priests, deacons should be named parish administrators (No. 37).

d. Concerning Hispanic women religious, it is proposed to establish a national center or program of comprehensive training (No. 38); that the communities allow its members to join *Las Hermanas* (No. 39); that congregations whose mother tongue is Spanish should be appropriately distributed throughout the country (No. 40).

e. Concerning foreign ecclesiastical personnel, the conclusions propose that they adopt a missionary style (No. 41);

that programs for training and inculturation be promoted (No. 42); that programs preparing candidates for the Hispanic apostolate be organized to enlist North Americans and non-Hispanic foreigners (No. 43); that regional training centers be formed (No. 44); that there be no economic discrimination (No. 45); that all candidates for the priesthood be required to study Spanish and Hispanic culture, and that this should be the case in intensified form in those dioceses with a significant proportion of Hispanics (No. 46).

(N.B. The concept of *foreigner* includes both non-Hispanic North Americans and Hispanics who are not North Americans.)

6. The fourth section is dedicated to lay apostolates and contains only two conclusions: No. 47, which refers to the establishment of centers for the training of laity offering the "necessary intellectual and pastoral training"; and No. 48, a call to make it a priority for the Church to provide assistance to lay directors overseeing programs of apostolic development.

7. The fifth section refers to the liturgy, putting it in the context of the concept of "unity within diversity," recognizing that the unifying core of each local Church is the Eucharist, as presided over by the local bishop. There are six proposals: to establish a national secretariat for Hispanic liturgy under the umbrella of the U.S. bishops' liturgical committee (No. 49); to establish an office for liturgical training and distribution of materials, including a magazine (No. 50); to establish a national institute for liturgical training (No. 51); to establish regional centers of experimentation (No. 52); to form regional and local commissions [dealing with the Hispanic liturgy] (No. 53); to recognize the right of access to and use of places of worship for the benefit of bilingual and multilingual celebrations (No. 54).

8. The sixth section is dedicated to religious education and the catechism. It opens with a declaration about the relationship

between faith and culture, and in five conclusions (Nos. 55 to 59) proposes to: develop programs that respond to cultural needs, "which should be an integral part of every true process of Christian liberation" (No. 55); that more Spanish-language educators be involved in the task (No. 56); that there should be a national structure [dealing with Catholic education for Hispanics] (No. 57); that there be programs for the education and formation of adults (No. 58); and that youth be able to count on diocesan economic support of their participation in training programs (No. 59).

9. The seventh section refers to Catholic schools (Nos. 60 to 68) and proposes that: everyone in the Church be informed of the cultural differences that characterize Hispanics (No. 60); the bishops encourage special funding for the Hispanics in their schools (No. 61); those in positions of responsibility support an equitable redistribution of economic and personnel resources for the schools (No. 62); subsidy for poor parishes become a national priority (No. 63); in schools attended by Hispanics, there be an annual evaluation of their achievements and difficulties (No. 64); officials in charge make possible the appointment of competent teachers for schools lacking funds (No. 65); the multiethnic situation requires that there be an intercultural plan for all Catholic schools to respond to the multiethnic reality, and that those schools serving a large number of Hispanic students put in place bilingual and bicultural programs (No. 66); corporations be formed to take advantage of federal funds earmarked for programs promoting ethnic and cultural identity on behalf of minorities (No. 67); a Hispanic should be named as Associate Director of the Department of Education at the bishops' conference (No. 68).

10. The eighth section tackles socioeconomic challenges and features six conclusions (Nos. 69 to 74). They propose that: everyone be informed of the discrimination against Hispanics and that resources be mobilized to denounce and combat these abuses (No. 69); the bishops' conference

establish an office for migratory workers (No. 70); that the Church throw its weight behind specific actions, such as the boycott of lettuce growers (No. 71); the Church help struggle against all unjust and discriminatory laws and rules, calling, for example, for the extension of preferential treatment given to Cubans as political refugees (No. 72); a scientific study be commissioned to study the situation of Cubans in the United States (No. 73); that all should be called upon to support the efforts to achieve a prompt and equitable administration of justice for the poor (No. 74).

11. The ninth and final section of the conclusions corresponds to four specific conclusions (Nos. 75 to 78): gratitude is expressed to all the non-Hispanic personnel of the U.S. Church who have been dedicated to the Hispanics (No. 75); gratitude is also expressed to Mrs. Encarnacion de Armas and to the Planning Committee (No. 76); there is a call, in preparation for the next *Encuentro*, that the First *Encuentro* be thoroughly evaluated (No. 77); and a committee is formed to clarify the conclusions and submit them to the National Catholic Conference of Bishops. The committee is composed of Bernardo Alvarado, Father Virgilio Elizondo, Isabel Erviti, Manuel Ferrales, Father Robert Stern, and Father Victor Torres-Frias (No. 78).

3

TAKING STOCK OF THE FIRST *ENCUENTRO*

3.1 REPORT OF THE AD-HOC COMMITTEE FOR SPANISH-SPEAKING PEOPLE

1. It is necessary to define a certain chronology:

   a. In August 1972, Cardinal Krol joins the Ad-hoc Episcopal Committee, reviewing the conclusions of the First *Encuentro*. The committee is presided over by Archbishop Joseph L. Bernardin. He is also joined by Archbishop Thomas A. Donnellan, Bishop Juan A. Arzube, Bishop John J. Fitzpatrick, Bishop Patrick F. Flores, Bishop Raymond J. Gallagher, and Bishop Edward D. Head.

   b. In October 1972, a meeting is held between the committee named by the First *Encuentro* and the Ad-hoc Episcopal Committee for the purpose of presenting the conclusions.

   c. In February 1973, the Ad-hoc Episcopal Committee prepares the first draft of a response to and an evaluation of the conclusions of the First *Encuentro*.

   d. In April 1973, a meeting is held in Kansas City (April 9–10) to discuss possibilities and strategies for implementing the conclusions. The committee named by the First *Encuentro* selects as co-presidents Father Virgilio Elizondo and Mrs. Encarnacion de Armas, replacing Father Robert Stern, who has gone to Rome.

29

e. In May 1973, the Ad-hoc Episcopal Committee presents a final report to the Administrative Board of Bishops. The report is published in *Origins*.

2. Concerning conclusions Nos. 1 to 18, which refer to the national and diocesan Church, the Ad-hoc Committee provides a number of notable suggestions:

a. What is important is not a bureaucratic change to the Spanish-speaking Department; what is needed is the department's direct access to the Secretary General of the bishops' conference. The two officials involved can make sure that happens (No. 1).

b. More Hispanics should be employed in the Church, and wherever possible, a data bank of this personnel should be maintained (No. 2).

c. As it gains experience, the Ad-hoc Committee can become a Permanent Episcopal Committee for Hispanic issues (No. 3).

d. The call for a larger number of Hispanic bishops goes beyond the competence of the committee; for the moment, there are not enough to fulfill the demand of conclusion No. 4; No. 5 would be useful, but a quota system is not viable.

e. Special funds are already available for the support of initiatives involving Hispanics (No. 6).

f. It is recommended that the Mexican-American Cultural Center of Texas become a pilot project and that the center receive funds from the Mission Board (No. 7).

g. A subcommission has already been established as part of the Committee for the Training of Priests to study the formation of Hispanic candidates for the priesthood (No. 8).

h. Concerning regionalization, experience has not been positive. The support of the Mission Board and the Committee for Social Development and World Peace is suggested (No. 9).

i. Regional *Encuentros* are a question of regional competence (No. 10), but are considered valid options.

    j. Pastoral institutes could evolve, but the Mexican-American Cultural Center should closely monitor their individual progress and advise accordingly (No. 11).

    k. Recommendations Nos. 12 to 18 are not within the competence of the committee, but it will recommend to ordinaries that they consider the possibility of naming episcopal deputies, within the limits of the Decree *Christus Dominus* 17 and the Letter *Ecclesiae Sanctae* 14, No. 4.

    l. Concerning the creation of an advisory group (No. 16), the committee thinks it useful and valuable, but insists that it has to be part of the Diocesan Pastoral Council or be closely connected to it.

    m. The Ad-hoc Committee believes a more efficient solution to the proposal made in conclusion No. 18 is the creation of a periodical that is entirely in Spanish.

3. Concerning conclusions Nos. 19 to 22, referring to the base ecclesial communities, the committee argues that such communities have always existed in the structure of the Church and should be encouraged—provided they be closely linked to diocesan and parish life. Lay leaders have a greater margin for adaptation [in response to particular pastoral needs], but ecclesiastical leaders are subject to the oversight of the permanent Committee for Training of Priests and Deacons (No. 20).

    With regard to the creation of personal parishes, the committee argues that they are not an essential requirement, although they may be of value. The circumstances differ in each diocese.

4. With reference to conclusions Nos. 23 to 46, the committee notes that the proposals with regard to bishops have already been addressed (No. 23) in its response to conclusion No. 5. Concerning other ministers of the Church, the committee responds:

    a. Candidates for the priesthood should be bilingual and bicultural. The Mexican-American Cultural Center is working to help, and the Josephinum Seminary in Columbus, Ohio, is prepared to take on this task (Nos. 24–25).

b. The Synod of Bishops of 1971 chose to maintain the celibate discipline for the priesthood (No. 26).

c. A dedication to Hispanics does not imply lack of care for the rest of the parish (No. 27).

d. There are already mixed pastoral groups and there is training available (No. 28).

e. Bishops are urged to have confidence in their Hispanic priests; these priests are encouraged to collaborate closely with their ordinary and all the clergy (No. 29).

f. It is recommended that Hispanic priests be allowed to continue their studies and broaden their competencies (No. 29).

g. A special coordinator is not considered necessary for the Hispanic deacons; instead, the committee calls for a greater coordination between the Office of the Permanent Deaconate and the Spanish-speaking Department. Training should be bilingual and of the highest quality (Nos. 30 and 34).

h. Concerning lowering the age required for deacons, the Holy See allowed it to be lowered to thirty-two-and-a-half years. The option of allowing for the marriage of widowed deacons is being studied. On the other hand, the marriage of single persons is not under study. In November 1972, norms were put in place governing the transfer of deacons from one diocese to another; these should be respected. This committee declares that it is not competent to determine whether deacons can administer penitence or perform the anointing of the sick, nor whether the Church could or should consider the ordination of women deacons (No. 35).

i. Deacons are part of the Church's pastoral teams (No. 36), but Canon Law does not invest them with a specific authority; however, they may be given specific responsibilities (No. 37).

j. Hispanic religious can take advantage of the resources of the Mexican-American Cultural Center (No. 38). As to their membership in *Hermanas* [Sisters], this recommendation (No. 39) should be put before the organizations of Major Superiors. The idea that religious should establish national lines of communication to serve the Hispanics is accepted; in fact, such is already the case at the local level (No. 40).

k. Foreign ecclesiastical personnel must be prepared to meet the needs of U.S. Hispanics. The Mexican-American Cultural Center offers training programs. Foreign Church workers should be adequately remunerated (Nos. 41–45).

5. Concerning the lay apostolate, the committee insists that the formation of lay leaders is crucial and that both dioceses and regional organizations should implement and oversee the process. The Mexican-American Cultural Center is held up as a valuable leadership-training institute (Nos. 47 and 48).

6. As regards the liturgy, the committee considers it counterproductive to create a separate secretariat for Hispanic-language liturgy; however, a Hispanic person will be added to the staff of the current secretariat and be in charge of collaborating with the Mexican-American Cultural Center. Conclusions Nos. 49 to 54 will be put before the Committee on Liturgy. Finally, the committee agrees that the physical facilities of the Church should be available to Hispanics.

7. With reference to Conclusions Nos. 55 to 59, the committee agrees with the need for greater emphasis on the religious education of Hispanics. Communication should be established between Hispanic religious educators and the Department of Religious Education of the bishops' conference, which has already agreed to the following:

a. Father Elizondo becomes a member of the editorial board of "Living Light," the journal of Church liturgy.

b. All Hispanic articles, research, and documentation can be incorporated in "Living Light."

c. Certain news items can be included in the bulletin "Nexos."

d. The National Congress of Diocesan Directors for Religious Education will be asked to ensure that the directors in those thirty dioceses where Hispanics constitute at least 35 percent of the Catholic community explore ways to improve the catechism of Hispanics.

e. Articles can also be included in the compendium *Enfoque a los Adultos* (Focus on the Adults).

f. The committee recommends that dioceses designate the necessary funds for the various activities.

8. Concerning Catholic schools, the committee supports the need for greater sensibility toward Hispanics, including their inclusion in the school councils and among diocesan and parish-based advisors (Nos. 60 and 61). In addition:

a. Recommendation No. 62 should be considered on a case-by-case basis, since solutions can be varied and broad.

b. The debate concerning help for the parishes that have lower incomes is complex; there is a variety of ways to subsidize poorer parishes (No. 63).

c. In Hispanic zones, the annual evaluation done by the diocesan school office and by schools themselves should include the participation of Hispanic personnel (No. 64).

d. It is recommended that the most dedicated and qualified teachers be assigned to poorer schools, both public and private (No. 65).

e. In the case of an overwhelming majority of Hispanics, bicultural programs should be put in place. These should work with those organizations that, through the ethnic minority provisions, can draw on federal support (Nos. 66 and 67).

f. The committee does not consider it practical or necessary that a secretary charged particularly with Hispanic concerns be appointed to the Department of Education of the bishops' conference (No. 68).

9. The committee responds in the following manner to the conclusions concerning socioeconomic challenges:

   a. It recognizes the presence of discrimination and condemns it (No. 69).
   b. It rejects the proposal that a separate office be established for migrant agricultural workers (No. 70).
   c. The committee does not support a lettuce boycott when such is not initiated by unionized harvesters (No. 71).
   d. The committee notes that much has been done to improve the migratory laws, especially in favor of family reunification (No. 72).
   e. The Spanish-speaking Department should concern itself with the problem of Cuban political refugees (No. 73).
   f. The Department of Cuban Affairs is preparing a document concerning reform in U.S. jails (No. 74).

3.2 IN THE WAKE OF THE FIRST *ENCUENTRO*

1. Following the presentation of the report of by the Ad-hoc Committee, the following series of events occurs:

   a. In June 1973, the report of the committee is sent to each Department Director and to each Episcopal Committee with a view to implementing the conclusions of the First *Encuentro*. The report is presented in the meeting of the Administrative Board of the bishops' conference, and the bishops vote that Archbishop Bernadin continue to lead the Committee for the Spanish-speaking peoples.
   b. On September 30 and October 1, a meeting is held in San Antonio with the leaders of the Mexican-American community with a view to observing and taking stock of the services and resources of the Mexican-American Cultural Center. Among those attending are Archbishop Bernardin, the Secretary General of the bishops' conference, and his assistant Archbishop Furey and Bishop Flores.

c. On October 6 in Chicago, the committee meets to review the progress of the implementation of the conclusions. It is noted that in some dioceses, the stepped-up participation of Hispanics in the pastoral activities has already begun.

d. In November, Archbishop Bernardin presents a report in which he urges the bishops to develop pastoral plans for Spanish-speaking Catholics. The report is well received.

e. In December in San Antonio, there is a meeting of the Hispanic Convention of representatives of the Spanish-speaking groups with the officials representing national Catholic organizations to determine collaboration in service of the Church.

f. In February 1974, the Ad-hoc Committee meets with the Committee for the Training of Priests to study the formation of Hispanic clergy. The Administrative Board of the bishops' conference names Bishop James Rausch as the new moderator of the Ad-hoc Committee.

2. Meanwhile, inspired by the First *Encuentro*, a number of regional *Encuentros* are held:

a. Southwest Regional *Encuentro*, October 5–8, 1972, in Houston, with representatives from Texas, New Mexico, Colorado, Nebraska, Kansas, Missouri, Louisiana, and Oklahoma (Arkansas and Iowa were originally to be included as well).

b. Midwest Regional *Encuentro*, January 17–19, 1973, in Chicago, with 125 delegates representing Illinois, Indiana, Ohio, Kentucky, Michigan, Wisconsin, and Minnesota (the two Dakotas were to be included).

c. West Coast Regional *Encuentro*, August 24–26, 1973, in Los Angeles, with three hundred delegates representing California, Oregon, Washington, and Nevada.

d. Northeast Regional *Encuentro*, October 1974 in New York, with representatives from New York, Massachusetts, New Jersey, Connecticut, Pennsylvania, Maryland, the District of Columbia, Rhode Island, Delaware, and Virginia (New Hampshire, Vermont, and Maine were to be included).

3. As a result of the Regional *Encuentros*, a number of subregional *Encuentros* are held as well. The most important are as follows:

a. The *Encuentro* of Denver, March 22–23, 1973, with some two hundred participants.
b. The *Encuentro* of Dallas, Texas, April 6–8, 1973, with seventy-five participants.
c. The *Encuentro* of Kansas, Nebraska, Missouri, and Iowa, June 15–17, 1973, with 150 participants.
d. The *Encuentro* of Rockford, Illinois, August 17–19, 1973, with just thirty representatives.
e. The *Encuentro* of Corpus Christi, Texas, September 14–16, 1973, with at least two hundred participants.
f. The *Encuentro* of Detroit, January 26, 1974, with two hundred in attendance.
g. The *Encuentro* of Chicago, November 8–10, 1974.

3.3 A LOOK BACK

We have already passed the fortieth anniversary of the First *Encuentro*. It will be fruitful to look back and measure the progress made in Hispanic ministry since then. Clearly, the First *Encuentro* made many positive contributions. Hence, this retrospective will honor that momentous achievement as one of the most important highlights in the history of the Hispanic people in the United States—an authentic experience of their Catholic faith lived out in the mother Church implanted in this great nation.

A proper evaluation demands being mindful of the danger of anachronisms; it also calls for an awareness of the historical-theological and theological-pastoral conditions that marked the First *Encuentro*. Against that backdrop, this analysis seeks to call attention to the most important new ground broken by the First *Encuentro*, the new perspectives it opened up as well as—easily spotted from today's vantage point—its evident limitations and weaknesses.

1. Danger of anachronism.

In spite of the number of years that have passed since the First *Encuentro*, in historical terms, it has not been that long, not even two generations. Yet so much has happened in those relatively short years as regards Hispanics in Church and society—there is a much greater awareness of all the complexities involved—that it would be easy to judge the First *Encuentro* solely by today's criteria. However, that would be an injustice.

In 1972, no one could anticipate, not even as a distant utopia, the crisis of the Marxist-Leninist regimes of Eastern Europe, let alone the demise of the Soviet Union. No one who participated in the First *Encuentro* could have dreamed of the fall of the Berlin Wall and the end of the Cold War. None of the organizers of the First *Encuentro* could have imagined Pope John Paul II—at Puebla, Mexico, in 1979—calling for a "new evangelization" that takes into account changing cultural circumstances, a call to action echoed in 1992 at the Fourth Council of Latin American Bishops. The two instructions on the Theology of Liberation issued by the Congregation for the Doctrine of the Faith had not yet been written. Meanwhile, the war in Vietnam was polarizing North American society, and there was intense, still violent debate about racial discrimination.

The organizers of the First *Encuentro* went about their task in good faith; they aimed to formulate what they considered the best thinking with regard to what was pastorally correct and most fruitful for Hispanic Catholics in the United States. Looking back, it is evident that the key players of the First *Encuentro* were faithful children of the Church. That was made crystal clear in their acceptance of the report of the Ad-hoc Committee and their enthusiastic preparation of the Second and Third *Encuentros*, whose deliberations and impact are chronicled in the pages following.

2. Historical-theological and theological-pastoral conditioning.

To put the First *Encuentro* in proper perspective, it is important to bear in mind that, in the same year, at the CELAM meeting in Sucre, Colombia, a majority of Latin American bishops set out—with the fervor of a crusade, as some would argue—to correct the direction taken by CELAM at Medellín, Colombia, site of CELAM's second plenary assembly (1968). At that groundbreaking earlier meeting, the bishops had largely endorsed the so-called "base ecclesial communities" and many of the tenets of liberation theology.

As often happens during generational change, the older leadership of CELAM was replaced by younger prelates eager to undo the direction set by their elders. One of the more valiant veterans quit CELAM and offered his services to the bishops' conference of the United States. His imprint is evident in many of the innovative conclusions of the First *Encuentro*.

What might have been the ideological and theological evolution of Bishop Raul Zambrano Camader remains a mystery: very soon after the First *Encuentro*, he died in an aviation accident, depriving the Colombian and Latin American Church of one of its more formidable intellects.

What this all means is that the First *Encuentro* was, in important respects, conditioned by theological thought patterns derived from what at the time was beginning to be called "liberation theology," the term coined by Peruvian theologian Gustavo Gutierrez. To judge this approach on its merits today would be an anachronism. Simply put, in 1972, it was believed to be the best approach for Latin America and, hence, for the Hispanic pastoral situation in the United States. The presentations, the chosen themes and the conclusions of the First *Encuentro* all point in that direction.

Behind the ferment of the deliberations of the First *Encuentro* was the increasingly influential thought of theologians like Giulio Girardi, who is unknown today, but who was a key forerunner of more famous names in the annals of liberation theology and its various causes: Hugo Assmann, Leonardo and Clodovis Boff, Juan Luis Segundo, Jose Comblin, Jose Marins, Segundo Galilea, the magazine *Christus*, Ignacio Ellacuria, Jon Sobrino, the theologians backing the *Sandinista* revolution in Nicaragua, and the admirers of the Cuban revolution. The list is long.

Certainly, 1972 was a year of major crisis in the postconciliar period; everything was being questioned and some very radical proposals had fervent defenders, such as the case made for the suspension of priestly celibacy and allowing women to be ordained. Not surprisingly, both issues turn up in the conclusions of the First *Encuentro*. In addition, liturgical experimentation had reached a peak level and it was believed that anything could be tried or any established practice modified. The same was true for the catechism.

Then there was the spotlight put on the "base ecclesial communities." Given the political repression in many Latin American nations, these communities provided the only public places that enjoyed minimal civic freedoms; they were seen as important bulwarks resisting military dictatorships and their unflinching pursuit of the "ideology of national security." Increasingly, church and state were seen to cross swords politically, making for passionate debates in the Church and in society at large. The First *Encuentro*, in key regards, was very much a creature of its time. Today, many of these then very hot topics have lost their edge, making room for today's handling of some of the same issues and themes in ways more spiritual and ecclesiastical.

In summary, the First *Encuentro* was definitely and inevitably subject to theological-pastoral and historical-pastoral conditioning as determined by the ecclesiastical situation in 1972. These were the waning years of the pontificate of Paul VI and what was, in many regards, the height of the crisis of the postconciliar period.

1. Great "intuitions" and insights.

Clearly, not all that was accomplished by the First *Encuentro* is time-bound and, therefore, relative. The First *Encuentro* also brought the Church a number of great "intuitions" and accomplishments. These can be summarized as follows:

a. It made the Hispanic pastoral situation an object of pursuit and study for the NCCB.
b. It triggered fresh support for the principle of unity of

Latin-rite North American Catholicism, within which the Hispanic pastoral situation is granted its particular space.

c. It clarified the meaning and use of the term *Hispanic,* which, up until that point, had been somewhat vaguely understood. Three characteristic meanings of the term stand out: the sense of a subculture transplanted from Latin America into North America, the sense of diaspora, and the ethnic-cultural identity of a linguistic and cultural minority.

d. The First *Encuentro* determined the overriding objective of Hispanic pastoral work: "integral human development" that clearly takes place "within" the U.S. Church—so that Hispanic Catholics do not go unrecognized and so that they are not seen as foreigners and outsiders.

e. Similarly, the ideal of Hispanic vocations was crystallized: the sense of belonging to the Hispanic community.

f. The First *Encuentro* helped instill in the U.S. Church a respect for and recognition of the importance of "culture," according to Vatican II's *Gaudium et Spes.*

g. It fostered respect for popular Hispanic religiosity and its value for all Catholics, overcoming the tendency toward cultural uniformity.

2. Ferment of perspectives.

The First *Encuentro* gave birth to a series of fresh perspectives and calls to action, which are not limited to the time and place of the event but allow for ongoing development and reflection. These include the following:

a. The importance of balancing the response to the pastoral needs of the Hispanic peoples, on the one hand, and faithfulness to the Church and the conservation of the juridical-pastoral integrity of the U.S. Church, on the other.

b. The crucial importance of reading the signs of the times and all that that implies for the Church's prophetic role in terms of speaking out against injustices and other societal ills.

c. A call for the awakening of the Catholic laity, stressing their vital contributions.

d. Putting the spotlight on the need for dedicated pastoral teams serving Hispanics.

e. Insistence on the "otherness" of the Hispanic peoples and, therefore, on the value of both similarities and differences.

f. Cultivation of support for permanent deaconate among the Hispanics.

g. A call for intensive training for Hispanic leaders, enabling them to collaborate more effectively to bring about social change and a greater cultural awareness of Hispanics.

h. Recognition of the value of the Cursillo movement, the Youth Movement, the Christian Family Movement, and the Society of Saint Vincent de Paul.

i. Acceptance of and support for Basic Ecclesial Communities.

3. Obvious weaknesses.

The First *Encuentro* had, not surprisingly, some significant weak points, some of which must be singled out here:

a. It was predominantly a clerical *Encuentro*: Of the 251 participants, 194 were clerics: bishops (8), priests (130), religious (56), making up more than 77 percent of the total. The remainder was comprised of forty-two men and fifteen women (just under 23 percent).

b. It was an *Encuentro* that spoke of inclusiveness, even though there were 182 men (just over 70 percent) and 69 women overall (less than 30 percent).

c. There was representation from throughout the country. However, given its location—Washington, DC—the Northeast was overrepresented with 151 participants, just over 60 percent of the total. The Midwest came in a distant second with thirty-four attendees; the Southwest sent eighteen participants; the Pacific Coast, fourteen; the Southeast, thirteen; and the Mountain Regions, just ten.

d. Nine states accounted for more than two-thirds of the participants, and one of them, New York, with its fifty-four delegates, represented more than one-fifth. New Jersey was next with twenty delegates; Massachusetts had nineteen; the District of Columbia, fifteen (including a number of Church officials); Florida, eleven; and Pennsylvania, ten. These figures do not accurately reflect the distribution of the Hispanic presence in the United States.

e. In the end, the First *Encuentro* failed to properly consider the pastoral needs of migrant workers, even though the subject was raised a number of times.

f. Similarly, the First *Encuentro* did not employ the principle of subsidiarity, despite discussion of that important principle of Church government.

g. Serious errors of ecclesial and disciplinary policy were in evidence as participants divided sharply over matters of Church tradition and discipline, the discussion of which clearly exceeded the competence of an assembly such as the First *Encuentro*: married priesthood, the ordination of women as deacons, the liberation of religious from their regimen of vows, the marriage of deacons who are widowers or single, and so on.

h. It was also an error—although a quite common one at the time of the First *Encuentro*—for liturgies to indulge in excess and display a lack of discipline.

i. Unfortunately, the First *Encuentro* did not achieve its goal of instituting provisions for bilingual and bicultural Catholic education.

j. Too much time was spent in the formulation of a list of excessively formal, bureaucratic petitions—most of them put forth by those who are already part of the church's institutional structure and who are not necessarily in touch with the wishes and needs of the grassroots.

k. In some cases, a certain naiveté was clearly evident, such as in the attempt to give universal application to a way of dealing with problems that is common to only Latinos and Hispanics in the United States. Nonetheless, a journey was begun—a sleeping giant was awakened.

II

THE HISTORY OF THE SECOND NATIONAL HISPANIC PASTORAL *ENCUENTRO*

Trinity College, Washington, DC (August 18–21, 1977)

1

TOWARD THE SECOND NATIONAL HISPANIC PASTORAL *ENCUENTRO*

1.1 CREATION OF THE SECRETARIAT AND CONVOCATION OF THE SECOND *ENCUENTRO*

Motivation

In the wake of the First National Hispanic Pastoral *Encuentro*, a number of critical circumstances are changing dramatically: the number of Hispanic bishops increases (from three in 1972 to eight in 1977); the Hispanic office—as part of the Department of Social Action at the bishops' conference—once dedicated principally to material assistance, is now pursuing pastoral integration, with an emphasis that includes the evangelization and education of Hispanics; the dialogue sparked by the evaluation and followup of the First *Encuentro* has prompted many bishops to embrace the Hispanic apostolate and the Hispanic people, becoming increasingly mindful of their dignity and importance.

Creation of the Secretariat (November 1974)

One of the deepest wishes of the Hispanic apostolate was for there to be a dedicated pastoral office. That was the thinking of Archbishop Robert E. Lucey when, in 1945, he established an office for Hispanics in San Antonio. In 1968, that office was for-

47

mally linked to the efforts of the National Conference of Catholic Bishops (NCCB), a move that greatly increases its scope of action.

The U.S. bishops, following a lengthy internal process, in November 1974 approves the elevation of the "Secretariat for those who speak Spanish" to become part of the "Division of Spanish-speakers," recommending the new secretariat be headed by Pablo Sedillo, Jr., who had already been working in the Division of Spanish-speakers. Subsequently, this Secretariat becomes the Secretariat for Hispanic Affairs at the NCCB/USCC.

Up and Running (January 1975)

The new Secretariat starts functioning in January 1975 and gradually begins to incorporate new staff mandated to attend to various aspects of the overall Hispanic pastoral plan. In this way, the Secretariat becomes associated with other Hispanic organizations as well as with the Regional Hispanic Centers.

Convocation of the Second Encuentro (November 1975)

Its first momentous activity, the Secretariat is responsible for presenting to the plenary session of the bishops' conference that fall all the materials that came out of the First *Encuentro*—and, thus, the case is made for a second *Encuentro*.

The U.S. bishops, meeting in November 1975, decide that the year 1976 will be dedicated to the pastoral preparation for the International Eucharistic Congress in Philadelphia held in August, an occasion at which Hispanics would be able bring to maturity their plans for a Second *Encuentro* to be held the following year.

1.2 THE HISPANIC MEETING IN PHILADELPHIA (AUGUST 3–5, 1976)

Framework of the Eucharistic Congress

Taking its cue from the pastoral decision of the bishops' conference, the Hispanic leadership wants to take full advantage of the International Eucharistic Congress. The leadership works hard to consolidate the Hispanic apostolate in the context of the spiritual renewal called for in the runup to the Congress. Hispanic leaders call for a national meeting a few days prior to the Eucharistic Congress.

Consultation with Hispanics

The National Secretariat wants to consult with its constituencies and prepares a brief questionnaire that prompts more than four thousand responses. The Regional Directors of the Hispanic Apostolate, the National Diocesan Directors of the Hispanic Apostolates, and the National Secretariat meet in Philadelphia, August 3–5, to study the research findings and make decisions accordingly.

Priorities

The meeting in Philadelphia settles two matters: first, that the priorities of the Hispanic apostolate and of the Second *Encuentro* will be will be threefold, focusing on: "Unity and Plurality," "Integral Education," and "Social Change," with the overarching goal to elicit greater respect toward Hispanic peoples; and, second, that work on each of the three priorities will be characterized by two emphases: leadership preparation and care for the young.

1.3 FIRST STEPS TOWARD THE SECOND *ENCUENTRO*

Selection of the Date

During the Congress, participants agree that the most convenient date would be the following summer in Chicago. But it is not until February 25, 1977, that Archbishop Joseph L. Bernardin of Cincinnati and now President of the NCCB definitively sets the date for the Second *Encuentro* on August 18–21, 1977, in Washington, DC, while proposing the same setting where the First *Encuentro* was held.

Constitution of the Organizing Committee

In 1976, the Committee for Hispanic Affairs names a tripartite organizing committee: it is composed of a team from the National Secretariat, the Coordinators or Regional directors, and the Directors of the Hispanic Apostolic Movements. Pablo Sedillo, Jr., director of the Secretariat, is named Coordinator. Four names are added to the leadership team: Father Edgar Beltran, Mrs. Mary T. Mahony, Father Frank Ponce, and Mr. Esteban Solis.

Regional Directors are six: Father Pedro Garcia for the West, Father Filiberto Gonzalez for the Northwest, Father Luciano Hendren for the Southwest, Mr. Mario Paredes for the Northeast, Mr. Rogelio Manrique for the Midwest, and Father Mario Vizcaino for the Southeast. Father Ricardo Ramirez from the Mexican-American Cultural Center also joins this team.

The Directors of the Hispanic Apostolic Movements are three: Father Manuel Martinez for PADRES, Sister Maria Iglesias for *Las Hermanas*, and Mr. Edward Kalbfleish for the *Cursillos de Cristiandad*.

Meeting of the Episcopal Committee (January 1977)

The Second *Encuentro* is an undertaking of the NCCB and, as such, falls under the aegis of the Episcopal Committee for Hispanic Community Affairs, presided over by Bishop James S. Rausch of Phoenix, and comprised of nine other bishops: the archbishops of Atlanta and Santa Fe; the ordinaries of Brownsville, Lafayette, and Pensacola-Tallahassee; and the auxiliary bishops of Los Angeles, San Antonio, Brooklyn, and Seattle.

Of these ten bishops, four are Hispanic: Archbishop Roberto Sanchez of Santa Fe, New Mexico; Bishop Rene H. Gracida of Pensacola-Tallahassee, Florida; Auxiliary Bishop Juan Arzube, of Los Angeles, California; and Auxiliary Patricio F. Flores of San Antonio, Texas. The meeting of the Episcopal Committee is held on January 13, 1977, in Washington, DC. It approves the preparation done so far and gives the green light to the work of the Coordinating Committee.

First Activities of the Coordinating Committee

The Coordinating Committee begins it work with great enthusiasm and immediately calls a meeting in Chicago on January 20, 1977, and another in Washington, DC, on February 4, 1977. At these two meetings, the Organizing Committee sees the benefit of holding the Second *Encuentro*, not in Chicago—as some have suggested—but in Washington, DC, in the same place where the First *Encuentro* was held. The President of the NCCB accepts the conclusions reached by the Committee and, following a rapid consultation with the Episcopal Committee, convokes the Second *Encuentro*, as noted, for the dates of August 18–21, to be held at the Trinity College in Washington, DC.

In these meetings of the Coordinating Committee, the methodology of preparation for the Second *Encuentro* was also put in place. It will hinge on a broad participation of the base, the people's views gathered and processed by the diocesan directors of the Hispanic Pastoral group.

National Meeting of Diocesan Directors of the Hispanic Apostolate (Tolentine, Illinois, February 21–24, 1977)

The Coordinating Committee and the Secretariat call a national meeting of the Diocesan Directors of the Hispanic Apostolate, which is held in Tolentine, Illinois, February 21–24, 1977. The meeting is attended by eighty-two Diocesan Directors—a significant increase, since a similar meeting preparing for the First *Encuentro* drew only thirty participants.

The meeting of the Directors has three objectives: to determine the theme of the *Encuentro*, put into action the preparation process, and take into consideration the role of the diocesan directors as well as the local church as a whole in the entire process.

The theme chosen is in agreement with the preoccupations of the universal Church, whose major concerns are underscored by the Apostolic Exhortation *Evangelii Nuntiandi* issued by Paul VI on December 8, 1975. Accordingly, the theme chosen for the Second *Encuentro* is Evangelization—to be studied in its own right and in five closely related subthemes: Ministries, Human Rights, Integral Education, Political Responsibility, and Unity in Plurality.

Each subject is to be studied in such a way as to produce concrete decisions and practical commitments.

The preparation process for the Second *Encuentro* aims for it to be an instrument for change, one that will transform the "Church of the masses" into a "Church of ecclesial base communities." The communities would be inserted into the diocesan church and also be coordinated at the regional level. These steps are meant to ensure that the Second *Encuentro* would truly be an event with national repercussions.

In the various meeting rooms, participants proclaimed that the process underway "would be a historical tool for the renewal of the Church throughout our world." That claim, surely, turns out to be an exaggeration.

No matter, undeterred in its push for the greatest possible success, the Secretariat appoints coordinators ad hoc in those regions that do not have any and the Committee begins to assign responsibilities.

1.4 MEETINGS OF THE COORDINATING COMMITTEE

First Meeting (San Antonio, March 10, 1977)

This meeting creates five operating subcommittees in charge of preparation; the theme of the Second *Encuentro* is chosen along with a hymn. The five subcommittees are designated as follows: general coordination, under Pablo Sedillo and the team from the National Secretariat; preparation of the "guides" and basic material used for consulting the grassroots, the Hispanic faithful at large, falls under Rogelio Manrique and the Midwest region; hospitality, under Mario Paredes and the Northeast region; communication and press, under Mario Vizcaino and the Southeast region; and liturgy and music are taken on by Pedro Garcia and the Western region, with the collaboration of the Southwest and Northwest regions.

The Northeast region, as host, is also called upon to set up six other complementary subcommittees: these will oversee welcome and reception arrangements, transport, first aid, social mixers, decoration, and exhibitions.

The theme chosen for the Second *Encuentro* is: "God's people are on the move." Echoing this theme, the composition of Emilio Vicente Mateu titled *Un Pueblo que Camina* ("A People who are on the Move") is chosen as the official hymn of the Second *Encuentro*. Fittingly, the composition expresses the significance of humanity journeying toward transcendence, along with a strong sense of social commitment. The hymn pays tribute to a driving force for "another city that lives on without end, without regret or sadness, an eternal city"—precisely the ambition of the second *Encuentro*.

Second Meeting (Chicago, May 3, 1977)

This meeting revises the work of the operating subcommittees and Father Frank Ponce of the Diocese of San Diego begins serving as Special Coordinator of the Second *Encuentro*. Additional minor subcommittees are created, and rules and procedures are put in place with regard to the participation and voting of the different "classes" of attendees. The First *Encuentro* had brought together 250 participants; the Second *Encuentro* is at first expected to double that number, to some five hundred. In the end, logistics are overwhelmed as the number of participants reaches twelve hundred.

The Coordinating Committee gets a sense of the number of people participating in the consultation process—they number more than one hundred thousand. Their diverse voices are channeled through the offices of the Hispanic apostolate in some one hundred dioceses, and further coordinated in six regions. The process is not perfect or always precise, but the results are quite interesting, giving organizers a good sense of the wishes, demands, and longings percolating at the grassroots level in the Hispanic Catholic community.

Third Meeting (Washington, July 5–6, 1977)

This meeting was held at Trinity College, which will be the site of the Second *Encuentro*. Participants finalize the agenda for the

Encuentro, allotting time for speakers and activities and assigning the many tasks involved in running the event. A count is made of the number of ecclesiastical dignitaries who have promised to attend. The participation of observers is unanimously embraced, with the stipulation that they can participate in the workshops but without voting power. By contrast, official delegates will have both the right to speak, and to vote in the workshops and during the plenary sessions. Three additional subcommittees are created, those overseeing the agenda, credentials, and rules of order.

In addition, the Secretariat takes on the responsibility to seek a site for the plenary sessions, while the hospitality subcommittee continues with its myriad preparations. The liturgy subcommittee is in charge of efficiently distributing all the material for the liturgical celebrations and the singing of hymns that will be part of the Second *Encuentro*. Finally, the Secretariat commits to publishing a bilingual edition of the Conclusions of the Second *Encuentro*. The members of the Coordinating Committee agree that remaining details will not require another meeting but can be handled by phone. (Needless to add, this was the pre-email era!)

2

THE PREPARATION PROCESS FOR THE SECOND *ENCUENTRO*

2.1 THE "GUIDES"

The Idea of the "Guides"

In order to reach the grassroots, the Coordinating Committee gives the green light to the production of a series of six "guides" in both Spanish and English, employing a user-friendly formula that relies on cartoon-style drawings, simple text frames, "slogans," pithy recapitulations of material, and simple questionnaires. From an artistic and methodological viewpoint, the guides are warmly received and contribute a great deal to the preparation of the Second *Encuentro*. However, it must be noted that—though their content is theologically correct, in general—the guides show a strong bias toward the Basic Ecclesiastical Communities, which they are clearly designed to strengthen.

That said, creators of the guides deserve a lot of praise. These materials have great pastoral value regardless of how they are used; given the generally weak state of the faithful's theological knowledge, the guides are used to awaken the faith and commitment of Hispanic members of parishes at large. Friendly in tone and highly accessible, the guides can play an important role in the catechesis of adults. An introductory guide introduces the others, describing the process and providing instructions on the methodology.

Guide 1, on Evangelization

This is the largest folder (twenty pages). It begins with an important question: What does Christ want from Hispanics in the Church? The Church is not some kind of supermarket of beliefs and rituals, nor is it just a building, and it consists of more than just the bishop, the priests, and the nuns. Rather, the answer is given, the Church comprises the Christian "people"; it is the voice of those who have no voice; it is leaven. Indeed, the Hispanic people—as the people of God on the move—should stir things up in the world in order to make it a better place. The Church should be a liberating force, following Christ as its example. It is a Church of the poor and a poor Church. It is an ecumenical Church, a Church of laypeople who pray and celebrate. It is a small and fraternal Church, comprised of the Basic Ecclesial Communities through which Hispanics are united even as they form part of the pluralism of the Church in the United States.

In fact, this guide says more about ecclesiology than evangelization, but it quotes abundantly from Paul VI's *Evangelii Nuntiandi* and seeks to make a comparison between yesterday's pastoral approach (preconciliar) and today's (conciliar). The purpose of this guide is to spark action with regard to the double need of Hispanics to both preserve their identity and to integrate in North American society. Logically, the guide looks on so-called Hispanic popular religiosity as a tool of cultural integration as it can make a contribution to Anglo Church culture.

Guide 2, on Ministries

This is a folder of typical size, eight pages long. It presents the notion of the Church as servant, a Church serving a people of God constantly on the move, requiring diversified ministries, each of which helps in the building up of the community. The most important task of this guide is to make the reader think about which services the community needs most, and in what way someone needs to dedicate or consecrate himself or herself to provide those services.

Guide 3, on Human Rights

This one also has eight pages and carries a strong message: it insists on the North American tradition of freedom and respect for human rights, which, the text notes, has been frequently violated. It reminds the reader about some of the anchoring articles from the Universal Declaration of Human Rights. These are held up in sharp contrast with the many injustices and acts of discrimination around the world. The guide holds each individual responsible for combating injustice wherever it is found.

The guide underscores the violation of the human rights of certain groups: Hispanic women, migrant farm workers, undocumented persons, prisoners, the elderly, Hispanic youth, and the disabled. It sets forth the general principle that all people have the same rights, because God has created all human beings equal as brothers and sisters in Christ.

Guide 4, on Integral Education

In eight pages, this guide presents the current educational system as a form of domestication that lays the groundwork for the "North American way of life"—a way of life that, the guide argues, in its optimism ignores many situations of capitalistic exploitation by the United States in Latin America. As an alternative, the guide presents a broader cultural concept of education for the benefit of Hispanics: one that is bilingual and bicultural and that hinges on the humanistic concept of integral education—education of the "whole" person—its principles linked to the kind of liberating education and formation that are part of the Church's mission.

Guide 5, on Political Responsibility

This folder opens with the Preamble of the U.S. Constitution and the principle that no one can shirk political involvement. Building on that concept, the guide defends a policy of participation based on the role of the Church in the political order, as specifically underscored by Pope John XXIII and the Bishops' Synod on Justice in 1971.

Guide 6, on Unity in Plurality

This is the last folder, which starts with a historical fact: that the United States is an ethnically mixed society, but one in which some groups have not been adequately integrated. This includes Hispanics, who themselves form a mosaic of peoples and traditions. They share the same language, some of the same attitudes toward life, a similar colonial past, says the guide, and a similar experience of exploitation and marginalization at the hands of the United States. Yet each Hispanic group is different as regards their country of origin, each of which has its own history following independence from Spain; their own systems of government and societal organization; their different histories of Church-state relations, and so on. The guide also notes that Hispanic migrants differ greatly in relation to their counterparts of urban or rural origin, particularly when it comes to education and economic means.

2.2 REGIONAL CONCLUSIONS

As part of the process of preparation for the Second *Encuentro*, each of the various regions hold local *Encuentros*. The deliberations reach some noteworthy conclusions.

The Northwest

On the subject of evangelization, six conclusions are drawn: the need for pastoral training of laypersons; the need for bilingual and bicultural training for the priests and lay leaders; the importance of making more use of modern communications media, and the need to produce more specific cultural resource material; establishment of mobile evangelization teams; the need for Hispanic priests and bishops steeped in Hispanic culture; the establishment of diocesan offices in charge of Hispanic affairs; and the creation of a regional Hispanic pastoral center.

The subject of ministries produced a number of conclusions, including, naturally, a call for more deacons and youth ministers. Interestingly, participants also request female catechists and insist on their bilingual and bicultural preparation; another innovation comes in the form of a call for the training of parents as youth ministers. In some cases, canon law is challenged, as in the call for women deacons.

The topic of Human Rights sparks several sharp calls to action, in particular, support for illegal immigrants, the elderly, the disabled, as well as the unemployed and those requiring medical care. Participants insist that education about these issues is provided to the community at large. There is also a call for the defense of the Spanish language and the right of Hispanic Catholics to practice their faith on Sundays. Finally, the text insists on the right to vote and express support for the unionization or organization otherwise of migrant farm workers.

With regard to Integral Education, six conclusions point to the need for bilingual and bicultural education; the importance of fairness in the distribution of scholarships and the appointment of Hispanic counselors and teachers; the need to overcome all forms of discrimination; the urgency of recognizing the value of Hispanic culture; the need for bilingual and bicultural personnel committed to both the parochial and public schools; and the demand that the clergy assume responsibility for the provision of integral education.

As regards Political Responsibility, participants call for more education on the subject; point at the need to build support for the election of Hispanic representatives and the creation of a stronger political block; stress the importance of voting; and insist on the strengthening of the political role of women and the encouragement of their political self-consciousness.

Finally, concerning Unity in Plurality, there is the general proclamation that unity in the faith is needed to encourage Hispanics helping one another to gain benefits for the entire Hispanic community. Other conclusions deal with the defense of Mexican identity, including a call for the Church to fight for its recognition as well as for the promotion of Mexican traditions. Participants note, however, that a Mexican majority need not result in the exclusion of other minorities, whether Hispanic or not, in parish life or in society at large.

The Far West

Regarding Evangelization, this regional *Encuentro* insists that three significant parameters be established: evangelization initiatives should carry to every Christian a message of integral freedom, a process in which both laity and religious participate alongside bishops and priests; plus, evangelization efforts must support Hispanic culture and employ the Spanish language. Finally, pointing at the lack of notoriety and influence of Basic Ecclesiastical Communities as ideal tools of evangelization, participants call for more creative and assertive use of the media. The region reaches five conclusions on the subject of Ministries: each baptized person has the obligation to be a minister according to his or her abilities; deacons should be properly trained, just as the community must learn about the deacon's role (ideally, each local Hispanic community will have its own deacon); the immediate priority of every minister is his own family, which he cannot disregard; farm workers, especially migrants, also need their dedicated deacons and ministers as well as missionary programs; lastly, participants insist that youth should be ministering to youth and must receive the proper training to be able to do so.

When it comes to Human Rights, the deliberations conclude with a few strong recommendations: the Church should celebrate and make known human rights, while strongly denouncing instances of their violation; pressure and lobby groups should be formed to denounce the support of dictators worldwide who receive U.S. support; finally, participants hold up three priority areas: appreciation and use of the prophetic voice of youth; service to undocumented workers and immigrants; and, controversially, relief from "oppression by the ecclesiastical hierarchy."

Integral Education is tackled as follows: participants point at Hispanics' lack of access to it; there is mention of the general lack of awareness of the benefits of a multicultural education; and the need for Catholic schools to support it. The text calls for Catholic education to be bilingual and of the highest quality.

With regard to Political Responsibility, participants insist that politics be an instrument for justice and serve the interests of the poor; they charge that the political system of the United States does not favor Hispanic participation. They point, however, at a number of Hispanic political groups in California that are meeting with some success: *Hermandad Mexicana* in Los Angeles, *Mecha* in Oakland, *Raza Unida* in San Francisco, *Mapa* in Fresno, *Lulac* in Orange, and Chicano Federations and *Campesinos Unidos* in San Diego.

The text calls for the creation of a lobbying group in Washington, DC, the establishment of local groups to provide political education to the parishes, the pursuit of national coalitions with other minorities, a get-out-the-vote campaign, funding for the candidates' campaigns, political training in the family setting, the organization of training centers, the organization of political groups comprised of parents, and the offering of classes on political and social leadership.

Regarding pluralism, this region makes four observations and recommendations: Hispanics are a diverse population, yet they want to maintain their general culture and language; the Church should offer Spanish-language programs for children and youth; Hispanics want to retain their own religious traditions—and unity with and within the rest of the Church depends on taking action.

The Midwest

Concerning Evangelization, participants proclaim that evangelization involves presenting Christ in a particular cultural context, triggering a process of growth in and toward full freedom. Success will depend on improving the education of adults and youth through training centers, and intensifying the spread of the knowledge and appreciation of Hispanic culture among non-Hispanics. The text calls on the institutional Church to better understand the Hispanic mentality as well as the risks of Hispanic Catholics being exposed to the proselytizing efforts of other Christian churches and denominations, and demands a careful review of the Hispanic movements to help prevent the movements from closing in on themselves.

Ministries, participants insist, should spring out of the commandment to love, a perspective that leads to the proposal of three policies: the formation of small ecclesial communities; the selection of candidates for the priesthood and other pastoral duties hinging on the candidates' identification with the community; and the creation of innovative formation programs, including an overall pastoral approach that promotes vocations among young people.

The importance of Human Rights is understood as springing out of the U.S. Constitution in four areas: on the social front, the Church should continue to struggle against discrimination; come out in favor of fair wages and proper rest for field workers; insist on respectful treatment of those without documents; and call for respect for Hispanic women, elderly, and youth. On the economic front, the Church should lend its weight to the creation of employment agencies, the development of programs for residences and scholarships for Hispanics, along with other provisions—all efforts supported with Spanish-language information. With regard to Education, participants demand that bilingual and multicultural education be provided in both Catholic and public schools, and that adults out in the fields or workplace also receive educational opportunities. Finally, when it comes to inner Church initiatives, participants recommend intensive programs designed to broaden knowledge about the Hispanic people—including Spanish-language courses and classes on various subjects—all as a means of overcoming discrimination.

To ensure success, participants argue that responsibilities be properly distributed: the bishops' conference should seek funds to facilitate integral bilingual and multicultural education that relies on adequate pedagogical resources and Hispanic personnel; the Hispanic community should commit itself to a greater participation in political decisions and the granting of scholarships. Much is made of staff at all levels being properly trained, which sparks a call on the state to make funds available for an increase in the number of Hispanic teachers.

Political Responsibility can only be properly exercised, participants reason, if the bishops provide adequate preparation to Hispanics, giving them the tools to support coalitions and help establish and enforce plans of affirmative action. There must also be adequate meeting places, which the Church can help provide. Participants insist that Hispanics should not allow themselves to be intimidated; what will make them strong in this regard is if they are well informed, present at election rallies and ready to vote, and well aware of the differences between candidates.

The region proposes two measures that are not legally viable: that legal residents be allowed to vote in local matters; and that legal residents be allowed to take certain government jobs. However, there are also proposals to speed up the naturalization process for legal residents. There is a reminder that Christians have the duty to care for migrants—a task that lends itself well to ecumenical efforts.

The section on Unity in Plurality starts with the proclamation that Hispanics feel proud of their identity and heritage. This leads to four recommendations: that every Hispanic have the opportunity to develop his or her cultural identity; that dioceses and other Church institutions promote interchange and dialogue with groups that have expertise in cultural pluralism; that popular religiosity be encouraged; and that the family be strongly supported in the conservation of its values.

The Southeast

This region starts with upholding a model of the Church as promoted through Evangelization: A Church that stands united is poor, is community-based, and has a missionary focus. There is a call to create a Hispanic center for pastoral research and for planning efforts at the regional level; such a center would be looked to for the formation of mobile pastoral teams and the organization of various pastoral and theological courses. The text proposes to create a Hispanic Apostolate Center in every diocese; these centers would have the mandate to encourage the deployment of bilingual and bicultural priests; make available basic catechesis in Spanish; engage with Hispanic apostolic movements; maintain contact with CELAM; and, last but not least, develop a strategy to enhance the awareness of Hispanic issues and culture on the part of non-Hispanics. Finally, there is a call for greater Hispanic representation at all levels of Church government.

The Church also should encourage Basic Ecclesial Communities, the text declares, as well as pastoral work in the service of migrant

farm workers, which could even include specially appointed ministries. These, moreover, should avoid all forms of paternalism.
Participants also call for other kinds of specialized pastoral work,
such as initiatives serving interparochial urban settings, prisons,
healthcare facilities, marriage preparation programs, divorced
people, missionary territory, and military personnel.

Concerning Ministries, the region proposes the creation of a
Pastoral Center that helps the Church make more effective use of
communication media; that assists the apostolic movements; that
supports the family, with special care for dysfunctional families;
that facilitates pastoral work in prisons and hospitals; and that
helps sustain sacramental pastoral work.

This approach implies the strong endorsement of contributions made by the laity; it insists on a distinct leadership quality
on the part of someone taking on a key role, including that of permanent deacon. Similarly, participants insist on support for work
with youth, including the promotion of vocations, which requires
a particular pastoral strategy.

Human Rights are viewed from a prophetic perspective. On the
practical level, this means that more energy must be put in the
dissemination of the Church's social teaching, that justice and
peace commissions be established, that undocumented workers
be granted amnesty, and that more resources must be made available to meet the needs of migrant workers.

There is also a proposal for the establishment of Regional
Centers offering leadership training with regard to calling attention to the plight of migrant workers. There is a call for Hispanics
to act in solidarity with six other minorities subject to various
forms of suffering: women, farm workers, political prisoners, the
elderly, those who are exploited by pornography, and those who
are denied the right to life (through abortion and euthanasia).

As concerns Integral Education, participants reaffirm the vocation of the Church as educator, alongside a reminder to the family to be aware of its primary responsibility to educate children.
Education should be, in all instances, bilingual and bicultural,
including, if not especially, the education offered to migrant farm
workers. The current system of educational policy falls short, the
participants charge. They call on dioceses to make better use of

the means of social communication—for example, by considering the model of the so-called radio schools of Colombia and Honduras.

Political Responsibility, participants declare, is a moral obligation incumbent on all members of the community—but there is a great need for Regional Centers to provide the appropriate formation. There is a call for encouraging Hispanics to become U.S. citizens, the support of honest Hispanic candidates, and the promotion of much-needed legislative changes. Participants propose the creation of committees for the dissemination of Hispanic values and the highlighting of those aspects of the political process that favor Hispanic participation. In that light, there is a call for the establishment of relations with organizations that promote Hispanic participation in the political process, such as Aspira, Image C.N.P.C., and others.

Concerning Unity in Plurality, the region is aware that there is a right to evangelize and to be evangelized in ways that are consonant with Hispanic culture, which includes Hispanic liturgical celebrations and specific Hispanic pastoral work to promote vocations. The integration in the dominant society is necessary, speakers argue, but this should not take the form of mere assimilation; the role of the means of social communication is crucial on that front, to keep the focus on crucial aspects of Hispanic culture and identity—but without letting the experience of one particular Hispanic people impose itself on other Hispanic national groups.

The Northeast

These participants view the evangelization process as best initiated in small communities, which should be encouraged, and its activities coordinated—with the clear understanding that young people are especially crucial for the Church's future and that they are a pastoral priority. There is a call for particular respect for and understanding of popular culture and piety; this means that all bishops must have an adequate formation when it comes to the values of Hispanic culture, including the crucial role played by young people. Here, as on so many other fronts, creative and assertive use of the media is crucial. Specifically, there is a demand for Hispanics' access—particularly the laity—to all levels of ecclesiastical responsibility. The Director of the Hispanic Apostolate, if he is a priest, should be an Episcopal Vicar. Moreover, clergy with a strong record of advocating on behalf of Hispanic concerns should be named bishops.

As regards Ministries in this region, participants uphold the premise that each one of the faithful should serve according to his or her gifts. They request that bishops be named who understand Hispanic matters and that special ministries be instituted to meet the needs of Hispanic Catholics—above all, youth, migrant workers, and the undocumented.

The region proposes that efforts concentrate, in particular, on the training of permanent deacons as well as the ministries of the Word and the Eucharist; women are said to be eligible for a full ministerial role. Youth should be organized and be the subject of pastoral planning; the same goes for other special groups: migrant workers, the divorced, the elderly, the infirm, prisoners, white-collar workers, students, prostitutes, gay people, and the disabled.

As regards Human Rights, participants call on the Church to do all in its power to defend these rights—particularly with regard to education, which will depend on the appointment of capable, qualified personnel. There is also a request that the Church train personnel for pastoral work in prisons and jails.

Concerning Integral Education, participants argue that bilingual and bicultural education are key for gaining access to the hearts and minds of Hispanics—provided there is no push for assimilation. In this regard, parents have a crucial role in shaping and maintaining Hispanic identity in the home. This region demands careful supervision of educational programs and the promotion of Spanish-language teaching, in particular. Closely linked to this orientation is the participants' proposal that Hispanics achieve an influential presence in the media, using them as a tool to create Hispanic coalitions for social and political purposes. The Church is encouraged to lobby the government for economic assistance to fund these various educational efforts benefiting Hispanics.

Participants also reflect on the right of the Church to expound its social doctrine to everyone, including the government. North

American democracy, they say, is in theory a framework that would allow Hispanics full political participation—but Hispanics need training in order to be able to occupy leadership positions; and all Christians must back this effort; the task ahead calls for research, marketing and promotion, and resources—all for the sake of appointing excellent teachers.

Finally, the region believes that authorities should provide facilities that would allow for the maintenance of Hispanic culture, and that pastoral work should embrace the ethnic-cultural pluralism that is characteristic of Hispanic believers. Participants call for annual folklore festivals that will do justice to the rich Hispanic cultural mosaic. Also, they say, bishops and their priests must give Hispanics a voice at the diocesan and parish level that corresponds to their numerical presence in the local church.

The Mexican-American Cultural Center (MACC)

Recommendations from MACC target three areas: Education, Human Rights, and Ministries. First, on the educational front, those who are going to do pastoral work among Hispanics should receive adequate training—which must be more than being able to speak Spanish; it also requires being able to appreciate and celebrate Hispanic culture. In addition, MACC officials say that Hispanics should be recruited as professors and administrative staff in seminaries and centers for leadership training, and all educational programs should feature appropriate bilingual material. There is a call for additional funds to support the training of those who will work with Hispanics; and religious formation, the officials add, should be provided in the mother tongue; furthermore, Hispanic seminarians should opt for study at regional seminaries, which gives them the best opportunity to develop tailored training programs.

Concerning Human Rights, MACC officials argue that the development and building up of a sense of Hispanic dignity should take the place of—or at least complement—programs of public assistance; homilies and catechesis should feature the social doctrine of the Church. There is a proposal that the U.S. bishops lobby the government for the abrogation of the "Right to

Work" law and the guarantee of the right of every person to choose his or his residence wherever adequate living conditions are found.

Concerning Ministries, the center recommends that the bishops and liturgical commissions become more flexible with regard to Hispanic liturgies, and that parish priests speed up the process of the formation of small communities and show greater regard for the competence of parish councils. Similarly, it is recommended that deacons avoid succumbing to new forms of clericalism; that Mother Superiors give Hispanic religious the option to work with Hispanics; and that they accept the basic document on popular religiosity as being relevant for pastoral work targeting Hispanics in the Southeast, New Mexico, and California.

2.3 THE WORKING DOCUMENT

Based on the recommendations of the regional groups, a six-part Working Document is put together that synthesizes and organizes the rich array of suggestions.

Evangelization

This section has four chapters: the introduction, reflections on the small communities, perspectives on Hispanic culture, and an elaboration on those who are to be reached through evangelization. The introduction is a call to conversion so that the Church might be united, poor, and also be community- and missionary-minded. The chapter on the small communities expresses their value, but here authors employ a controversial ecclesiological principle: the argument is made that it is somehow inherent in the kingdom of God that it must be initiated in small groups. A more mainstream approach to that mysterious process does not use such concrete language. For example, data from the New Testament—keeping in mind the limitations of speaking in such terms—speaks of mass conversions, such as the three thousand said to have been converted at Pentecost (Acts 2:41) and the five thousand converts mentioned in Acts 4:4.

The Working Document proposes a pastoral plan that coordinates key initiatives across the board: the formation of an interregional mobile team, and greater and more efficient communication between key groups. There is mention of the goal of breaking down parochial, diocesan, and regional church jurisdiction barriers. But this would be hard to square with Canon Law, except in the cases of personal prelacies, diocesan-wide rites, and military ordinariates. Not surprisingly, there also is an exhortation on the crucial role of Hispanic youth.

The document then proceeds to discuss Hispanic culture, arguing that the institutional Church should take it into greater account. It proposes the creation of additional Regional Centers that can provide stepped-up training for Hispanic leaders, with a focus on promoting the use of communication media and offering courses on pastoral renewal. In those dioceses where there are a significant number of Hispanics, the document argues, there should be local training centers. Hispanic bishops and priests should be involved in their native culture, and popular religiosity should be cherished. Indeed, there is a call for the promotion of Hispanic culture among non-Hispanic clergy and laity as well. Finally, there is a firm demand for the promotion of dialogue with CELAM.

The last part of this section on Evangelization refers to those served by pastoral efforts. Here, the—admittedly problematic—creation of an ordinariate is requested to specifically serve farm workers. There is also a call for increased pastoral initiatives serving prisons, hospitals, engaged couples, divorced persons, missionaries, and the military.

Ministries

This section of the Working Document opens with a chapter on the calling of all the faithful to participate in the Church's ministry. This given, this reality should lead to the formation of small ecclesial communities with their own leaders; an accompanying recognition of the value of the laity, including their ministerial abilities; insistence on the ordination of more Hispanics as permanent deacons; and respect for the role of women and other ministries; as well as recognition of the competence and duties of parochial councils.

The introduction concludes with a request for the appointment of more Hispanic bishops, more bishops who understand Hispanics, more Hispanic priests who are committed to their heritage and people, and more Hispanic religious who want to work with Hispanics.

The second chapter bears the title "Selection and Training of Ministers." It spells out the requirement that candidates for ministry have a good reputation; that they identify with the community they are to serve; that their family commitments be respected; and that their candidacy be considered without regard to age, sex, or educational level. Their training should be bilingual and multicultural. Clearly, the text insists, this effort requires an education of all the Hispanic people.

The third chapter tackles pastoral work serving youth, saying it must be dynamic and proactive, well-planned, and focused like a true ministry. There is a call for youth to have their own leadership, the creation of a youth organization, and the promotion of a broad-based youth pastorate. The chapter also stipulates that young people should have their own workshop at the Second *Encuentro*.

The fourth chapter deals with special ministries, such as those serving families and migrant workers. There is a call for Hispanic liturgy to enjoy greater flexibility and an endorsement of the demand that the basic document on popular religiosity, as approved by the Southeast, New Mexico, and California, be accepted across the board. The chapter ends by repeating a list of pastoral challenges, such as service to the divorced, elderly, retired, undocumented, sick, imprisoned, and so on.

Human Rights

In a brief introduction, this chapter recalls the obligation of all people to defend human rights. Specifically, there is a call for the protection of the undocumented—along with a plea for a highly unlikely general amnesty; better care for migrant workers, including fair wages, medical care, nondiscrimination, the right to organize and to rest, freedom to practice their religion, and so on. The Church is called upon to establish Commissions of Justice and Peace that are to become active in this domain and to provide these commissions with proper funding. Finally, there is another call for the establishment of Regional Centers that provide leadership training.

The next chapter opens with what is called a prophetic call for the awakening of people's awareness of all forms of oppression, including the injustice involved in U.S. support for Latin American dictators. More stipulations are made for pastoral work in prisons, in defense of women, against the pornographic exploitation of children, to protect life from beginning to end, and to serve the needs of the poor.

There is also a section dealing with human rights in the economic and social spheres. It calls for the creation of specialized centers that offer workshops and training to help raise the public's awareness of the most important issues in this area. The following chapter deals with the right to adequate bilingual and multicultural education, both in public and in Catholic schools. The Church, it is proclaimed, should even guarantee the education of Hispanic adults and provide classes teaching English and information about human rights.

The final chapter concerns intra-ecclesial affairs and requests that evangelization efforts be in Spanish and that all discrimination against Hispanics be eliminated. Here, too, is an insistence on establishing intensive programs tackling Hispanic culture, the preaching and dissemination of Catholic social doctrine, and the establishment of Hispanic vocational programs and Spanish-language courses in the seminaries. Finally, there is a call for the proportional increase of Hispanics at all levels of the Church's institutional structure.

Integral Education

This section of the Working Document is divided into six parts: the first sets the overall goal and insists on bilingual and multicultural education and what is loosely called a dimension of "liberationism." These overall demands are presented as remedies for the still dominant approach to the education of Hispanics that aims strictly at assimilation.

The second part makes recommendations in four key areas: programs, supervision, personnel, and funds. Concerning programs, there is a call for public, private, and parochial schools and preschools to be established in a manner that is firm and stable, setting students on a steady course—from primary school onward to secondary school and the university level, in addition to adult education. There is also a call to establish schools near the fields where the migrant workers are laboring, a petition for a program of political education, and the demand for a plan to study new educational models. Concerning supervision, there is the insistence that public and Catholic schools offer bilingual and multicultural programs. With reference to personnel, there is mention of the need for the recognition of a special vocation for educators who value Hispanic culture and bilingual education. There is a call for more Hispanic counselors and teachers as well as for the development and growth of exchanges on the educational front with Latin America.

Finally, with regard to funding, the text calls for fairness and equality in the distribution of scholarships and the appointment of specialized personnel to help Hispanics to identify resources and to make sure that state-mandated funds be appropriated to increase the number of Hispanic educators.

The third part refers to the responsibility of the Church and requests that the Catholic schools establish multicultural programs, just as public schools are doing. The Church is asked to lobby for changes at the federal, state, and municipal levels so that some public funds will be available to Catholic schools; clergy are called to commit themselves to this ideal.

In addition, there are a series of recommendations pertaining to the training of seminarians and other personnel who will work with Hispanics (again, there is the premium put on bilingual education, appreciation and study of Hispanic culture, regional Hispanic seminaries, and so on.).

The fourth part deals with religious education for Hispanics. The bishops' conference is petitioned to provide funds and the necessary Hispanic personnel. This would allow dioceses and parishes to promote religious education in Spanish as well as enable Church-run communication media to contribute to the effort.

The fifth part deals with parents' responsibility, insisting that they must emphasize Hispanic identity, the values and customs of their culture, as well as their own religious practices. The creation of Hispanic school clubs is suggested, along with the building up of community life and so on, and the overall facilitation of parents' effective participation in school programs. Among other suggestions, the Hispanic community is called upon to provide scholarships to outstanding students.

The sixth and final part deals with means of social communication—the media—and proposes that a more influential media presence be built in the interest of Hispanics; such efforts would help form and sustain "Hispanic coalitions" backed by the diocese, and would be capable of offering adequate media content that disseminates Christian values, such as is done by the so-called radio schools of Colombia and Honduras. Asking for the impossible, there is a demand that migrant farm workers get their own radio and television programming as well as their own periodical.

Political Responsibility

The Working Document opens this section recognizing the democracy of the United States—adding, however, that, due to discrimination, the lack of training and the absence of leadership, the Hispanic community is relegated to the margins of society.

The text then insists on certain conditions for political participation. For example, Hispanic candidates should be honest and responsible; political figures (Hispanic or otherwise) should be competent and charismatic; legislation should favor the human person; citizenship should be a prime concern of all people; a Hispanic political block should be formed; the rights of women should be insisted upon; parents should create alliances among themselves; and Hispanics should not allow themselves to be intimidated in the political arena.

The text also calls for Hispanics' political training and education, insisting that the Church commit itself to this process by organizing diocesan and parochial centers or schools to train Hispanics;

requiring that key political documents be promoted and disseminated at a popular level; and providing meeting places for Hispanics to study the political process. The text also calls on Hispanic organizations to offer classes in political leadership.

The fourth point deals with the responsibility of the Church to facilitate the active participation of Hispanics in the political process. This could take the form of helping build coalitions of the faithful at all levels; to help particular groups petition the government on behalf of affirmative action, for example; and to put the institutional power of promotion behind such efforts. Especially with regard to easing the plight of migrant workers, the Church should act in unison with other denominations, the text says, and seek contact with existing Hispanic organizations.

The fifth and final point addresses the right to vote. On this score, there is, again, a request for something legally unthinkable in the United States: that all legal residents should have the right to vote, at least with regard to local issues. In addition, the text takes up the request for the promotion of programs that encourage naturalization and calls for campaigns to seek to allow legal residents to be employed in certain government jobs.

Unity in Plurality

The final section of the Working Document begins with a declaration reaffirming Hispanic identity in the context of full integration, while rejecting all forms of assimilation. The text expresses the hope that this proposal will be accepted by the Church at all levels. Each Hispanic group has a right to its own identity, the text argues; non-Hispanics should be exposed to Hispanic cultural history; and dialogue should be established with groups that advocate on behalf of other minorities.

Second, there is a reference to "unity among plurality" as characteristic of the Hispanic community at large, a dimension that should be encouraged, the text says, adding that Hispanic unity hinges, among other things, on popular religiosity. Finally, there is reference to the family as the source and guardian of the deepest Hispanic values.

3

THE SECOND NATIONAL HISPANIC PASTORAL *ENCUENTRO*

3.1 GENERAL ASSEMBLY ELEMENTS OF THE SECOND *ENCUENTRO*

*Convocation by Archbishop
Joseph L. Bernardin*

On February 25, 1977, Archbishop Joseph L. Bernardin of Cincinnati, President of the National Conference of Catholic Bishops of the United States (NCCB/USCC), delivers the official convocation for the Second *Encuentro*.

A highlight of the inauguration ceremony, the Convocation is a beautiful address, which the prelate begins by underscoring the honor granted him as President of the Episcopal Conference to sponsor a Second *Encuentro*—five years after the First *Encuentro* that had given such a great boost to Hispanics, creating a variety of new structures and greatly increasing sensitivity toward Hispanic issues.

Considering the needs of the moment, the archbishop says, he is happy that the theme of evangelization has been chosen, giving to this Second *Encuentro* a distinct and unique character. It will confront a number of practical problems, he adds, saying this is not only appropriate but necessary. What will distinguish the Second *Encuentro*, in particular, proclaims the archbishop, is the dimension of faith in Jesus Christ and the faithful's identification with him through baptism—according to Galatians 3:36–39.

That same idea that was elaborated by Saint Paul, the prelate continues, is presented by the Pope in his encyclical concerning evangelization, which proclaims that salvation in Jesus is at the center of the Christian message (*Evangelii Nuntiandi* 27).

The Church's message of liberation should be preached in light of that perspective, the archbishop says, and the Catholic community should do everything possible, in accordance with the demands of justice, to help all those who are marginalized. This effort, according to the prelate, cannot be separated from the Gospel, just as Paul VI said (see *EN* 34).

On the other hand, Hispanic culture and tradition are a gift for the Church, contributing to its rich diversity, adds Archbishop Bernardin. All too familiar with suffering, Hispanics have faced injustices and have had to expend considerable efforts to make known their presence and their needs, he says; this has created tensions, but what Hispanics have done shows their faith and love for the Church, the archbishop insists. Society, he proclaims, needs the testimony of Hispanic Catholics, their respect for life, love for the family, their human warmth, and devotion—and especially their great love for the Virgin Mary.

Just as Saint Paul prayed for the Philippians (see Phil 1:9–11), Archbishop Bernardin asks that the present deliberations may bear mature fruit, and that the Lord complete the work that he has begun in the participants of the Second *Encuentro*.

The prelate assures his hearers that all the bishops have a great love for Hispanics and see their own role as Paul saw his own task to Titus (see Titus 1:7–9): they want to be near, to encourage and to support. It is in that spirit that the archbishop formally convokes the Second *Encuentro*, asking the Lord to bless its work.

Welcome by Bishop James S. Rausch

The bishop of Phoenix and president of the Episcopal Committee for Hispanic Affairs, in a brief welcoming address, emphasizes that "no subject could be more appropriate at this time than the one you have chosen": evangelization. He expresses gratitude for the efforts of the Coordinating Committee and prays that, as the Second *Encuentro* begins, everyone will pursue unity in Christ as their overriding objective. The bishop acknowledges that difficult and sensitive subjects are on the table, insisting that participants, as did the leaders of the ancient Church, show that they love one another. This search for solutions implies sacrifice, the bishop says, and all involved must work with patience, avoid fragmentation, overcome all pride, and try to find the best way to serve God.

Therefore, concludes Bishop Rausch, these days of the Second *Encuentro* should, in the first place, be days of prayer and constant petition for the presence of the Spirit.

Address by Pablo Sedillo, Jr.

The Director of the Secretariate for Hispanic Matters of the NCCB and President of the Coordinating Committee of the Second *Encuentro* gives a motivational speech.

He emphasizes that the effort to get to know so many brothers and sisters from throughout the country is very worthwhile. Seeing them, he says, is like contemplating the face of Christ, wearied by his travels. The heart of everyone is filled with love, there is no rancor—all want to work for a better world, says Sedillo, and all those present are committed. The speaker notes that many are delegates from local Churches, that others are observers, and that there are even some bishops from Latin America.

The difficulties are nothing compared to the response, insists Sedillo. He proclaims to be a witness to the dedication of so many, reporting that many bishops have stimulated the process; that diocesan committees have spared nothing; that the various regions have communicated their conclusions; and that their meetings have been a true anticipation of the fellowship of the Second *Encuentro*.

Pablo Sedillo is visibly moved and gives thanks to God, saying he sees many sacrifices now crowned with success. He is sure that nothing obscures the image built up from the base of the Church, from the grassroots. The voice of that base will not be distorted, he declares. Surely, his talk is emotional if not substantive. His speech is committed to the by now familiar scheme of things, in line with a very particular theological and pastoral outlook.

Message of the Holy Father Paul VI

Bishop Thomas C. Kelly, OP, Titular Bishop of Tusuro and General Secretary of the NCCB—who had been consecrated on August 15, just three days before the opening of the Second *Encuentro*—has the task of introducing the greetings that the Holy Father delivers to those participating via a recorded message. The pope expresses his joy that the diverse aspects of evangelization have been chosen as the theme for reflection at the Second *Encuentro* and encourages all to find appropriate ways to pursue that goal. The pontiff insists that the Gospel should illuminate and penetrate all situations and circumstances (see *EN* 29); this is a task to which Hispanic Catholics should apply themselves by developing their own creative identity, according to their own specific needs—working closely with their pastors and in collaboration with others and in accord with a pluralism that brings integral freedom to all people.

The pope concludes by insisting on the duty of Hispanic Catholics to conserve their heritage and help it flourish, adapting it along the way, but without forgetting or neglecting popular religiosity. He calls on Mary, "the star of evangelization," to guide and protect those to whom he imparts his apostolic blessing.

Keynote Address by Archbishop Roberto F. Sanchez

Archbishop Roberto Fortune Sanchez of Santa Fe, New Mexico, delivers the keynote address on the theme of the Second *Encuentro*: Evangelization. He opens his address with a text from Saint Luke, in which the Lord says that the Spirit is upon him, basing these words on Isaiah (Luke 4:18–19). Archbishop Sanchez proclaims that these words have a "magnetic force."

Each person present is representative of a particular [local] church, the prelate says, but knows that the Church is one—that all the faithful share the same faith, the same Eucharist, the same baptism. The talk then unfolds by focusing on three points:

the Church united, the Church differentiated, and the Church as servant.

The Unity of the Church is a matter of mind, heart, and soul; the faithful meet in the Lord's name. Their unity is forged and maintained in faith, love, and action. This Church is experiencing a new Pentecost—in bringing together many traditions, but just one people, with a common heritage, under the guidance of the pope's presence. Such is the Catholic Church in the United States, according to the archbishop.

Yet, at the same time, it is a pluralist Church, he says; it is not uniform, and cultural diversity is not an imperfection, just as Paul VI stated in *Evangelii Nuntiandi*. The First *Encuentro* made the U.S. Church aware of the Hispanic presence, says the archbishop, and showed that even though Hispanics are different, they are not inferior. This Second *Encuentro* should reveal the same regarding Hispanic popular religious traditions, the prelate continues, adding that Hispanics should preserve their identity and their heritage—and in doing so preserve their faith.

Then the archbishop speaks of evangelization as a dramatic and energetic concept; a word that should be on everyone's lips and a word that, according to the prelate, "resists every effort to define it." The content is the good news of Christ; it should lead to commitment, to proclamation, and to testimony through action.

Based on this perspective, the archbishop continues, evangelization should transform an indifferent and egotistical society into a people filled with love and concern for others; evangelization can transform structures, illuminate the future, and make the world more just, he proclaims.

Evangelization is directed toward all, he notes, but in a special way, it is aimed at those who suffer from injustice and sin. Accordingly, Catholics must examine their relationship with those who live outside the Church and also be willing to critically examine their own lives. The Church, the archbishop insists, should ask itself: How should believers confess their sins and ask for forgiveness? How should they defend human rights and justice? How can they channel resources toward the neediest areas?

How can they establish a neutral sphere where there is no discrimination?

With deep insight, Archbishop Sanchez counsels his audience not to rush to the judgment of others, without examining themselves and their own actions first. Christ's values, he says, are not the values of the world. People must come to know Christ first and listen to him before bringing him to others. "Our own imperfections should not discourage us," the prelate insists.

With the Second *Encuentro*, Hispanic America is ready to take on the task of evangelization, proclaims Archbishop Sanchez. Hispanics are convinced that they are capable of identifying with the poor; they can be a leaven; they are a cordial people who love celebrations and fiestas. The prelate calls on all Hispanics to help evangelize all of society, echoing the words of Saint Paul to the Romans (see Rom 8:35–37), and concluding with the Saint's exhortation to the Philippians (see Phil 1:3–10).

Special Presentation by Monsignor Eduardo Boza Masvidal

Adding an exceptional note to the Second *Encuentro*, there follows an address by the late Bishop Eduardo Boza Masvidal, Titular Bishop of Vinda, formerly Auxiliary Bishop of San Cristobal, in Havana (Cuba, 1960–1963); exiled from Cuba by the dictatorship of Fidel Castro, he later served as the Vicar General of the Los Toques Diocese in Venezuela. Monsignor Boza directed the bulk of his apostolic efforts in service to the Cuban Church in exile.

The subject chosen by Monsignor Boza is that of Unity in Plurality. He begins his discourse by arguing that the Second *Encuentro* does not have the goal of making Hispanics into a separate group, nor of encouraging the development of vague forms of nationalism. On the contrary, the overriding goal is to build unity in plurality, says the bishop. God makes all people brothers (and sisters) and each person is unique and different, the prelate insists; there is no "standard" type. Among Hispanics there is great diversity, he says, but that, he adds, is not an obstacle. Unity is different from uniformity, as is true in the case of families as well.

The meeting of two cultures produces enrichment; on the other hand, when there is assimilation, the people are impoverished, says Monsignor Boza; identity and values are lost. Hispanics have much to learn from North Americans, he adds: their practical nature, their sense of organization, their commitment to work. But they also have much to give: spontaneity, a deeper sense of family, devotion to Mary, and so on. These riches must not be lost, the prelate insists.

The conservation of the Hispanic language is important, he continues, as it is there where the soul of a people finds expression. To "remember" implies, in Spanish, to conserve the mind; it is a word that carries a different connotation from one language to another. When a clock is damaged, Spanish-speakers say it stopped working, since they take things more calmly. In English they prefer to say "stopped running" because that's the way Americans are. To lose your own language, he tells Hispanics, is to be unable to clearly express who and what you are—and to speak with God believers need the greatest spontaneity, he says.

He goes on to argue that it is a false query to ask: Do I integrate or do I continue to consider myself a Cuban? People must do both, and at different levels, he insists, stressing that the Church is one and the bishop is the shepherd. Saint Paul in Ephesians, the bishop points out, reminds us: "one Lord, one faith...." But the message of Christ must be lived out within each culture (see AC 22), even as the faithful must remain open to the needs and witness of the entire world (see GS 1).

The bishop calls on Hispanics to reject the temptation to remain a closed group; he calls on them to be a leaven in the world. Hispanics must have very clear ideas and criteria of their own, even as they learn to respect those of others. They must be open to all, especially the poor and oppressed. In Latin America, he charges, many are exhausted, tortured, and so on, suffering under dictatorial regimes or in similar oppressive circumstances. People must not be strict with one ideology and complacent with another, the bishops says, stressing that believers' commitment must be to Christ, justice, and the truth. The prelate calls on his audience to reject what he calls the false alternatives of Marxism and capitalism. The faithful, he proclaims, are with the poor and oppressed, traveling with Christ in the adventure of bringing about the redemption of the world—an adventure that begins in the heart of each person, so that love and freedom might unite all people.

Unity in plurality is a new pathway, the bishop continues, facing three possible attitudes: to do nothing (egotism, cowardice, taking the easy way out), to raise our fist (hate, division, conflict), or to open our arms (love, service, surrender). Then the prelate tells his hearers to overcome weariness and discouragement by opening their arms wide. That is the ideal of Christ that enlightens Christians' lives, he affirms, and the Second *Encuentro* should help all to walk along this path.

Final Presentation by Bishop Patricio F. Flores

Bishop Patricio F. Flores, in his homily at the closing Eucharist, presents the final message of the Second *Encuentro*. (Bishop Flores is, at that time, Auxiliary Bishop of San Antonio; several months later, when the documents of the Second *Encuentro* are published, he is Bishop of El Paso, staying on in that city for only a brief time [March 1978 to August 1979].)

The homily of the bishop is titled "A People Full of Hope," and he begins by reminding of the Lord's phrase in Saint Matthew, "Be valiant, do not fear, it is I" (Matt 14:27). He calls the Second *Encuentro* "a new sun" for Hispanics in the United States. He compares it with the First *Encuentro*, which had 250 attendees—the Second *Encuentro* counts more than 800; the First saw 5 bishops attending, one of them Hispanic; the Second *Encuentro* boasts 40 bishops, of whom 8 are Hispanics. Here, abbreviated and in paraphrase, are the bishop's words: We are no longer a sleeping giant—the people are on their feet ready to take the lead, but with arms open wide. The people have been oppressed, but they are not resentful. We are not a troubled people—we have great and youthful power. All of us have suffered. We have struggled to avoid losing our identity: the Castilian language, popular religiosity—we are resisting the philosophy of the "melting pot."

We have not given validity to violence, because it is not God's offspring; nor have we sought vengeance. Some things have been accomplished: improvement of the conditions of those who work the fields, much of education is bilingual and bi-cultural; walls have come down, our vote has been recognized. In recent years, we have had two governors, mayors of small towns, council and district members, congressional representatives, judges, the director of immigration, eight bishops and the head of the [Hispanic] secretariat. Most of this has happened in the last eight or nine years.

We are happy, but not satisfied. For that reason we will continue so as to obtain 25 more times the representation we have today. Hope challenges us. If we have seen a glimmer of light, we expect to see the greatness of the sun. There is a temptation to divide, for people to struggle alone and to lose hope. Therefore we remember the Lord's word: Do not be dismayed.

The Lord wants us to be united (John 17:21–23) and to share in his work (Matt 28:19–20). Our response should be: we are ready; we are a people full of hope.

Poem: Somos un Pueblo Hispano *(We Are a Hispanic People) by Juan Alvarez Cuauhtemoc*

The author points out that his inspiration comes from many, but above all, from the participants in the Pre-Second *Encuentro* regional meeting of the Midwest held on July 15, 1977, one month earlier. The poem has fourteen stanzas of varied lengths. It speaks of geographic extension and the relationship between earth and dream. There is reference to three races that become integrated as Hispanic; then it speaks of the ambivalence of a people being both conqueror and conquered, liberator and oppressor. Juan Diego and Guadalupe as well as Saint Martin de Porres make an appearance. The poem affirms what the Hispanic people were and are: the children of three races. Then it surveys a number of countries, from Mexico to Argentina, emphasizing that which unites all Hispanics: language and religion.

There is a tribute to various nationalities and colors, and an entire stanza is dedicated to the United States. Another speaks of a people mindful of the conflict-ridden situation in which they live. There is mention of Protestants and the final stanza speaks of being the people of God.

Hymn: Un Pueblo que Camina (A People on the Move) by Emilio Vicente Mateu

The Second *Encuentro* has chosen this hymn as its official song of praise, since it reflects the dimension of hope and unity, of journeying and of transcendence, of overcoming difficulties and of finding freedom. It also asks for the light of God's Word to guide people's steps. It is a poem that reaffirms the dimension of struggle and of unity, that speaks of the desire for peace and liberty, and that reflects on weariness and the assurance of rest.

3.2 UNPACKING THE SECOND *ENCUENTRO*

For the Record

Although Bishop Flores speaks of eight hundred participants, the organizers claim an actual attendance of twelve hundred, including observers.

The Secretariat prints a total of forty-two thousand pages to provide all attending with all the documents. Full-time staff grows to a number of twenty, while during the *Encuentro* there are thirty workers, taking on more than five thousand hours of work. A number of them are volunteers.

The Second *Encuentro* features twenty-eight workshops, sixteen of which are on Evangelization, three on Ministries, three on Human Rights, and two each for the other three principal subjects. Each liturgy has a dedicated team. Five persons take eighty hours facilitating the participation of each region in the various teams, while three hundred hours are spent to accommodate the twelve hundred attendees, taking into account their preferences and the distinctive nature of each region.

The liturgies reflect diverse Hispanic cultures and are all conducted in Spanish, with two exceptions. The Holy Father delivers his message in Spanish and many of the bishops do so as well; (a total of fifty bishops are in attendance at various times, although not all them can stay for the entire *Encuentro*).

The Working Document, the fruit of six hundred hours of preparation, is distributed prior to the *Encuentro* to the five hundred individuals formally enrolled; later, all in attendance are offered a copy at the beginning of the Second *Encuentro*.

The Final Document is prepared in nine steps, including the drafting of the original copy in Spanish and its translation into English. Included are all the discussions, modifications, plenary presentations, style corrections, and so on. The schema for the process of compilation is: Base—Diocese—Region—National Synthesis (The Working Document)—workshops—plenary sessions—coordinating committee—publication of Final Document—translation.

The Agenda

On Thursday, August 18, from 9:00 a.m. to 4:00 p.m., the normal reception of all participants is handled. The proceedings are prolonged for many hours because of flight delays and last-minute inconveniences.

At 4:30 p.m., the inaugural session is set to begin, led by Pablo Sedillo as moderator. But things first get underway with the hymn *Un Pueblo que Canta*. Then Archbishop Bernardin, as president of the bishops' conference, offers the official convocation. Then a word of welcome by Cardinal William Baum of Washington, DC, is delivered by his Auxiliary, Bishop Thomas Lyons. Next, Bishop James S. Rausch, Bishop of Phoenix and President of the Episcopal Committee for Hispanic Affairs, gives his greeting. Finally, comes the motivational message presented by Pablo Sedillo in his double role as Director of the Secretariat and President of the Coordinating Committee. Afterward, Father Frank Ponce, Special Coordinator of the *Encuentro*, makes the necessary housekeeping remarks.

The papal message is heard with rapt attention following the introduction by Archbishop Thomas C. Kelly, OP, General Secretary of the bishops' conference, and a few words of welcome by Archbishop Jean Jadot, the Vatican's Apostolic Delegate to the United States.

Next up is a para-liturgy titled "Called to Participate," prepared by the Midwest Region and presided over by Bishop Gilberto E. Chavez, Auxiliary of San Diego, California. The day ends with dinner and a period of fellowship hosted by the Northeast Region.

The main focal point of day two, August 19, is the presentation on Evangelization by Archbishop Roberto F. Sanchez of Santa Fe, New Mexico. A subsequent recess is followed by the presentation on the chosen themes by each of the regions; next up, sixteen separate workshops begin their deliberations on Evangelization, taking turns to break for lunch. These workshops continue until past 4:00 p.m. Mass, presided over by Cardinal Terrence Cooke of New York, begins at 4:30 p.m. Auxiliary Bishop Juan Arzube of Los Angeles and Auxiliary Bishop Raymundo J. Peña of San Antonio—who delivers the homily—assist the Cardinal. Roberto Chavez serves as deacon, representing the Southwest Region.

Following the Eucharist, dinner is served, and until 7:00 p.m., there is another plenary session to approve the conclusions concerning the principal theme of Evangelization. Sister Palmira Perea, OLVM, from the Midwest Region, serves as Coordinator. This session ends with a prayer service.

On Saturday, August 20, following breakfast, the plenary session is led by Bishop Raymond J. Gallagher of Lafayette, Indiana. Rogelio Manrique, Regional Director of the Midwest *Encuentro* committee, is the moderator. Following prayer, prepared by the Southeast Region, Father Frank Ponce makes a series of observations to launch the other twelve workshops, each of them identified by a color: blue, for the three workshops on Ministries; purple, for the three on Human Rights; green, for the two on Integral Education; black, for the two on Political Responsibility; and orange, for the two on Unity in Plurality. The workshops continue until after noon, at which point the groups take turns for lunch.

After a rest, the Eucharist is presided over by Cardinal Humberto Mederos, Archbishop of Boston, with Archbishop

Edward McCarthy of Miami as principal concelebrant and Bishop Ricardo Antonio Suriñach Carreras, Auxiliary of Ponce, Puerto Rico, delivering the homily. Rafael de los Reyes, from the Southeast Region, serves as deacon.

That evening, following dinner, a beautiful festival is held, called *Arco Iris Hispano* (Hispanic Rainbow), coordinated by Mario Paredes, the first Executive Director of the Northeast Region, and Father Seán O'Malley, OFM, Cap. (now the Cardinal Archbishop of Boston), the second Director of the Hispanic Apostolate of the Archdiocese of Washington, DC. The festival has three parts: an audiovisual presentation titled *Nosotros Hispanos* (We Hispanics); the words of Bishop Eduardo Boza, the former Auxiliary of San Cristobal, Havana, under the heading *Unidad en pluralismo* (Unity in Plurality); and, finally, there is a musical program.

The final day of the second *Encuentro* is August 20, with the plenary session beginning after breakfast under the presidency of the late Bishop Francis J. Mugavero of Brooklyn, with Alicia Marill from the Southeast Region moderating, and the opening prayer prepared by the Northeast Region.

Conclusions are presented concerning Integral Education, coordinated by Rosa Maria Zarate from the Far West Region; those on Political Responsibility, coordinated by Leonardo Anguiano on behalf of the Southwest Region and the Mexican-American Cultural Center; and those on Unity in Plurality, coordinated by Maria Iglesias of the national team of *Las Hermanas*. Immediately afterward, participants make their way to the National Basilica of the Immaculate Conception for the final Eucharist. It is presided over by Cardinal William of Baum, Archbishop of Washington, DC. Bishop Patricio F. Flores, Auxiliary of San Antonio, gives a homily on the theme "A People Full of Hope." Serving as deacon is Aquilino Gonzalez from the Northeast Region. The Mass formally concludes the Second *Encuentro*.

3.3 CONCLUSIONS OF THE SECOND *ENCUENTRO*

Regarding Evangelization

The conclusions come in seven parts: No. 1 serves as introduction and defines *Evangelization* as a continuing process relying on Christ and his Gospel. It implies conversion and testimony. All the participants of the Second *Encuentro* declare themselves responsible for Evangelization in the United States.

No. 2 is titled "Call to Conversion" and calls for a united Church, one that is poor, committed to the community; a Church missionary and just—and with bishops committed to this ideal. No. 3 deals with Basic Ecclesial Communities, which, the text insists, must be forces of evangelization and liberation. There is a proposal to support them, form mobile pastoral teams, ensure better communication, and an efficient sharing of resources; there also is a call to encourage and strengthen family, support for youth, as well as the development of an international work plan.

No. 4 is dedicated to Hispanic culture and insists on the right of Hispanics to be evangelized within their own culture. There is a recommendation that regional centers be created where none exist as yet so that leaders can be trained in the use of communications media; these centers would also offer courses in what the text calls integral pastoral renewal. There is a call for the coordination of diocesan Hispanic pastoral work and the appointment of more Hispanic bishops as ordinaries of dioceses, alongside a call for more Hispanic parish priests and deacons, and so on. The text also calls for the appreciation and validation of Hispanic popular religiosity and the overall raising of awareness of the meaning of Hispanic culture. Hispanic apostolic movements are recommended, as is greater dialogue with CELAM (here referred to incorrectly as the "Conference" of Latin American Bishops; it is the "Council").

No. 5 is dedicated to those who are the target of evangelization efforts, as distinct from the Basic Ecclesial Communities. The focus is especially on migrant workers, on interparochial groups serving dispersed Hispanic populations, on those incarcerated, the sick, the elderly, the family, those who are engaged, the divorced, widows, military personnel, intellectuals, white-collar workers, artists, the poor and all those on the margin, the undocumented, and all those in society who are oppressed.

No. 6 is dedicated to young people, featuring the recommendation to create what is referred to as a National Youth Work Team. This team would be a point of contact and a lifeline for those who are addicted to drugs, victims of pornography, and so on. Conclusion No. 7 recommends that this initiative be implemented within three years.

Regarding Ministries in the Service of Evangelization

A noteworthy change in the recommendations is to make explicit each theme's relationship to evangelization. This second chapter has thirteen parts, No. 1 being an introduction in which the ministry of all is accepted, alongside a variety of ministries. No. 2 is dedicated to the small communities, the Basic Ecclesial Communities, which are held up as privileged forms of ministering. No. 3 refers to lay ministries, calling attention to the value and validity of the lay state. There is the insistence that there be no discrimination and that these various ministries begin to function forthwith. There is also the spotlight put on service to migrant workers—who, the text says, need more leadership; and there is a reminder of the value and importance of parish councils.

No. 4 is dedicated to permanent deacons; there is a call for more Hispanics to join their ranks; and the demand that these candidates come from the grassroots; that a new Hispanic clericalism be avoided; that an accommodation for service in the military be allowed; that both single and married deacons be embraced by the Church; that they be helped economically; and, finally, that deacons can serve throughout the diocese, rather than just doing service in one particular parish.

No. 5 insists on the active participation of women, calling for complete equality between the sexes. No. 6 refers to the other ministries—those related to the Eucharist, catechesis, and special groups. No. 7 refers to the bishops and priests, calling on prelates to ask for more Hispanics priests, and calling all non-Hispanics to show more commitment to the wellbeing of Hispanics. No. 8 deals with Hispanic religious and requests that they be allowed to work specifically with Hispanics.

No. 9 refers to the selection of ministers, who, the text insists, must have a good reputation, have ties to community, give priority to the family, avoid discrimination, and be recommended for their role by the community. No. 10 is dedicated to the training of ministers, requesting that their formation be bilingual, multicultural, practical, feature a social dimension, and so on. To make this happen, there is a proposal for the creation of both diocesan and regional entities, and the Church should overall employ more Hispanic personnel, support associations of Hispanic seminarians, and revise programs already in place to make them more flexible and more responsive to the Hispanic reality.

No. 11 is dedicated to the pastoral needs of young people and requests that the National Youth Work Team mentioned above make youth ministries a priority. There also is call for the creation of a national organization, a center for the training of ministers, and the overall promotion of vocations, both clergy and lay.

No. 12 discusses the liturgy and stresses the importance and vitality of popular religiosity. Greater flexibility and creativity are sought on the liturgical front, along with the creation of more liturgical commissions, support for the document approved by the Southwest and California, and a greater sacramental awareness on the part of all the faithful.

No. 13 is titled "Special Ministries and Other Pastoral Areas." There is reference to pastoral care for both the family and migrant workers as well as pastoral attention for a number of other groups, including those in the military. There is a call for ministers to serve the "divorced, students, prostitutes, gay people, disabled, drug addicts and alcoholics." There is mention of the importance of the use of media and the crucial role of the apostolic movements. Obviously, this final section is a real "potpourri" or "cocktail" of pastoral ideas.

Regarding Evangelization and Human Rights

This chapter has eight parts, beginning with an introduction in which the Second *Encuentro* petitions the U.S. bishops' conference and the Third General Conference of the Latin American Episcopate (CELAM), which was due to meet in 1978 in Puebla— in fact, due to the deaths of Paul VI and John Paul I, the Latin American bishops would end up meeting in January 1979—to ensure that "the pastoral emphasis on liberation and the defense of human rights be maintained, both in civil and ecclesiastical matters."

No. 2 is devoted to the undocumented. There is a call for a full amnesty as well as a denunciation of discriminatory laws; there is a proposal that migrant workers be helped to regularize their documentation, alongside an expression of opposition against the restoration of programs pertaining to the "import of workers." The text denounces the lack of justice brought against those accused of torturing undocumented workers in Douglas, Arizona, and a call for the complete revision of the immigration system. There is the insistence on the right of families to reunite all their members, documented or not, and the demand that all workers gain access to labor union benefits (union organization, Medicare, and so on) and representation. Finally, the texts call for the simplification of the paperwork involved in acquiring citizenship.

No. 3 addresses the plight of migrant farm workers; the text argues that they are entitled to a just salary, medical attention, and better living conditions. There is the call for a stipulation that those under age sixteen are not allowed to work. There is a demand for the recognition of the right to organize a field workers' union, alongside a plea for support for the United Farm Workers of America (UFWA), the Farm Labor Organizing Committee (FLOC), the Texas Farm Workers (TFW), and so on. In the same way, the text calls for respect for the workers' right to appropriate rest periods and the right to practice their religion. The Church is called to commit to making Catholic social doctrine better known, to support the diocesan justice and peace committees with more funding, and to establish regional centers for leadership training in this domain.

No. 4 deals with the human rights of other groups and minorities; the text calls for the commitment to denounce the human rights violations of any regime, including those outside the United States; it expresses support for the Red Cross, the International Commission of Jurists in The Hague, the Netherlands, and the UN Commission on Human Rights. There is a strong denunciation of those U.S. government agencies that "sell and betray the rights of refugees and exiles who work and struggle for the freedom of their native countries."

Curiously, the Second *Encuentro* personalizes the issue and expresses support for Puerto Rican nationalist Lolita Lebron, who at that time has spent twenty-three years in prison. There is also a charge of human rights violations by the police in the Northeast; plus, there is a call for pastoral outreach to prisons; and for the defense of women, the elderly, the disabled, children, and so on—care for all who are subject to discrimination and exploitation. In a similar vein, abortion and euthanasia are condemned, along with plans to sterilize minorities, and so forth.

Finally, this section demands respect for the rights of all poor, all the racial minorities, and so on. The bishops' conference is petitioned to lobby the President and the Congress to launch an investigation of the matter of "land grants" in the Southwest. To make all this happen, the Second *Encuentro* proposes that the Church use all its power and resources, and that the "official ministers" abide by criteria that make a priority of service to the poor and minorities, and that they "review some of the criteria currently in place that favor privileged classes and vested interests."

No. 5 refers to economic and social issues; there is a proposal to establish work centers at the diocesan level that can coordinate with bilingual and multicultural specialized personnel, providing motivation and training to the underemployed or unemployed as well as undocumented Hispanic workers. The text insists that the Church should seek to obtain federal funds to provide workers with adequate living quarters, while also supporting the development of a program that works toward creating conditions of full employment.

No. 6 insists on the right to an adequate education, which should be bilingual and multicultural in the public schools. The Church should also provide such education in its own schools as well as offer adult education, especially for migrant farm workers.

No. 7 tackles a sensitive intra-ecclesial area: here, the Second *Encuentro* affirms that "the Hispanic people have felt a certain oppression and incomprehension on the part of the ecclesiastical hierarchy." As a remedy, it is proposed that evangelization efforts be done in Spanish, that Hispanic ministers be given full respect and recognition, that the discrimination against women be eliminated, that programs be established for teaching bishops about Hispanic culture, and so on. There also is a demand that the Church's social doctrine be made better known, that Hispanics be better represented at all levels of the Church, that programs to promote Hispanic vocations be put in place, and so on.

At this point, the conclusions of the Second *Encuentro* tackle concrete cases, insisting "that a response be made—breaking the silence—to the Christian who investigates or asks about injustices and the structures of the Church, as has happened in correspondence directed to the NCCB/USCC concerning the layoffs of lay personnel in their offices." This section concludes with the request that the Secretariat for Hispanic Affairs employ staff of different Hispanic national backgrounds.

No. 8 makes two special declarations: one, in support of the International Campaign for Human Rights, as promoted by the Peace and Justice Service in Latin America in observance (in 1978) of the thirtieth anniversary of the Universal Declaration of Human Rights; and another in protest of military governments that persecute the Church. The language here, as could be expected, is strong and confrontational.

Regarding Evangelization and Integral Education

This set of conclusions has seven substantial parts. The first is introductory and defines Integral Education as having three key characteristics: it attends to the total person; its goal is liberate the individual; and it promotes a creative pedagogy. Its fundamental objective is captured in the phrase, "To be evangelized in order to evangelize."

No. 2 presents the goal of Integral Education as found in five characteristics: bilingualism, multiculturalism, freedom from prejudice, appreciation of other cultures, and esteem for one's own values. This education does not exist for Hispanics, the text charges—the Church is not helping Hispanics in this vital realm.

No. 3 makes some practical recommendations to achieve a system of Integral Education. This section requests that all schools establish bilingual programs, give Hispanics the opportunity to be trained and educated, provide for adequate scholarships, and so on. It insists on special training for migrant farm workers. It also proposes a meeting with the bishops' conference, calls for education in prisons and ordinary people's political formation, the development of new educational models and permanent programs, and the guarantee of educational equality. As regards supervision, the conclusions here insist that leadership safeguard the particular philosophy of the education. Regarding the leadership, it is recommended that they receive bilingual and multicultural training, that there be an exchange of practices and ideas with Latin America, and that more qualified administrators be appointed. Finally, there is a call for fairness and equality in the distribution of scholarships, for transparency in the administration of the funds involved, that parents be informed about their rights, and that the number of Hispanic teachers be increased.

No. 4 refers to the Church's role, requesting that these recommendations be fulfilled by 1980: bilingual and multicultural programs in the Catholic schools, no school closings in Hispanic areas, a firm pursuit of obtaining public funds, and the Church taking responsibility for providing integral education. There also is a call to establish programs geared toward Hispanics in Catholic universities such as Georgetown, Fordham, the University of San Diego, Marquette, Notre Dame, and so on. The Church is also called upon to do more to promote the role and liberation of women, including the right of Hispanic women to participate in the planning of faith-related activities and the like. This requires, the text says, that the clergy and Church personnel who work with

Hispanics have adequate training, which must involve much more than language training. In a similar vein, there is a call for the hiring of more Hispanic personnel, and that funds be made available to that end as well as for their adequate training. The Church is also petitioned to ensure the distribution of Hispanic seminarians by regions.

No. 5 refers to the religious education of Hispanics, which, the text insists, should be bilingual, multicultural, and aim for the total or integral liberation of the human person—and the bishops' conference is called upon to provide the necessary funds. Dioceses and parishes are asked to provide religious education in Spanish, while the diocesan Departments of Education should support the conclusions of the National Conference of Diocesan Directors concerning Hispanic education. There is a call for the promotion of Hispanic religious art, especially works depicting the Virgin Mary.

No. 6 tackles the responsibility of parents for education in the family setting, their role in conveying a sense of Hispanic identity to their children, promoting their culture, and so on. There is a call for special programs to train parents, the creation of Hispanic school clubs, putting parents together with teachers, and so on. Parents are urged to actively participate in the schools, and the text insists that all meetings they participate in be bilingual. Also, the Hispanic community at large is called upon to make a commitment to defending integral education, participate in political decisions, and help grant scholarships to capable students.

No. 7 is dedicated to the communication media and recommends that the Hispanic community make a push toward having a strong media presence; that Hispanic media coalitions be formed; and that these be aware of available Hispanic programs, including content targeting military personnel. Hispanic media, the text urges, should accentuate the values of Hispanic culture and promote programs that fulfill the requirements of the Federal Communications Commission (FCC). Finally, there is a demand for media content that serves migrant farm workers, along with a call on Catholic publications to feature adequate Spanish-language and Hispanic-oriented content.

Regarding Evangelization and Political Responsibility

This theme is tackled in five chapters, the first being introductory. It recognizes that democracy in the United States presents—in theory—the means necessary for the political participation of Hispanics; in practice, however, it is noted, discrimination, the lack of training, and the system itself do not favor Hispanic participation in the political process.

No. 2 calls for the active participation of the Hispanic Christian community in the political process, reminding the faithful that their fundamental responsibility to join the process is born out of faith. Specifically, the text calls for Hispanic political candidates to be honest, responsible, and capable. All political figures, whether Hispanic or not, should also be competent and live according to Gospel values, the text continues; all Hispanics who are able to do so should acquire citizenship and register to vote; what's more, a "political block" should be created to denounce injustice and combat oppression and discrimination. The text demands that that block be supported by the Church. Here, too, are calls to promote legislation that truly liberates individuals and to politically organize groups of parents; to press for full respect of women's rights; to form political unions; and to ensure economic support for Hispanic candidates. Specifically, the text insists on three crucial stances for any Hispanic political effort: to not give in to intimidation, to not accept a denial as a final response, and to be present in whatever arena in which Hispanic interests are at stake.

No. 3 is dedicated to political training and education, which the text calls an obligation, and hence, support is requested from the National Conference of Catholic Bishops. There is a call for a four-pronged strategy: that all Hispanic centers and schools encourage political training in Spanish, that reading materials be accessible to a popular readership, that meeting places be provided, and that leadership classes be available.

The active participation of the Church in support of Hispanics is the objective of No. 4, which features a number of recommendations and demands: the creation of coalitions on the national and diocesan levels as well as on level of the Basic Ecclesial Communities, application of affirmative action within ecclesiastical institutions, Hispanic participation in all the structures of the NCCB, commitment to use social communication media, and intervention when any of these principles are violated. There, again, is a call for the protection of migrant farm workers as well as for collaboration with Hispanic organizations that facilitate Hispanic political participation. The bishops are urged to recognize these organizations, in addition to supporting the undocumented and denouncing what are called the abuses of the "Grand Jury."

Finally, No. 5 makes three recommendations: that the NCCB present Congress with a petition that all legal residents be given the right to vote on local issues, that educational programs on how to apply for citizenship be available in Spanish and that the citizenship test might be taken in Spanish, and that legal residents be entitled to occupy government posts.

Regarding Evangelization and Unity in Plurality

This section also has five chapters, including the introduction that expresses pride in cultural identity and heritage, along with the affirmation that the country's internal cultural diversity is a treasure, and that Hispanics are part of a pluralistic reality. There is the reaffirmation of the need of Hispanics to integrate in U.S. society—but assimilation is rejected because it is an impoverishing factor given the inherent loss of Hispanic identity.

No. 2 is dedicated to integration and proposes a number of action steps: that all offices of the Church apply the concept of integration—rather than assimilation; that each person and each group might develop their own identity openly; that Hispanics awaken the awareness of non-Hispanics about Hispanic culture; that a dialogue with other ethnic groups be established; that the Church promote the notion of "unity in plurality" by means of the communication media; and that bishops and parish priests include Hispanics in all structures, in proportion to the size of the Hispanic population.

No. 3 refers to unity among Hispanics, making a number of recommendations on this front: the creation of campaigns to boost awareness of the various different Hispanic cultures, histories, and traditions; and help for families to promote knowledge and appreciation of Hispanic family life and culture at home. The Church is called not to concentrate on the experience of only one Hispanic people, but to promote activities that confirm Hispanic identity, to develop themes that promote Hispanic unity, to encourage a creative interchange among Hispanic groups, and to organize an annual folkloric festival that would celebrate the rich mosaic of the various Hispanic cultures.

No. 4 studies Hispanic unity on the level of faith and religiosity, proposing several strategies: the study and celebration of religious traditions; preservation of customs; awareness of the Hispanic contributions to Catholic life in the United States; programs for the re-evangelization of adults; and the development of an overall Hispanic pastoral approach that includes catechesis, liturgies, pastoral work to promote vocations, and so on. Last but not least, there is a call to establish religious programs to serve youth.

Finally, No. 5 refers to the family, making two recommendations: the creation and development of an educational system that helps the family to preserve and deepen its cultural values, and a request that this cultural dimension be taken into consideration as a potential addition to educational programs already underway.

3.4 EVALUATION OF THE SECOND *ENCUENTRO*

Balance

In establishing some of the data regarding the Second *Encuentro*, there was mention of the sharp increase in the number of attendees, compared to the First *Encuentro*, a quantitative note. More important, however, is the articulation of the process that starts with the overall preparations, moves to the regional

Encuentros, from there to the Working Document, and culminating in the publication of the Final Document. Certainly, that aspect of systematization and superb organization make the Second *Encuentro* an organic whole hinging on the central axis of Evangelization. However, it must be noted that, given the theological-pastoral circumstances that prevailed at the time, the Second *Encuentro* is marked by a particular theological tendency and pastoral methodology. This fact is neither good nor bad a priori, but it limits the flexibility of the Final Document and the process that went into its creation because of the adherence to this particular theological and ideological orientation. This orientation was determined by a bias toward liberation theology and all its implications for both theology and pastoral practice, and sets the tone for the overall foundation of the Second *Encuentro.*

Does this invalidate all the proposals made? No, but this fundamental orientation conditions them, obliging us to consider them anew today and reformulate them as necessary. Some things continue to be very positive: consultation with the grassroots and the need for a systematic approach to the larger Hispanic pastoral challenge. On this score, it is worth mentioning a white paper that both complements and reflects on the Second *Encuentro.* It is the work of Moises Sandoval, published in 1979. Another document of note is a demographic study published in 1982.

A Special Task

In 1978, Moises Sandoval, with funding from the Alicia Patterson Foundation, published a treatise on the "Latinization" of the United States. In December 1979, Pablo Sedillo explains in a preface that the work of Sandoval has been commissioned by the Secretariat for Hispanic Affairs as a response to some of the recommendations made at the Second *Encuentro.*

The ninety-two-page document is titled "Hispanic Challenges to the Church," featuring an introduction and six parts. The introduction surveys some of the great changes in the Hispanic landscape. For example, Mexican-Americans have become urbanized in the past thirty-five years; numbering just seventy thousand in 1940. Puerto Ricans have seen their total swell in the United

States to 1.8 million, which is equal to 37 percent of the population on the home island. The Great Lakes region now counts more Latinos than Colorado, New Mexico, and Arizona combined. These trends have created a subculture of poverty and rendered a part of California as seemingly belonging to the "Third World."

Of the four remaining chapters, one deserves particular mention: the second. It follows an opening chapter that compiles by now familiar and interrelated themes: the challenges of Hispanic immigration, deficient education of Hispanics, their economic disadvantages, the specter of police violence toward Hispanics, the destruction of the family, lack of leadership, cultural alienation, and institutionalized violence in the Hispanic communities. The second chapter, however, breaks new ground. Titled "Imperatives of the Second *Encuentro*," it concentrates on what is of the highest interest in the wake of the Second *Encuentro*. Claiming that he wrote this chapter based on the input of 100,000 people, the author highlights five conclusions of the Second *Encuentro*, those he considers the most significant.

Those five conclusions are: the urgency of awakening the national conscience with regard to the Hispanic question, the insistence on help for the undocumented, the call for the elimination of economic disadvantages and all forms of oppression hurting Hispanics, the need for the defense of an integral education for all Hispanics, and the demand for the development and building up of Hispanic leadership.

The third chapter deals with the way the Church has made changes, referring to the very beginnings of the Hispanic pastoral effort; the chapter features plenty of data, percentages, comparisons, and so on. Here, Sandoval also gives an in-depth analysis of a number of case studies, such as that of San Jose Parish in Saginaw, Michigan; that of San Timoteo in San Antonio; that of COPS (Spanish acronym for "Organized Communities for Public Service"); that of the late Father Bryan Karvelis in Williamsburg, Brooklyn; and that of the apostolic initiatives in Miami.

The fourth chapter presents a series of comparisons involving the demography of Hispanics (national groups, concentrations, and so on), their economic situation, psychological factors, challenges of acculturation, a picture of the racial mosaic, and a consideration of popular religiosity.

Next, chapter five presents a broad selection of graphics and projections, comparisons, and so on, among which stands out a snapshot of Hispanic participation in the structure of the Church. At the time, there are eight Hispanic bishops among 320 bishops total; 1,415 Hispanic priests among almost 59,000; 1,500 Hispanic women religious among a total of 135,000; 120 brothers among 8,625; and 167 seminarians among almost 9,000. Finally, there is an extensive bibliography.

This work of Moises Sandoval well captures the situation of the Hispanic Catholic community in the United States in the immediate aftermath of the Second *Encuentro*; it provides all the data affecting and shaping the Hispanic pastoral situation at this concrete moment in time. It would be worthwhile to revisit all these data again and take note of the dramatic changes that have taken place since Sandoval's writing.

Demographic Complement

In January 1982, the Secretariat for Hispanic Affairs published a demographic document comparing 1970 and 1980, under the title "Hispanics and Catholics in the United States: Some Preliminary Demographic Observations and Comparisons between 1970 and 1980 Figures." Among the data presented, some are worth highlighting, in particular: the U.S. population jumped from 203 million in 1970 to 226 million in 1980; there are 44,800,000 Catholics in 1970 (22.1 percent of the population) and 47,500,000 in 1980 (21.0 percent); the figures indicate that the Catholic share of the population has shrunk somewhat, contrary to normal assumptions. These data are close to the numbers found in *The Catholic Directory*, which puts the Catholic population at 47,800,000 in 1970 (23.6 percent of the total) and at 49,800,000 in 1980 (22.0 percent).

The decline in the Catholic share of the population is especially striking in light of the fact that, in the same period, the Hispanic population in the United States grew considerably: from 9 million in 1970 (4.5 percent of the population) to 14,600,000 in

1980 (6.4 percent). In other words, out of the 5,600,000 additional Hispanics counted in the United States by 1980, fewer than 2,600,000 are counted as Catholics—and that supposes the unlikely fact that the period saw no other growth in the U.S. Catholic population drawn from other ethnic groups or new arrivals. This same oddity shows up in regional and state statistics. This means that either the majority of Hispanics are not Catholic, or that Hispanics are not properly accounted for in the statistics of the U.S. Catholic Church.

In summary, this document sheds further light on the situation of the Hispanics with regard to the U.S. Church; it also seems to validate the reasoning behind many of the observations made at the Second *Encuentro* as well as tenor many of its conclusions, that Hispanics are underappreciated and underserved. The document's findings also put in doubt the reliability of the census data of the period.

3.5 PERSPECTIVE AFTER TWENTY-SIX YEARS

Changes Compared to the First Encuentro

The years between the First and Second *Encuentro* (1972–77) are turbulent years in Latin American theological development, strongly affecting the theological schools of thought that reach the Hispanic Catholic world in the United States; positions have become radicalized; the interpretation of the documents of Medellín is the object of fierce controversy; the most celebrated and radical liberation theologians pass across the scene; there is a ferment of new theological and pastoral language, sparking oft-repeated proclamations and slogans—though often without substantial content.

For example, there are references to the "Church of the masses" and the "popular Church"; the Basic Ecclesial Communities are considered the "only" form of the postconciliar Church. There is a demand that the Church "should" begin in small groups. The Church is told to "commit itself," often to causes that are emotional and fleeting. There are even charges of "oppression" suffered at the hands of the hierarchy. All of this is reflected in the execution of the Second *Encuentro*, which, in comparison with the First *Encuentro*, is much more systematic, organized, and methodologically prepared. There is a degree of popular consultation, but the "guides" most often serve as ideological straitjackets that do not allow departure from a particular way of thinking—a dominating leftist point of view that is quite rigid and dogmatic, a way of thinking that excludes different points of view, and that involves everything, controls everything, and predetermines everything.

In the five years that passed between the First and Second *Encuentros*, the consolidation and triumph of a certain model of the Church is evident, at least on the theological plane—and it is a model that clearly does not coincide, nor could it, with the traditional and well-established Church model that derives from the Irish, Italian, Polish, and German mentality of the nineteenth century and beginning of the twentieth.

What is disconcerting is that this new Church model is readily assumed to be a fit and even a requirement for the Hispanic pastoral situation. Although this model has not been lived out or widely accepted, the Second *Encuentro* calls for its praise and defense. The Second *Encuentro* was so systematic in its approach, so comprehensive in its execution—so tightly prepared by the regional *Encuentros* and the Working Document—that at its conclusion, in the Final Document, there are no surprises. There is very little fresh thinking. In reality, there is much, very much, of the same.

We cannot doubt the good faith of those who prepared the Second *Encuentro*, nor their organizational capacity, which is quite superior to that of the First *Encuentro*. They worked diligently and helped put the spotlight on the Hispanic pastoral challenge as centered on a permanent theological theme: Evangelization. In that sense, the Second *Encuentro* has definite value as, at least, a partial reading of the exhortation *Evangelii Nuntiandi*.

Benefits of a Systematic Approach

The Second *Encuentro* has an as yet unexplored richness in presenting a vision of the whole—thanks to the efforts that were made to systematize its process and the uniform style of its recommendations. It is a systematic exhibition of the Hispanic problem.

There may be some missing pieces—but the final result is complete and harmonious in its parts. Rather than a practical tool, it could very well serve as a model for teaching various constituencies about the complex needs and rich contributions of the Hispanic Catholic community in the United States.

The six principal themes of the Second *Encuentro* show a pastoral tendency that is somewhat horizontal, in that five of the topics involve practical concerns and that the sixth, Evangelization—although treated on the theological, vertical level—is presented as fundamental to the operability of the other themes. It is quite a curious case in which, while seeking to explore the roots of Hispanic cultural and spiritual identity, a scheme emerges that is hardly Hispanic. It is rather coldly pragmatic, an approach that Pius XII might have labeled a "heresy of action."

The Second *Encuentro* does not ignore the liturgical, the catechetical, or the spiritual dimensions of the faith—but it but does not focus on them as being central to the life of the Church. The world of the Second *Encuentro* is social, but understood not in the light of the Church's social teaching, but in the context of the Cold War. In this landscape, the United States is not seen as supporting democracy and human rights, but as lending its support to Latin American dictatorships and their anticommunist stance, their ideology of national security. According to this policy, the only dictator who can be condemned is Cuba's Fidel Castro, since he is both pro-Soviet and anti-American. In its political stance, the Second *Encuentro* clearly takes positions that are diametrically opposed to those of the U.S. government. Of course, the Church has a right to oppose policies that are contrary to natural law, to true justice, and to Church teaching.

On the other hand, when it comes to intra-ecclesial affairs, in the five years since the First *Encuentro*, strong calls have emerged demanding an end to priestly celibacy; there have been a host of small scandals, of individuals leaving the priestly and religious life. This trend certainly had an impact on the preparation and execution of the Second *Encuentro*, and that is quite evident in some of its conclusions.

Persistence of Weaknesses

In summary, the Second *Encuentro* repeats the error of taking sides in questions that go beyond its competency, such as its petitions for a married priesthood, women deacons, major changes in canon law regarding deacons, and so on. Also, just as was the case at the First *Encuentro*, too much time is spent in the drafting of overly detailed formulations of petitions and lists of pastoral priorities. The great challenge is to make all these actionable.

III

THE HISTORY OF THE THIRD NATIONAL HISPANIC PASTORAL *ENCUENTRO*

Catholic University, Washington, DC (August 15–18, 1985)

1

TOWARD THE THIRD NATIONAL HISPANIC PASTORAL *ENCUENTRO*

1.1 THE NATIONAL COORDINATING COMMITTEE

Integration and Launching

As a result of the Second *Encuentro*, a National Advisory Committee was created with the mandate to advise the Secretariat for Hispanic Affairs; as of May 1983, this becomes the National Coordinating Committee of the Third *Encuentro*. The committee is made up of the Director of the Secretariat, a representative of each of the Regional Centers or Offices, a Diocesan Director of the Hispanic Apostolate chosen in each region, the representatives or directors of the national apostolic movements, the pastoral institutes, representatives of immigrants, youth ministry leaders, and members of the main Hispanic pastoral organizations. The launching of the National Coordinating Committee of the Third *Encuentro* is driven by a guiding principle and the design of a process that aim to engage "the masses of Christians who are not in the Church, [while] seeking the broadest possible participation." The overriding objective will be for participants in the Third *Encuentro* to be "reflecting on a model of the Church as missionary and participatory."

How much time was spent in order make this particular model a reality? Certainly, the careful design and organization of the proceedings bear witness to great effort; considerable creative ability; and many hours of study, preparation, and meetings on the part of the organizers. Certainly, the National Council Committee of the Secretariat and the Secretariat team merit recognition of their efforts and considerable talents.

The Proposal (June 1982)

In June 1982, the National Council Committee officially presents the Secretariat for Hispanic Affairs with the proposal for the Third *Encuentro*. The document contains two parts: a justification, or "rationale," and a proposed process.

In terms of the rationale, the proposal opens with the statement that five years have passed since the Second *Encuentro* and that the period has seen both highs and lows.

Highlights include the fact that many bishops now better understand the dimensions of Hispanic ministry, that several concrete pastoral strategies have been embarked upon, that steps have been taken toward the inculturation of the liturgy (the text refers incorrectly to "acculturation"), that appropriate lay ministries have been initiated, that there is more hope for vocations among Hispanics, and that the wholesome influence of the apostolic movements is being felt. These and other signs have been very encouraging.

But there also are some "shadows": a lack of communication with Hispanics who are outside of the Church, particularly those who are at risk of joining other Christian churches or denominations; a lack of leadership in the Hispanic Catholic community; a pastoral crisis caused by the lack of appreciation of Hispanic popular religiosity; and Hispanics are still not present in the most important levels of the Church's structure and feel like failures because they are not able to contribute significantly to the Church in the United States, due to persistent cultural barriers.

However, the proposal also mentions that the bishops of the province of Santa Fe, New Mexico, at the beginning of 1982, took note of a decrease in the level of Hispanics' participation in political life and found that they were benefitting less from the socio-economic structures available—all this in the context of an overall threat to traditional Hispanic Christian values.

For all these and other reasons, the National Advisory Committee considers that it is time an inventory be done of both progress and remaining challenges, and that fresh hopes be raised; this, the authors argue, can only be achieved with a Third *Encuentro*.

The proposed process has four major purposes: pastoral training of leaders, evangelization, bringing about a commitment on the part of the grassroots, and a focus on *Encuentros* at the diocesan and regional levels. To facilitate things, the proposal presents a calendar marking the series of various stages and proposes, as already noted, that the National Council Committee become the National Coordinating Committee for the Third *Encuentro*.

The Diocesan Pastoral Teams (EPDs)

The launching of the preparation for the Third *Encuentro* is to happen simultaneously with the formation of the EPDs. These, the document suggests, should be formed between May and October 1983 through the mechanism of the Diocesan Assemblies or the Hispanic Pastoral Councils, "or, where such organisms do not exist, [the EPDs should be formed] by the Directors (of the Hispanic Apostolate) of the Diocese."

No valid documentation is at hand to ascertain how many dioceses organized the EPDs through assemblies and so on, or by means of the Directors of Hispanic ministry. Moreover, it is not clear how many EPDs actually began functioning. A further investigation of this matter would undoubtedly be fruitful and interesting.

During that time (May to October 1983), the EPDs have the task to review and evaluate the implementation of the Second *Encuentro* in their respective dioceses, and to focus on those aspects that had not been implemented. The result in each case is unclear, but in light of the later development of the process, it becomes clear that the EPDs are able to implement little beyond what had already been initiated.

At a later stage, from October 1983 to April 1984, the EPDs are tasked with creating awareness at the grassroots level of the campaign to prepare for the Third *Encuentro*, doing so through the use of "appropriate means of social communication," the specifics of which are not spelled out. In the end, it is not clear if local media were actually used.

During the same period, the EPDs are asked to form groups within the Hispanic community in order to "consult with the base" concerning the principal pastoral issues, as identified by the same Hispanic community. This work is not to simply be an "inspection"; rather, it is described as a process of "pre-evangelization." The speaker or animator for the local group is urged to present a "personalized image of the missionary Church." The National Coordinating Committee is to prepare materials for this purpose.

Finally, the EPDs, during this same stage, are to organize a "diocesan workshop for reflection" that would study the conclusions reached thus far. Five key points from these deliberations are then slated to be put before the National Conference of Diocesan Directors and others who are responsible for Hispanic ministry.

It is not known how many dioceses actually held these workshops nor in how many dioceses the Diocesan Director, after apparently minimal consultation with his or her closest team, extracted the five key points or conclusions reached at the workshops. It is conceivable that a number of the participants at the National Conference of Diocesan Directors joined the proceedings without having prepared any conclusions and simply participated in the regional groups.

In hindsight, the concept of the EPDs would seem, as with so many good initiatives, to have had only a brief life, given the fact that their existence was tied to certain facts on the ground or circumstances that are fleeting. Nevertheless, a number of teams did capture and record concerns, hopes, and projections that helped launch and find expression at the Third *Encuentro*.

1.2 EVALUATION OF THE SECOND *ENCUENTRO*

The Pastoral Letter "The Hispanic Presence: Hope and Commitment" (December 12, 1983)

At the plenary assembly of the National Conference of Catholic Bishops of the United States (NCCB), held April 29 through May

1, 1980, in Chicago, the subject of pastoral care for Hispanics is dealt with in a detailed manner. Four documents presented on that occasion deserve special mention; they were published by the Hispanic Catholic Center of the Northeast in 1980 and reedited and reissued in 1981 under the title "Hispanic Catholics in the United States."

The first of these documents consists of introductory remarks by Archbishop Roberto F. Sanchez, Archbishop of Santa Fe, New Mexico, chairman of the Ad-hoc Committee for Hispanic Affairs. Then follows a panoramic, sweeping survey titled "Hispanic Catholics in the United States," written by Father Frank Ponce. Third is a document titled "Christian Identity and Mission of Hispanic Catholics in the United States," written by Father Virgilio Elizondo. Finally, there is a beautiful homily by Archbishop Patricio F. Flores of San Antonio.

This was the Bishops' Conference's starting point for the lengthy process of preparing a Pastoral Letter, which—following a number of drafts and debates—was published December 12, 1983, under the title "The Hispanic Presence: Hope and Commitment." The document, in section 18, calls for the Third National Hispanic Pastoral *Encuentro*.

The letter consists of four main parts. The first is a call for Hispanic ministry, as practiced in response to the reality on the ground, including the socioeconomic conditions affecting the Hispanic community. The second part lays out the achievements of Hispanic ministry in the United States. The third deals with the most urgent pastoral needs and challenges, based on the mission of the Church and the Hispanic presence in the United States. It highlights, in order: the liturgy, homiletic renewal, catechesis, vocation and formation of lay ministries, vocations to the priesthood and religious life, Catholic education, communications media, ecumenism, Hispanic youth and family, migrant farm workers, social justice and social action, prejudice and racism, ties to Latin America, popular Catholicism, Basic Ecclesial Communities, and other possibilities.

The fourth chapter is a declaration of commitment: to universal Catholicity as well as to a response to temporal needs and available resources. It is joined to a call to recognize the Hispanic reality, in the form of the convocation of the Third *Encuentro*, and the announcement of an overall Pastoral Plan. Summing up, this Pastoral Letter can be considered an evaluation of the Second *Encuentro* and the effective launching of the Third *Encuentro*.

Case Study: Evaluating the Second Encuentro in the Northeast (January 1984)

The Northeast region, like the other regions, pursued an in-depth assessment of the Second *Encuentro*. The team is comprised of Maria Rivera and Amanda Polania; Eduardo Kalbfleish, national secretary of the Cursillo Movement; Fathers (subsequently Bishops) Alvaro Corrada del Rio, SJ, and Roberto O. Gonzalez, OFM, with the collaboration of Father Eric Ruggiano, CSC; then there is the staff of the Hispanic Catholic Center of the Northeast, comprised of Mario Paredes, Carmen Castro, Freddy Cintron, Dina Escobar, and others. The team prepares an evaluation of the Second *Encuentro*, which is analyzed by Father Roberto O. Gonzalez, OFM, and tabulated by the seminarian (at the time) Freddy Cintron. The questionnaire was earmarked for 180 potential interviewees, among whom are included the 100 individuals who had been delegates from the Northeast to the Second *Encuentro*; the 46 who had attended as observers; and another 34 chosen from among Diocesan Directors and consultants associated with the Center but who had not attended. However, in the wake of some potential interviewees having moved to other areas of the United States, to Puerto Rico, and to Spain, the questionnaire was sent out to 149 individuals, of whom 83 or 56 percent responded, a high rate of response for this type of poll.

Those who responded were twenty-four women (29 percent) and fifty-nine men (71 percent). The majority (55 percent) is between thirty and forty-nine years of age; 40 percent were over fifty and 5 percent under thirty. From a hierarchical point of view, 47 percent were priests and 7 percent were deacons, plus laypersons (35 percent) and women religious (11 percent). Overall, 57 percent of those who responded had participated in the Second *Encuentro*; among them 43 percent were priests; 9 percent, deacons; 4 percent, women religious; and 44 percent, laypersons.

When asked whether the recommendations of the Second *Encuentro* had been implemented or not in their diocese, 52 percent gave a significantly positive response; 37 percent said the recommendations were implemented only in a limited way, and the remaining 11 percent said they did not know.

The importance of safeguarding the Hispanic language and culture was strongly emphasized by the Second *Encuentro*; not surprisingly, 69 percent responded that both (language and culture) were very important in their diocesan and parish pastoral programs targeting Hispanics.

It should be pointed out that only twenty of those polled responded that Basic Ecclesial Communities (BECs) were established in their area. Only sixty-seven responded that they had some kind of program for Hispanic youth; and only five said they did not know of any. As could have been expected, the feast days of *Providencia, Caridad del Cobre, Altagracia*, and Our Lady of Guadalupe were pointed out as the most significant Marian festivities. It appeared that, generally, all the parishes feature a procession of palm leaves on Palm Sunday as well as the procession of the Cross on Good Friday. Also celebrated are the *Posada*, the *Aguinaldos* Mass, *el Dia de los Reyes Magos*, and the feast of John the Baptist.

Among the groups and movements most often mentioned were the Cursillos, followed by the Prayer Groups or Circles, the Ladies of the Sacred Heart of Jesus, the Legion of Mary, the Society of the Holy Name of Jesus, the Daughters of Mary, biblical study groups, Pre-Cana programs, and the Spanish-language choirs. Twenty-five respondents reported that there is bilingual education in the Catholic schools of their diocese. Half of those who responded affirmed that local workshops on political responsibility for Catholic laity had been offered—but that many of them were only conducted in English.

Almost 40 percent of respondents reported that Hispanics faced difficulties in being accepted, while 11 percent, by contrast, indicated that Hispanics were widely accepted. A majority affirmed that there is cooperation among the diverse Hispanic groups. However, 7 percent said that they were not aware of such cooperation.

The conclusion reached by the report is that the recommendations of the Second *Encuentro* have been broadly implemented and that there has been a definite, ongoing effort on the part of the Church to evangelize the Hispanic community. However, the well-known Basic Ecclesial Communities are only in a beginning stage of their development. Many of the pastoral activities have been carried out in Spanish, among them many kinds of retreats and other events targeting youth. The emphasis on cultural identity does not seem to be significant, although that is not the case when it comes to Marian devotions and the important seasons of Advent, Christmas, and Holy Week. The same is true for rosaries and novenas said for the deceased.

Nearly three-quarters of respondents affirmed that the subject of Hispanics' human rights had been highlighted in dioceses and parishes—but with limited effect. In addition, for the most part, bilingual education has not been provided in the Catholic schools of the Northeast region. Some Hispanics have experienced tension with other ethnic groups, although this does not take away from important examples of cooperation.

For the record, the poll was conducted by telephone, after Father Alvaro Corrada del Río [now Bishop of Mayaguez, Puerto Rico] sent interviewees a memorandum assuring them of confidentiality. The results of the poll were published in 1984.

Theological Reflection (February 1984)

At the same time that the poll was taken, small groups engaged in theological reflection on the two *Encuentros*. This reflection was guided by three themes: a history of salvation, a deeper study of the Christian vocation, and some elements of ecclesiology. A synthesis of these discussions was published in the February 1984 issue of the bulletin *Noticias de la Región XI* (News from Region Eleven). The principal conclusions are as follows:

1. The history of salvation involves questions of conscience, in accordance with the tenets of liberation theology, which establishes a parallel between the history of the Hispanic people and the history of the liberation of Israel. The faith of Hispanics, transmitted by their ancestors, must be seen in a historical perspective, with an awareness that Hispanics are

both an "oppressed" and a dispersed people. They have dignity and identity as a people, a people with its own culture; Hispanic Catholics, by virtue of their baptism, have the right to be ministered to by the U.S. Church.

2. The Christian vocation of the Hispanic people leads them to accept their journey as pilgrims, pursuing a continuing conversion and a transformation of their situation as part of their search for the kingdom of God. From an ecclesiological perspective, Hispanics must cease considering themselves as simply a "mass" of persons in order to develop an awareness of their identity as a people. The Hispanic people have an important prophetic role, as, from the grassroots up, they denounce all manner of wrongs—a witness that must be accepted, respected, and integrated into the work of the Church.

3. This movement from the base up, says the text, should inform the development of a Pastoral Plan, a plan that favors the relationship between faith and culture, that identifies with those who are marginalized, and that maintains the parallel between Our Lady of Guadalupe and the Church. There should be a coordinated pastoral effort, one that favors the multiplication of ministries, with very special attention paid to youth and the poor—a Pastoral Plan that is the personification of Christ Himself.

1.3 NATIONAL CONSULTATION IN ROSEMONT, ILLINOIS (APRIL 4–7, 1984)

What Is Involved?

In May 1983, as previously noted, the process of preparation for the Third *Encuentro* begins in earnest. In November of the same year, the U.S. bishops officially convoke the Third *Encuentro* and, in order to prepare for it, call for a National Planning Conference, which is held in Rosemont, Illinois, April 4–7, 1984. Convened by Cardinal Joseph Bernardin, Archbishop of Chicago, more than 450 representatives from around the country participate.

In Rosemont, two Hispanic bishops address the gathering: Archbishop Roberto F. Sanchez of Santa Fe, New Mexico, and Bishop Placido Rodriguez, Auxiliary Bishop of Chicago. The job at hand is to evaluate proposals made by all the dioceses and arrive at the formulation of the five principal themes of the Third *Encuentro*.

According to the scheme of Rosemont, it is determined that in those dioceses without a Director of Hispanic ministry, a member of the EPDs would step in and represent the local Church in preparing for the Third *Encuentro*. Similarly, it is requested that each region engage three migrant workers, three young people as well as regional representatives of the apostolic movements.

The Approved Process

The meeting in Rosemont also stipulates that each diocese hold a second meeting of the community at large—between April and December 1984—to study the subjects chosen for the Third *Encuentro*; the meeting also calls for a second "workshop" for reflection and the election of delegates to participate in the Regional *Encuentro*.

Regional *Encuentros* are scheduled to be held between January and May 1985, with the participation of representatives of each diocese and, of course, with the approval of each respective ordinary.

Finally, the Rosemont conference decides that the Third *Encuentro* will be held in August 1985, again in Washington, DC— just as the First and Second *Encuentros*—and that a National Hispanic Pastoral Plan would be formulated based on the deliberations of the Third *Encuentro*.

1.4 PREPARATORY MATERIALS

Manual to Serve as a Guide for the Formation of the Diocesan Teams of Promotors (EPDs)

The twenty-six-page, eleven-chapter document features: an expression of commitment to unity and service of the Hispanic Pastoral Institutes, an instrument for the formation of the

Diocesan Pastoral Teams (EPDs), a pedagogical resource to facilitate work at the grassroots, and the outline of the process leading to the Third *Encuentro.*

Following the introductory chapter, the second chapter deals with the EPDs and offers a series of guidelines. For example, the participants at the diocesan or parish level are representative leaders from the different areas of pastoral work—laypeople, priests, or religious; the responsibilities and tasks of the EPD are mentioned to determine the criteria to be used in the selection of its members. The chapter then explains the purpose of the national consultation, and provides practical information regarding accreditation and so on.

The third chapter explains the method for analyzing the reality "on the ground," using the schema of "See-Judge-Act": *See* implies that EPDs introduce themselves into the reality in order to transform it; *Judge* insists that this should be done from a theological perspective, while *Act* calls for concrete pastoral action and periodic evaluation. This chapter is the most important, not only from a theoretical or ideological perspective, but also with regard to methodology. It features the questionnaire that will assess people's experiences and thinking in order to inform three key objectives: to identify the most urgent needs of Hispanic Catholics; to create evangelization tools for EPDs, which will also allow them to reach out to the un-churched; and to generate interest in participating in the Third *Encuentro.*

It is expressly requested that the questionnaire not be sent by mail, that it also be given to nonparticipants, that it be administered by the EPDs, and that the findings inform a day of reflection. The chapter concludes with two appendices: one featuring a guide to conduct surveys and another that provides norms for effective dialogue.

The fourth chapter sets six priorities: the strengthening of leadership and its orientation toward service, that organizers make effective use of a communication network, that effective coordination keep the focus on the overall vision and facilitate the sharing of tasks, that all content focus on integral evangelization, that the target of all efforts is the Hispanic community—the people whose voice should be heard—and that the focus be on the theological-pastoral foundations of the entire enterprise. These are the Bible, the Magisterium, and tradition as well as the history of the Hispanic people. As regards these foundations, ample support is found in the documents of the U.S. Bishops' Conference and the Council of the Latin American Bishops (CELAM).

The fifth chapter further explains the "tradition," emphasizing the oral tradition as a crucial guardian of the people's memory. The Latin American peoples, the text says, "have a rich tradition of struggling for freedom that is expressed in historical movements of emancipation and independence—[pursuing goals] still unattained today, yet always present in the people's *memory*." There is also a substantial section devoted along similar lines to "history."

The sixth chapter tackles potential "reactions and conflicts," foreseeing difficulties with diverse outlooks. Here, the text insists on a spirit of "conversion," as well as on the broadest possible openness to an "invitation." Chapter seven is dedicated to spirituality, based on the reading of Exodus as a story of liberation. The text then goes on to explain how to "celebrate" the Hispanic journey, how to overcome dualisms, how to find ways of identifying and meeting fresh challenges, and how to rescue Hispanic traditions and take advantage of their cultural riches. The text emphasizes the core importance and value of the Eucharist and the Marian cult as well as the entire sacramental life. The chapter concludes with a selection of songs from the Second *Encuentro*.

The remaining chapters are brief. The eighth chapter gives a list of the seven "Pastoral Institutes"; the ninth assigns to Sister Rosa Martha Zarate M., SJS, and Maria Pilar Aquino the responsibility as editors. The tenth discusses various liturgical materials that can be used, and the eleventh features a very brief bibliography in which the only book cited apart from the Bible is a history of the Church in Latin America written by Enrique Dussel, a noted exponent of liberation theology.

Guide for the Diocesan and Regional Encuentros

The guide opens with a declaration that its objective is to encourage, invite, and promote a sense of community among the

Hispanic people; it insists that it does not seek to control nor limit creativity, nor impose a particular way of proceeding. It declares its commitment to find a balance between local creativity, on the one hand, and parochial, diocesan, regional, and national unity, on the other.

The guide then reminds the reader that the Third *Encuentro* is convoked by the NCCB, by way of item No. 18 of the Pastoral Letter titled "The Hispanic Presence: Hope and Commitment." Therefore, the guide suggests, the diocesan bishop is the one who should convoke the Diocesan *Encuentro*, just as, by way of the regional organizations, the local bishops in question will convoke the Regional *Encuentros*.

Third, the manual notes that the goal of the Third *Encuentro*, according to item No. 19 of the Pastoral Letter, is to produce material for a National Pastoral Plan for Hispanic Ministry. For their part, the diocesan and regional *Encuentros* "are the channels through which the prophetic voice of the grassroots reaches the national level."

Stressing the importance of the *Encuentros* as part of the historical process of developing a comprehensive pastoral strategy in the service of Hispanics, the guide refers to the Third *Encuentro* as a moment of grace within that process. It adds critical objectives for the diocesan and regional *Encuentros*: creating awareness among the community, amplifying the prophetic voice and discerning the role of prophecy in the process, gathering the contributions of the people, developing practical proposals and drawing firm conclusions, choosing the participants for the Third *Encuentro*, and confirming the creation of EPDs.

Next, the manual sets the criteria for choosing participants at the various *Encuentro* levels: he or she must have participated in a reflection or study group, have a clear commitment to evangelization among Hispanics, have an ability to work well with others, and demonstrate a knowledge of the Hispanic reality. The process of selection is stipulated as follows: the Diocesan Promotional Team selects those who will participate in the Diocesan *Encuentro*, which, in turn, will choose the individuals to attend the Regional *Encuentro*, provided they are mandated by their local bishop. Finally, diocesan delegates to the Third

Encuentro are chosen from among those who attend the Regional *Encuentro*.

The guide spells out nine categories of individuals who may participate in the Diocesan *Encuentro*: the bishops; the Hispanic vicars and parish officials; priests; male and female religious; members of reflection groups; members of the EPDs; members of the mobile work teams; members of parish organizations and movements; personnel of the diocesan chancelleries, if convenient; members of the regional team or office; plus, "any other person that the EPD believes it is useful to invite."

When it comes to the regional level, the guide suggests that, first of all, the bishops of the respective dioceses should participate; next, come the diocesan directors of Hispanic affairs and those chosen by the diocesan *Encuentro*. This last group, the guide stresses, should allow for substantial representation from youth, farm workers, blue-collar workers, and women.

At the national level, ideally, seven participants per diocese are foreseen. Depending on the size of the Hispanic population in the dioceses in question, the number of participants per diocese can differ, provided the regional total represents the equivalent of seven participants per diocese. In each diocese, there should be at least four participants: the bishop, the diocesan director overseeing Hispanic affairs, and two laypeople. Again, the guide calls for the participation of youth, migrant farm workers, and women, noting that a migrant female youth could fulfill all three categories.

The manual then revisits the functions of the Diocesan Promotional Team (EPD); it calls for the setting of a date for the diocesan *Encuentro* as well as a selection of a location. It also outlines the process of selecting participants; lays out the various tasks; and indicates how to gather and analyze the deliberations of parish reflection groups that will feed into the diocesan *Encuentro*; and, finally, it suggests ways of how to effectively broadcast information about the local *Encuentro* throughout the diocese.

In the wake of the diocesan *Encuentro*, the EPD is charged with sending its recommendations to the Regional Office and helping to implement deserving proposals at the diocesan level. A local editorial team is put in charge of drafting the conclusions. The EPD is also charged with eventually communicating the conclusions of the

Regional *Encuentro* as well as the Third National *Encuentro* to the grassroots. In the end, the EPD is also put in charge of encouraging the implementation at the diocesan level of all the directives and commitments formulated in the various *Encuentros*.

Similarly, the committee in charge of organizing the Regional *Encuentro* is asked to pick a place and time for it, assign the various tasks, and compile the results of the diocesan *Encuentro* that will inform the regional proceedings. Also, the committee must ensure that information about the Regional *Encuentro* is properly distributed, making especially sure that all the bishops of the region are informed as well as those in charge of the Third *Encuentro*. The committee is in charge of continuing this process in the wake of both the Regional *Encuentro* and the Third *Encuentro*.

The guide goes into further detail—in very exhaustive, some would argue tiresome, fashion—regarding the mechanics of the diocesan and regional *Encuentros*. Their execution and success hinge, says the text, on four different orientations, which are labeled as: objectives, *la mistica*, methodology, and *iluminación*. These are offered as simple suggestions for group discussions.

Nonetheless, the guide provides a great starting point for creating an ecclesiastical environment in which various groups are integrated. The text also carefully outlines the process of formulating proposals coming out of the deliberations, using five criteria to evaluate them: the conclusions are to be prophetic, global, urgent, replicable, and applicable.

The guide also provides valuable information on the way to organize a session dealing with *la mistica*; suggestions regarding the selection of participants; counsel on how to pursue theological illumination as part of the proceedings; directions on how to evaluate deliberations; and, finally, ways of celebrating and proclaiming the conclusions.

In a similar vein, the guide suggests activities that can be pursued in the wake of the diocesan *Encuentro*. In the first place, these concern the participants in the Regional *Encuentro*. There are a number of "suggestions" as to how to evaluate the Diocesan *Encuentro* as well as with regard to getting the EPD started with its tasks. The guide features seven annexes as well as an English version of the entire text.

In summary, this manual is a very serious guidebook on methodology, reflecting careful thought and design. However, in its very precision and detail—which run so contrary to a typically Hispanic approach to tackling issues—the guide also becomes a kind of straightjacket that risks strangling spontaneity and inspiration.

1.5 THE MEETING AT COLLEGEVILLE (JUNE 12–13, 1985)

Evaluation of the Regional Encuentros

In San Antonio, Texas, on February 14, 1985, a first evaluation, leading up to Collegeville, is held. First off, a significant Hispanic presence was reported in 164 dioceses, which are divided into 8 regions. Among them, there was a report on active engagement by regional offices in 126 dioceses, of which 119 had already had or were about to have a Diocesan *Encuentro*.

However, it proves impossible to determine the number of Basic Ecclesial Communities, although the number of guides that were produced exceeds twenty-four thousand, and they have clearly been widely used. There was talk of 177 Diocesan Pastoral Teams, which, if each represented a single diocese, would mean that an even greater number of dioceses had gotten involved in the process.

With regard to the Regional *Encuentros*, it is reported that at least 175 individuals have participated in each, while in total some 450 people have taken part, making for a total number of participants of 2,290. Some nine or ten bishops have taken part, for a total of fifty-six prelates; between 1 and 26 migrant workers joined in per region, for a total of 160; between 15 and 34 young people took part per region, for a total of 240. Based on these figures for the Regional *Encuentros*, it is estimated that the Third *Encuentro* can count on the participation of more than one thousand people.

Armed with these data, the meeting in Collegeville convenes on the afternoon of June 12 and the morning of June 13, 1985.

This meeting is heated and lively, as participants consider a series of reports on the process leading up to the Third *Encuentro* and tackle evaluations of the Regional *Encuentros*. The proceedings culminate with the presentation of the Working Document, prepared by Father Mario Vizcaino, and the document known as the "Guide for Facilitators," written by Sister Dolorita Martinez.

The Collegeville meeting also fine-tunes and sets the agenda of the Third *Encuentro*, building on some excellent preparatory work: the outline of structures and committees presented by Father Juan Diaz Vilar, and the draft of a tentative agenda prepared by Sister Consuelo Tovar. The organizational chart of the Third *Encuentro* is also confirmed, with its coordinator reporting to the Secretariat for Hispanic Affairs as well as the National Coordinating Committee and its Executive Committee known as EPN, the *Equipo Promotor Nacional* (the National Team of Promoters).

Committees for the Third Encuentro

The committees had already been established at a meeting at Whitefriars, in Washington, DC, on September 5, 1984. In Collegeville, the committees present their work done to date and firm up their respective responsibilities. There are twelve organizing committees involved in the Third *Encuentro*:

1. The Finance Committee is responsible for managing all economic resources and paying all expenses, especially those incurred by the involvement of Catholic University.
2. The Committee for Accommodations is responsible for finding lodging for the participants at both Catholic University and Trinity College, where the first two *Encuentros* were held. The committee is to coordinate its efforts with those of the two hospitality teams at the schools.
3. The Transportation Committee is responsible for facilitating the arrival and departure of the participants at the two airports that serve Washington, DC, as well as transporting them every day between meetings and their lodging. The

committee is also responsible for transporting dignitaries and any special guests who require assistance.

4. The Reception Committee is responsible for welcoming all participants, providing them with the necessary information, helping them find accommodations, and so on. This committee must work in coordination with the security team of Catholic University as well as with various student organizations.

5. The Registration Committee is responsible for checking in participants, all of whom should already be preregistered. This committee must collaborate with the credentials committee.

6. The Credentials Committee provides each participant with identification badges, following his or her registration. The committee is comprised of staff from various regions, and thus, its members can be expected to be acquainted with their own delegates.

7. The Hospitality Committee is responsible for creating an atmosphere of celebration and *fiesta*. Its mission includes being particularly sensitive to the needs of dignitaries in attendance as well as to the needs of participants with disabilities, elderly persons, and youth.

8. The Press Committee is responsible for keeping the communications media informed, providing them with precise and timely information, steering clear of sensationalism, and showing sensitivity to the needs of various media outlets.

9. The Secretarial Committee is responsible for the transcription of all presentations and deliberations to be recorded and reproduced; it is comprised of a group of highly skilled professionals.

10. The Translations Committee, first established in Rosemont in April 1984—a different one from the one deployed at the Second *Encuentro*—is responsible for all translations, be it from English into Spanish or vice versa.

11. The Documents Committee, comprised entirely of staff based in Washington, DC, is in charge of compiling all the information about the Third *Encuentro*, including statistics.

12. The Liturgy Committee, appointed by the National Hispanic Liturgical Committee, is in charge of all the liturgical celebrations of the Third *Encuentro*, including music, morning and evening prayers, Masses, and so on.

Clearly, the organizational infrastructure for the Third Encuentro is quite complex and—from a methodological point of view—highly practical, comprehensive, and efficient.

127

2

THE WORKING DOCUMENT

After a lengthy process, as was foreseen, the Secretariat for Hispanic Affairs published—along with a letter sent out on July 15, 1985, one month prior to the Third *Encuentro*—a bilingual version of the comprehensive Working Document for the Third *Encuentro*.

2.1 INTRODUCTION

The document opens with a number of introductory elements, to which a brief description of the methodology is added.

Letter of Presentation

The letter is signed by Sister Consuelo Tovar, DC, who explains that the document has three main parts: the proposals, the pastoral context on which these are based, and an overall theological reflection. She adds that the document expresses the "voice" of the Hispanic people from throughout the eight regions of the United States.

The Presentation salutes the work of the Editorial Committee, which, following the meeting in Collegeville—where a draft was presented—was able to very quickly edit and polish the text and send it off in timely fashion to all the participants of the Third *Encuentro*. (The document is to be distributed only in advance and will not be available at the *Encuentro* itself. Hence, each recipient is urged to bring along his or her copy to the *Encuentro*.)

There is a call for participants of the Third *Encuentro* to hold diocesan meetings in advance—to study the various proposals, focus in particular on the most prophetic elements, and begin preparing for the commitments to action on the part of the local Church. Participants are also urged to review the agenda of the Third *Encuentro* and are reminded that the pastoral guidelines for the National Plan should emerge from the deliberations at the National *Encuentro*.

Illumination: "Prophetic Voice"

This section begins by recalling the prophetic tradition in the Old Testament of speaking in name of "someone"—the Lord as well as the believing community. The prophecy comes from God, but it needs to be incarnated. The "prophetic voice" implies that the speaker is not speaking in his or her own name, but is inspired by the Word of God and the teaching of the Church—but all the while the prophet bears in mind the joys, suffering, and the hopes of the community. Concretely, that voice should be a reproof of all that impedes the coming of the kingdom; and a proclamation of the deliverance offered by God as proclaimed by Jesus Christ.

Methodology

The Working Document presents five subjects that were chosen during the carefully methodological process of reflection; each subject features a section A, which is labeled "Proposal"; a section B, labeled "Reality"; and a section C, called "Theological Reflection," which includes a brief theological compendium containing references to the Bible and other, mostly ecclesiastical, documents.

2.2 THE CHOSEN SUBJECTS

Evangelization

Section A features ten proposals:

1. To renew the evangelizing mission of Hispanic ministry—this includes catechesis at all levels, including the adult level; the promotion of the Hispanic culture using bilingual

and bicultural methods; and a missionary effort that reaches those who are estranged from the Church and/or marginalized in society, such as immigrants, the undocumented, and refugees. There is also a call for the formation of leadership teams (6 regions).

2. Evangelizing the family—this means putting the focus on family unity; encouraging and prompting parents to educate their children in the faith; offering families orientation programs; creating support programs for divorced or separated persons as well as for those who are living together without the sacraments; and stimulating apostolic movements, such as Marriage Encounter, the Christian Family Movement, Family *Encuentro*, and so on (6 regions).

3. Evangelization for the sake of justice—which includes cultivating respect for the dignity of the human person and preventing the violation of this dignity by abortion, sexual abuse, and the exploitation of children. This section also insists on respect for women, the elderly, and those who are sick and without resources, while adding that such concern for human dignity should reach beyond the borders of the United States (1 region).

4. Evangelization through social communication media— this, the text suggests, must be done in accordance with Hispanic culture by way of appropriate radio and television programs; there is a call to ban pornography and other forms of immorality in the media; these efforts, says the text, will require special funding and well-trained professionals (6 regions).

5. Evangelizing migrant workers—an effort supported by a comprehensive program that includes Bible study, liturgy, respect for human rights, a focus on the country's laws, and the formation of leadership. Such a program would be enhanced by various civic and cultural activities (1 region).

6. Preparing pastoral agents who recommend themselves to the bishops by their Hispanic values and their knowledge of Spanish and Hispanic culture—this will ensure that Church documents are published in Spanish or in a bilingual edition, not just translations. Finally, there is a call for

the promotion of Hispanic vocations to priestly and religious life, along with an insistence that those who serve the Church full-time receive adequate salaries (7 regions).

7. Creating, supporting, and maintaining Basic Ecclesial Communities (BECs)—to promote Hispanic culture: to develop a proper appreciation of the Church among Hispanics; to attract those who are estranged from the Church; and to encourage prayer and reflection. To make this happen, members of BECs are called to "serious" study. The text also asks for the creation of interdiocesan and interregional mobile pastoral teams providing pastoral care for Hispanics. These are called to share experiences, support parish priests, use social communication media, and "recruit" Hispanic priests and deacons who understand the dynamic of the BECs and are fully dedicated to Hispanic ministry and to the formation of the laity (7 regions).

8. The creation of bilingual diocesan, regional, and national Pastoral Centers that attend to all Hispanics, including those who are marginalized and undocumented—these would organize groups of agents of evangelization, prepare continuing programs of integral formation, and assist parishes by providing Hispanic personnel (6 regions).

9. The preparation of a joint Pastoral Plan to which each bishop can commit himself and which he can adapt for his local use—this would require the creation of a diocesan Hispanic Pastoral Council with specific functions, such as providing direction to the BECs. Any such Pastoral Plan must take into account the specific reality on the ground, prioritize its activities accordingly, lend missionary emphasis to all efforts, guarantee continuity, and so on (7 regions).

10. Supporting Spanish-language liturgies, even for small groups—if such is the case, suggests the text, the priest should read the Mass in Spanish and delegate the homily to a properly prepared member of the BECs (2 regions).

In the second phase, B, the "reality on the ground" is studied from a number of critical perspectives, the most extensive of which refers to ecclesiastical structures. Here, the spotlight is put

on those structures needing conversion, those lacking inculturation or grounding in the Hispanic culture, and those that lack a
spirit of love and a sense of community. The text also questions
the value of local evangelizing agents who have plans but no concrete commitment to Hispanics, and who do not know the
Hispanic reality. The same goes for those local Church situations
that lack pastoral integration and effective diocesan directors, a
situation that makes for a neglect of Hispanics and opens the
door for the proselytizing of other Christian Churches and
denominations. These include dioceses in which Hispanic ministry lacks sufficient support from the hierarchy; where pastoral
leaders have little pertinent training; where there are few Hispanic
priests and few Hispanic vocations; where Hispanics lack appropriate locales to gather; where there are no BECs; where there are
no bilingual programs; and where there is no biblical formation
geared toward Hispanics (8 regions).

Other problem areas include a lack of media that supports the
interests of Hispanic Catholics (3 regions); families that do not
evangelize within the home (4 regions); social injustice in the
United States and in underdeveloped countries (1 region); and
discrimination of Hispanic immigrants, who, moreover, lack
organization as a group (1 region). Finally, the text expresses a
sense of discouragement, charging that the First and Second
Encuentros failed to produce concrete results (1 region).

The third and final phase, C, is expressed by way of eight
strands of theological reflection (one for each region): evangelization as the central mission of the Church, the need for conversion and renewal, the importance of recovering the missionary
dimension of the Church, the promotion of the evangelizing mission of the family within the context of a prophetic Church,
encouragement of the family as a natural promoter of unity,
appreciation and use of the Bible as the interpreter of reality, and
the imperative to protest against all forms of oppression that
impede the coming of the kingdom. The section concludes with
five citations from the Old Testament, thirty-three from the New
Testament, twenty-one from Vatican II documents, thirteen from
Evangelii Nuntiandi, ten from CELAM's deliberations at Medellín,
twenty from those at Puebla, sixteen from the Second *Encuentro*,

fourteen from the "Hispanic Presence" Pastoral Letter, three from the Code of Canon Law, and one from *Nican Mopohua*.

Integral Education

In the first phase, A, fifteen proposals are presented:

1. The Church's integral promotion of the individual and the family (8 regions)—success will depend on the presence of four essential elements: communication within the family, an awareness of Hispanic culture, a sense of both the history and current experience of the Hispanic peoples, and the creative and liberating mission of faith.
2. Planning to fulfill the pastoral obligation of providing education to Hispanics in every diocese—which means establishing programs of integral education in the parishes (3 regions).
3. The creation of a series of programs to serve the Hispanic community—including those that provide: biblical formation (4 regions); promotion of Hispanic cultural values (7 regions); promotion of family unity (2 regions); moral education tackling the subjects of sex, drugs, and alcohol (2 regions); human rights education (3 regions); political education (6 regions); and civic education (1 region).
4. The establishment of training centers for those in charge of evangelizing the Hispanic community—these should not simply be copies of such centers dealing with English-language ministry (4 regions); such centers could be inter-diocesan and serve various jurisdictions at the same time.
5. The creation of teams that will be responsible for integral education and rural evangelization (3 regions).
6. Offering seminars and workshops dealing with specific, practical problems—including discrimination, lack of documentation, and so on (2 regions).
7. Providing literacy training for adults (2 regions).
8. The creation of Offices for Hispanic Ministry at the diocesan level (3 regions).
9. Making available funds to acquire and produce audiovisual

programs and to make use of media in the integral education of Hispanic Catholics (4 regions).

10. Providing access to communication media that are committed to the development of bilingual programs that, in accessible language and style, transmit Christian values and do not harm the family or support immorality, and so on.
11. The participation at the diocesan level of Hispanic pastoral agents (2 regions).
12. Creating programs for pastoral agents, ministers, and professionals that build up their awareness and increase their sensitivity regarding crucial aspects of Hispanic life.
13. Involving the Church in the national educational system—in particular, in the reform of the Catholic school system, with a view to: overcoming discrimination (2 regions); admitting Hispanics to advanced levels of education (3 regions); providing financial aid to students (3 regions); making available bilingual programs, including those that deal with the Hispanic language, history, and culture (8 regions); hiring Hispanic professors and teachers (2 regions); encouraging collaboration with Latin America (1 region).
14. Maintenance and increase of the financial aid and scholarships available to Hispanics in both the public and Catholic school systems (3 regions).
15. Creating committees to help identify sources of funding for scholarships and training programs for the benefit of Hispanic students and teachers (3 regions).

In the second phase, B, again the reality "on the ground" is studied, leading to thirty-eight specifications: Hispanics seek integral education (1), which is understood as a comprehensive, holistic formation (2), and an awakening (3); it must be bilingual and bicultural for everyone (4), make use of social communication media (5), and serves as a counterweight to assimilation and discrimination (6).

This education, the text insists, should be given great importance, given the situation of immigrants, especially the undocumented (7). To reach these individuals, this education should begin at the grassroots (8) and also to seek to increase political awareness (9), while denouncing all forms of discrimination (10).

This integral education should encourage solidarity (11), the text argues; Hispanics should also be granted the possibility of pursuing advanced levels of education (12), about their faith (13) and their values (14). The text charges that programs for Hispanics are too few (15), because advocates for them are lacking in schools and state governments; overall, the educational system is unfamiliar to Hispanics (16), partly because the system is unfamiliar (17); as a result, education is denied to many Hispanics, though it is their right to be educated (18).

Basic education should be guaranteed to all Hispanics (19); and integral education in particular makes possible their emancipation (20), since it helps them gain self-awareness as "historical subjects" of God's plan (21). The process leading up to the Third *Encuentro*, the text notes, has not reached everyone (22); many parents have little formal education (23) and there is a great need for the education of the entire family (24); indeed, all people have the right to be educated and to be treated as human beings with dignity (25). Hispanic youth, the text insists, need Catholic formation (26).

In many places there is no integration of Anglo and Hispanic priests and their activities (27), says the text, adding that many parish priests and religious education directors do not know what to do with Hispanics (28), due to the fact that many Hispanics have not had an up-to-date integral education (29); moreover, charges the text, the government and the educational system show no respect for human rights (30).

The Hispanic clergy, the text continues, help the fight against assimilation and support integral education (31), which is an urgent need for groups such as the undocumented (32). In many dioceses, the charge goes, Hispanic culture is not accepted and programs for Hispanics merely copy those designed for English-speakers (33); moreover, Hispanics have but little access to the use of media in the Catholic schools, especially if the Hispanic students are very poor (idem).

The integral training of leaders is an urgent need (34). It is also noted that economic conditions are among the principal factors hampering the education of Hispanic people (35). For this reason, it is argued, integral education is much needed (36), and the Church needs to be aware of this (37). The lack of such an education causes Hispanics to lose a sense of their values and gives them a diminished appreciation of themselves; as a result, many Hispanics are ashamed of their roots, believing that they are inferior (38).

The third phase, C, offering a theological reflection, revolves around two poles: the first is the missionary dimension of the Church, which is open to all cultures and which requires an integral education that allows Hispanics to emerge from spiritual poverty. The second pole again concerns the concept of integral education, this time as found in the papal encyclical *Populorum Progressio* (No. 14), and reaffirmed by the Second *Encuentro*. These arguments are strengthened by one citation from the Old Testament, ten from the New Testament, twenty-two from Vatican II's documents, six from *Evangelii Nuntiandi*, fourteen from other papal documents, eleven from CELAM's deliberations at Puebla, seven from the Letter "Hispanic Presence," and six from the Second *Encuentro*.

Social Justice

This begins with phase A, featuring fourteen proposals:

1. Committing the Church to a position of solidarity with the poor (2 regions).
2. The Church should struggle for justice (1 region).
3. Justice must be upheld and lived out in the Church (4 regions): especially through the Church's teaching on social justice and with programs that support the undocumented, refugees, and migrant workers. The text expresses a desire that the institutional church be the first to concretely stand up for justice for the Hispanic community.
4. Getting the Church to promote human rights (4 regions)— specifically civic, electoral, and labor rights as well as guarantees for the rights of the individual. Such an initiative must go hand-in-hand with concrete actions, such as

denouncing injustice, respecting the integrity of creation, and especially, steps that fight the discrimination of Hispanics.

5. Making the practice of and respect for justice a reality on the part of all the clergy and laity (2 regions).
6. Hispanics are called to be the prophetic voice of the Church (2 regions).
7. Awakening the conscience of the people—especially with regards to all forms of injustice, since fighting for social justice is an integral part of evangelization. Accordingly, the text calls on the bishops to take a number of concrete steps to support this process (6 regions).
8. Creating centers that will promote social justice and feature a range of related activities—centers will express solidarity with the victims of racism (2 regions); provide training for those committed to aid these victims and defend their rights (2 regions); and include a legal office to defend victims of racism, including prisoners, for whom the center will develop special programs such as initiatives providing illegal immigrants with "sanctuary" and other services provided by ecumenical efforts. The text also urges the support of commissions for justice and peace (1 region) and a range of programs responding to the needs of Hispanics (1 region). There is also a call for the creation of cultural centers, which can help improve the negative image of Hispanics; plus, the document argues on behalf of putting pressure on the U.S. government with regards to the war against leftist movements in Central America (2 regions). To bring all this about, the Church is urged to train "prophets" (1 region) as well as deploy mobile teams at the diocesan level that can organize parish workshops and promote awareness of Hispanic needs, while also providing training and shelter to those who have just arrived in the United States (1 region).
9. Committing to the defense of immigrants (1 region).
10. Recognizing the role of women (1 region).
11. Forming migrant farm workers' unions (1 region).
12. Establishing pastoral care for ex-prisoners (1 region).

13. Pressuring the government to introduce new, milder laws pertaining to immigrants, migrant farm workers, the undocumented, and so on (2 regions).
14. Integrating catechesis and liturgy in the pursuit of justice (1 region).

Phase B, dedicated to the "reality-on-the-ground," hinges on nine vital points: the first is a reminder that the Church has defended human rights and stood for social justice throughout the centuries; therefore, it should now commit itself anew in support of Hispanics. The second point is the importance of the participation of Hispanics at all levels. The third rejects the global arms buildup, in particular, the war in Central America, and the situation of the poor. The fourth point is a reminder that in God's plan all human beings are equal. The fifth describes the terror plaguing the lives of undocumented workers. The sixth point stresses that many Hispanics are poor, do not speak English, lack training, and do not earn fair salaries. The seventh notes other forms of discrimination and oppression—including those parishes where immigrants still feel like strangers. The eighth point insists on equality and respect for all, which, in part, depends on better communication. The ninth reaffirms that it is the Church's duty to back Hispanics in their struggle against all forms of discrimination.

Finally, phase C, dedicated to theological reflection, explores what it describes as the systematic oppression of the Hispanic people, which, it is argued, should lead Christians to struggle for social justice in accord with Vatican II's call for such a response. The text argues that this call is an echo of the one that brought the Israelites out of Egypt, as they demanded their liberty. The Gospel, the document continues, insists on Christians' mission to bring the good news to the poor, and charges that racism is a sin that must be strongly denounced. All these arguments are anchored in nine references to passages in the Old Testament, twenty-eight references to the New Testament, fifteen to documents from Vatican II, seven to *Evangelii Nuntiandi*, twelve to the deliberations at Medellín, thirty-five to those from Puebla, four to material produced at Second *Encuentro*, and three references to letters issued by the National Conference of Catholic Bishops (NCCB).

Youth

The first phase, A, presents fourteen proposals:

1. Recognition of the importance of putting the focus on Hispanic youth calls for a formal pastoral declaration, in addition to specific programs that help young people integrate into Anglo society, even as they teach respect for Hispanic culture—all in the context of an overall commitment to the struggle against injustice experienced by children and youth in both the United States and the developing world.
2. Giving preferential treatment to Hispanic youth.
3. Formulating a National Pastoral Plan for Youth as part of an overall pastoral plan for Hispanic Catholics, which will feature a range of programs that promote the representation and support of youth, especially keeping in mind the importance of their relationship with the family.
4. Establishing a National Hispanic Pastoral Office for Youth, staffed with personnel and a budget provided by the NCCB—such an office would publish a bilingual periodical or magazine; convoke annual conventions; run programs that increase awareness of priests, deacons, and ministers; and establish a national training institute that features mobile teams.
5. Establishing the post of a regional coordinator for ministry to Hispanic youth.
6. Also establishing the post of a diocesan coordinator for ministering to Hispanic youth.
7. Providing each parish that has a significant Hispanic population with a full-time, salaried, adult bilingual and bicultural advisor overseeing the integral development of youth.
8. Establishing centers and programs for the training of youth and adult advisors—those serving adults should be bilingual, bicultural, and sensitive to the Hispanic situation;

they must know how to challenge Hispanic youth to participate in public life, and be able to respond to the needs of youth—chicanos, *cholos*, latinos, and ex-prisoners. This task requires a substantial preparation for all pastoral agents, especially seminarians.

9. Creating a mobile youth team.
10. Establishing diocesan youth training centers.
11. Facilitating and supporting both academic and integral education.
12. Emphasizing the creation of programs targeting parents and children, which are oriented toward promoting family unity.
13. Supporting youth ministers—including ensuring their participation in diocesan and parish councils.
14. Giving special attention to the following youth: those who have left home, ex-prisoners and others who need rehabilitation, pregnant girls, the *cholos,* the jobless, drug addicts, those with suicidal tendencies, school drop-outs, the undocumented, refugees, and migrants.

Phase B, examining the "reality-on-the-ground," raises a number of critical issues: the first is a reminder that youth constitute the majority of the Hispanic Catholic community—but 99 percent of them "are outside the Church." More than half of Hispanics are under twenty-five years of age and these young people have many problems. Next, the text embraces a preferential pastoral option to serve youth, pointing to the difficulties of their socioeconomic situation as well as the shame of being Hispanic so many experience. There is a call for a National Pastoral Plan for Youth to be integrated into an overall pastoral plan for Hispanics. The text demands the establishment of National Pastoral Office for Youth, led by a coordinator who would oversee the promotion of programs that study and celebrate Hispanic cultural identity. There also is a call for the creation of a diocesan youth pastorate, along with the warning that many young Hispanic Catholics participate in programs offered by other denominations, which are often better organized and more attentive to the Hispanic culture. The text strongly denounces the fact that, in many parishes, youth are barred from being part of the parish council.

Next, the text raises the issue of the lack of trained adult advisors, including priests. There is a call for more training and mention of the need for guidelines for the encouragement of vocations. There also is a call for programs serving parents and children. A demand for youth ministry is accompanied by a lengthy discussion about proclamation and denouncing abuses. This section concludes with a call for youth to bridge the two cultures—Anglo and Hispanic—taking the best of each. There is a claim that just 1 percent of Hispanic youth are involved in Catholic youth groups, but this might be an exaggeration. The section concludes with another call for the rehabilitation of youth who have fallen on hard times.

Phase C, dedicated to theological reflection, offers five brief commentaries: one draws on Scripture to counsel the avoidance of pride; Vatican II is cited in commenting on the modern world's influence on youth; there is reference to CELAM's deliberations at Puebla on youth; there also is reference to the U.S. bishops' Pastoral Letter on Racism; and a quotation from the Pastoral Letter of the Hispanic Bishops, "The Bishops Speak with the Virgin." The section also includes a quotation from the Old Testament, seventeen citations from the New Testament, another nine from Vatican II, three from *Evangelii Nuntiandi*, nine from Medellín, twenty from Puebla, twenty-two from the Second *Encuentro*, six from the letter "Hispanic Presence," and one from another ecclesial document.

Formation of Leaders

In the first phase, A, ten proposals are made:

1. The creation of programs for leadership training (6 regions).
2. Coordinating the work of ministry teams (8 regions).
3. Choosing leaders who understand the people, live with them, and have a personal relationship with Christ as well as a number of other personal qualities—somewhat arbi-

trarily, the text affirms that "for this leadership to be authentic in its commitment and service...it should follow the line of authentic basic ecclesial communities." There also is the mention of the importance of the role of women (8 regions).

4. Creating training institutions—these should include a National Mobile Pastoral Institute, a training center for leaders or schools of ministry, and a promotional team; the training offered, says the text, should be prophetic, using appropriate language and formats, and paying special attention to certain preferred groups (8 regions).

5. Establishing training programs for leaders who are bilingual, respect and celebrate Hispanic culture, and feature use of the Bible, the liturgy, the sacraments, ecclesiology, and so on, plus a host of other secondary sources.

6. The continued training and education of leaders already in place (3 regions).

7. Ensuring that Hispanic leaders participate in overall pastoral planning (4 regions).

8. Requesting that bishops, priests, and religious live more closely with Hispanics, and especially, that bishops take into account the particulars of each pastoral context when deciding on the appointment of ministers, especially priests.

9. Giving more pastoral cooperation to the leaders of movements, promoting vocations, and insisting that formation should be sensitive to the Hispanic cultural needs: there is a strong call for the promotion of the permanent diaconate among Hispanic Catholics.

10. Identifying leaders in each diocese and local community.

Phase B, tackling the "reality-on-the ground," has six chapters: the first affirms that Hispanic participation in the Church's life is lacking. The second chapter points at the lack of leaders, beginning with priests and religious. The situation is considered particularly urgent, given the lack of publicity and promotion of the various services available to Hispanics and the absence of adequate training due to educational deficiencies. The text charges that "the majority of leaders do not have the necessary qualities to be effective."

The third chapter continues to deal with the lack of training and affirms that adequate programs are lacking, that there is no standard methodology for working with people, and that training is poor because of the lack of specialized centers. The fourth chapter points at the need for awareness on the part of bishops and priests; accommodation on the part of diocesan structures, and so on. But there are many instances of a lack of cooperation. Also, there are too few leaders, says the text, and there is not enough participation on the part of the laity; also, Hispanic leaders do not understand what their role is and they don't know how to delegate. The fifth chapter stresses the need for youth leadership, and the sixth again stresses the shortage of leaders who are capable of serving the marginalized sectors of the Hispanic population.

Phase C, providing theological reflection, stresses seven key points: First, the Diocesan Promotional Teams (EPDs) have helped to train leaders. Second, the text calls attention to the prophetic commitment, catholicity, and ecumenical cooperation. The third is a reminder of the parable of the talents. The fourth insists on a model of the Church that is open to all people. The sixth offers a reading of the passage of Galatians 3:28–29, and the seventh reiterates the words of Archbishop Sanchez of Santa Fe, New Mexico, delivered in a homily at the Second *Encuentro*, in which he reflects on evangelization. This rather insubstantial section features twenty-two references to the New Testament, eleven citations from *Apostolicam Actuositatem*, one from *Evangelii Nuntiandi*, eight from Medellín, seven from Puebla, one from the Second *Encuentro*, eleven from the Letter "Hispanic Presence," and eight from the Code of Canon Law.

3

THE THIRD NATIONAL HISPANIC PASTORAL *ENCUENTRO*

3.1 COMMON ELEMENTS

This content is presented on different occasions or featured in various documents that pertain to the Third *Encuentro*. Some are published as introductory to the entire *Encuentro*; others, as introductory to the commitments or conclusions; and still others are appendices to the same.

Focus

This is a kind of welcome that was given out with the notebook of the Third *Encuentro*; it begins with a surprisingly formal, solemn formula that affirms: "In the name of the Holy Trinity, and in response to the invitation [more correctly, convocation] of our bishops, we are meeting these days in Washington, DC, starting on the date of the feast of the glorious Ascension of our Mother Mary, to celebrate the Third National Hispanic Pastoral *Encuentro*."

This is followed by an articulation of what the *Encuentro* is called to be: an experience that creates and deepens the awareness of the Church; a study of and reflection on the Hispanic reality, Catholic doctrine, and proposed action—all according to the conclusions of the Regional *Encuentros*; and a discernment with regard to the five principal themes or priorities guiding the entire process of the *Encuentro*.

Obviously, the strong focus of the Third *Encuentro* established from the outset becomes a kind of straitjacket, with the very methodology of the process leading inexorably to certain conclusions. This effect can be considered either positively, as a valuable piece of planning or, negatively, as a regrettable form of manipulation.

Relationship to the 500th Anniversary of the Evangelization of the Americas

On October 12, 1984, in Santo Domingo, Pope John Paul II had begun the novena of nine years in preparation for the fifth centenary of the beginning of the evangelization of the Americas. He presented each bishops' conference in both North and South America, including the United States, with a large wooden cross modeled on the one planted when Christians set foot in the Americas for the first time.

Participants at the Third *Encuentro* are given small replicas of that cross, along with material about the meaning of the anniversary. This substantial dossier begins by reminding readers in the United States that—according to CELAM—the observance is of enormous importance: at the invitation and urging of the Pope, it is a fitting occasion to embark on a "new" evangelization; also cited are the exhortations of the Pontifical Commission for Latin America (CAL). The text also states that the U.S. Church cannot remain indifferent to what other bishops' conferences and Church institutions are considering to be crucial, noting, as an example, the commitment to observing the anniversary on the part of the Spanish bishops' conference.

Next, the document features a formula for the novena of nine years to prepare for the Anniversary: three years dedicated to faith (1984–86), three to hope (1987–89), and three to charity (1990–92). The novena of years is to start on October 12, 1984, in Santo Domingo. There also is a papal message, which includes John Paul II's fervent request to the Church in the Americas to be persistent in prayer during those nine years.

A further section is dedicated to the cross as symbol of celebration, while a special hymn is included as well. The Jubilee Year is announced: originally planned for October 12, 1991, to October 12, 1992, it will be observed, more logically, from October 12, 1992, to October 11, 1993. Next, it is indicated that the Pope will be petitioned to convoke the Fourth General Conference of the Latin American Episcopate. Finally, the dossier announces the issuing of various publications, while also listing the programs of celebration and observances of each of the bishops' conferences in the Americas.

Preface

Upon publication of the final document of the Third *Encuentro*, Pablo Sedillo, as Director of the Secretariat of Hispanic Affairs, presents the document formally in the preface, adding a few additional items and thanking the Ad-hoc Editing Subcommittee for Hispanic Affairs, comprised of Archbishop Roberto F. Sanchez of Santa Fe, New Mexico; Archbishop Roger Mahony of Los Angeles; Bishop Peter A. Rosazza, auxiliary bishop of Hartford, Connecticut; and Bishop Ricardo Ramirez of Las Cruces, New Mexico.

There is also mention of the National Editing Committee, comprised of Fathers Ricardo A. Chavez; Jorge E. Crespin; Juan Diaz Vilar, SJ; Domingo Rodriguez. ST; Rosando Urrabazo, CMF; Mario B. Vizcaino, SchP; Jose Marins; Sisters Soledad Galeron, Dolorita Martinez, Dominga Zapata, Carolee Chanona, and Teolide Trevisan; and Mrs. Maria Luisa Gaston. This committee enjoyed the full support of the Secretariat team led by Father Vicente O. Lopez, OP, who is assisted by Mrs. Rosalva Castañeda and Mrs. Carmen Etienne.

The preface concludes by affirming the hope and expectation that the document would provide encouragement to the delegates, to all those who participate in the *Encuentro*, and to all those who are involved in the pastoral care of Hispanic Catholics.

Introduction

The introduction briefly underscores the importance of the historical context, introduces the commitments and the theological reflections, while urging that the Third *Encuentro* be studied closely—as the present text is committed to do—taking into account the Working Document and the guides.

Historical Context

This section opens with a well-argued clarification that the Third *Encuentro* is not an isolated occurrence, but the continuation and the fruit of a long line of antecedents: the history begins in 1915, in Philadelphia, when Hispanics first became the subject of official pastoral attention; then, there was the creation of the Hispanic Office in San Antonio, Texas in 1945; the First *Encuentro* in 1972; the establishment of the Mexican-American Cultural Center in the same year; the Eucharistic Congress of Philadelphia in 1976; the Second *Encuentro* in 1977; the publication of the Letter from the Hispanic Bishops in 1982; and the U.S. bishops' Pastoral Letter "Hispanic Presence: Hope and Commitment" in 1983.

There also is mention of the founding of PADRES in 1970, plus the establishment of *Hermanas* in 1972 as well as the creation of the regional offices serving the Midwest in 1968, and those in the Southwest and the Northeast all the same year, 1974.

Prior to the First *Encuentro*, the text recounts, there were only three Hispanic bishops; between the First and Second *Encuentro*, five more were ordained, and between the Second and Third, nine more were appointed, which increased the total to seventeen, of which eight are ordinaries and nine auxiliaries. In 1978, the regional office of the Southeast was created; in 1979, that of the Far West; and in 1981, the office in the Northwest; in 1982, the office for the Northwest began getting set up, and in 1984, the Mountain states were added to the ranks.

During the Second *Encuentro*, the National Youth Task Force was created, which later became the National Hispanic Youth Pastoral Committee. In 1978, the National Council Committee (NAC) was created as part of the Secretariat for Hispanic Affairs; this committee would become the organizer of the Third *Encuentro*.

In 1979, the Southeast Pastoral Institute (SEPI) is opened; in 1981, the Midwest Hispanic Ministry Institute is set up; in 1983, the Northwest Pastoral Institute opens its doors; and in 1984, the California Hispanic Catholic Institute was given its go-ahead.

The very particular methodology that has been forged over the years projects a model of the Church that is one of fellowship and participation. The process leading up to the Third *Encuentro*—the product of excellent teamwork—and its eventual execution is coherent with this model. The methodology consists of eleven critical steps:

1. Formation of the EPDs and the Mobile Work Groups.
2. Evaluation of the Second *Encuentro*.
3. Promotion of the Third *Encuentro* through the media.
4. Consultation with the grassroots by way of a system of direct personal contact.
5. Reflection at the diocesan level and selection of principal subject matter; the first diocesan meeting.
6. National Meeting of Diocesan Directors.
7. Study and reflection of the grassroots concerning the chosen themes.
8. Second diocesan meeting.
9. Regional *Encuentros*.
10. Third National Hispanic Pastoral *Encuentro*.
11. National Hispanic Pastoral Plan.

The Third *Encuentro*, at the outset, has four objectives: evangelization, leadership training, raising awareness at the grassroots level, and a focus on necessary action at the diocesan and regional levels. To these objectives a fifth is added: the provision of materials that would provide the foundation for the National Hispanic Pastoral Plan. A further, sixth objective—added after considerable discussion—is the participation at the Third *Encuentro* of an EPD member for each of the country's dioceses.

The theme of the Third *Encuentro* is "Hispanic People: Prophetic Voice," which derives from the U.S. bishops' pastoral letter "Hispanic Presence: Hope and Commitment." The theme is settled upon at the National Consultation in Chicago in April 1984.

The Third *Encuentro* draws an attendance of 1,148, representing 134 dioceses; attendees include 56 bishops and Major Superiors,

168 priests, 125 religious, and 799 laypeople. Participants include 545 women, 153 youth, and 47 migrant farm workers.

The Third *Encuentro* takes place in five halls, with more than two hundred people in each. Attendees are divided into groups of forty-five, which subsequently are split up into groups of fifteen. The dialogue format facilitates consensus building. The "prophetic pastoral lines" are giving shape to the overall orientation and strategy of the Hispanic pastoral program. In the end, the "commitments" illustrate the decisive "will" of the participants and guarantee a high degree of continuity as expressed in the practical action steps that are proposed to implement the Third *Encuentro*.

Prophetic Pastoral Lines

These are considered to be the most important result of the Third *Encuentro*, its richest fruit; they should serve as basic guides for pastoral action, indeed, they are a "necessary reference for all pastoral work." They reflect a coordinated pastoral methodology designed to harmonize all pastoral efforts; provide an integral education to Hispanics—enabling them to build up an evangelizing and missionary Church that promotes justice, a justice reflected in its inner workings. This prophetic thrust lays out nine different "paths," which, taken together, are as one:

1. Making the family the first priority of pastoral work.
2. Choosing preferentially in favor of solidarity with the poor and marginalized.
3. Choosing preferentially in favor of Hispanic youth.
4. Developing and executing an overall pastoral plan.
5. Becoming an evangelizing and missionary Church.
6. Promoting a committed leadership that is rooted in Hispanic culture.
7. Promoting a form of integral education that is sensitive to cultural identity.
8. Building up a Church that promotes and provides examples of justice.

9. Recognizing the value of women's contributions, and defending their equality and dignity.

Creed

This is a summary of the "beliefs" expressed in a variety of ways on the morning of August 18, 1985. Participants proclaim the creed was adopted "in a process similar to that followed by the Christians in the primitive Church." In practice, they define the creed as the "colors, lights and tones that integrate the rainbow of our alliance with God."

In formal terms, the creed has seven parts:

1. "We believe in the Holy Trinity." The text acknowledges the creed as the "powerful work in our people" and holds it up as a model to follow, and as a way to imitate and connect with the three Persons of the Trinity. Upon referring to the Father, the creed affirms that He delivered us "from the slavery of discrimination [and led us to] the freedom to be united." In referring to Jesus Christ, the creed centers on an invitation "as a people to [contribute to the] construction of the Kingdom." With reference to the Holy Spirit, it speaks of "inspiration and strength given to our leaders" and of the spiritual fruits produced by the Third *Encuentro*.
2. "We believe in our identification with Christ," and therefore, "we support and collaborate in the struggle of the poor, the humiliated and marginalized"; there also is an affirmation of a belief and confidence not only in the leadership of the pastors, but also in the work of political leaders. Similarly, the creed proclaims belief in the role of women, in an integral and just education, and in the need for a process of conversion and study.
3. "We believe in the Catholic Church," a proclamation accompanied by an affirmation of the discovery of "the love of our pastors, our mission as laypersons and the greatness of being Catholics." There is a reflection on the catholicity of races and cultures, and a statement of their pursuit and commitment of common goals—which for

Latino Catholics means to feel accepted as Hispanics in the U.S. Church, while opening their hearts to be evangelized.

4. "We have faith in our people," which poetically adds that the Rio Grande and the Caribbean are God's instruments to fertilize the land that has received the Hispanics. Here is the belief that the U.S. Church is being renewed thanks to the contribution of Hispanic faithful. There is an expression of trust that Hispanic believers will overcome all frustrations and that a commitment to service is the best way to evangelize within the Catholic ethnic mosaic of the United States.

5. "We believe in the gift of the prophetic voice," a voice that commits the Hispanic faithful to the text at hand, a text that gives hope, that seeks fellowship, and so on.

6. "We believe in this National *Encuentro*" and in all aspects of the process involved in all three of the *Encuentros*. Bonds have been formed that will not break, the text says; the voice of Hispanic Catholicism has been expressed, its prophetic force manifested in the Third *Encuentro*'s five principal themes. Here follows an affirmation that Latino Catholics have faith in their leaders, in their own ability to perform the tasks at hand, in their ability to take on the commitments required, and so on.

7. "We believe in Mary, our mother"; the Virgin has embraced Hispanic culture, interceded on behalf of Latino believers, and is clearly on their side. The creed concludes with a final expression of gratitude and an "Amen."

Theological-Pastoral Reflection

This takes place after the conclusion of the Third *Encuentro*, but it is part of the overall evaluation. Its content appears as an appendix to the Conclusions. As a result of a meeting of thirty-five pastoral agents from throughout the United States, in Seattle on October 1–4, 1985, the text is later reviewed and worked on by the seventeen bishops of the Ad-hoc Committee for Hispanic Affairs in a meeting in Tucson, Arizona, January 21–22, 1986. It has four parts:

1. "God acts in our favor." It argues that while the plan of salvation is universal, the Hispanic people have become aware
   of God's active presence among them because he has made
   a preferential option for the poor and has called the
   Hispanic people to a prophetic vocation.
2. "Jesus in the *Encuentro*," affirms that the Third *Encuentro*
   was a *kairos* moment (a moment of grace) thanks to its
   recognition and uncovering of the presence of the Lord
   incarnate in Hispanic history and culture. Hispanics, by
   appreciating the value of their way of being as well as their
   suffering, have a greater sensitivity toward the needs of others, and thus, a closer or privileged approach to Jesus of
   Nazareth and the Risen Christ. In addition, says the text,
   the Third *Encuentro* is an affirmation of the dignity of the
   human person, which is expressed in its outreach to those
   who are estranged or marginalized, women, migrants, the
   undocumented, refugees, and prisoners. The *Encuentro*, the
   text continues, also was the occasion for Hispanic Catholics
   to create and embark on a common project; simultaneously, the *Encuentro* provided the spur to consider the
   majesty of the kingdom, and prompted conversions of the
   heart. Also, this section concludes, the kingdom confronts
   Hispanic Catholics with a challenge to make the best use of
   their freedom and creativity.

   By convoking the people, the Third *Encuentro* has given
   them the opportunity to experience Jesus and his work,
   while embarking on the creation of a new social order;
   learning how to work as a team; exercising authority as a
   form of service; and collaborating with other sectors of
   society. The enterprise is difficult and poses numerous
   risks, but taking these risks is a form of participation in the
   death and resurrection of Jesus. The *Encuentro* proposes a
   demanding pathway—it is a *via crucis* that leads to peace
   and a new creation, holding the promise of the emergence
   of a new model of the Church.
3. "A new style of Church." This shift is considered one of the
   richest aspects of the Third *Encuentro*—the proclamation of
   a new model for the Church, one "in which the prophetic

dimension is preeminent," a model that empowers the Hispanic faithful to not only be a particular "voice" in the community of faith, but to go still further and to articulate prophetic commitments in the face of formidable obstacles. Obviously, this shift challenges more traditional forms of ministry and evangelization that are common in the Church at large.

This section reiterates the demand that evangelization efforts and the Church's missionary dimension be directed primarily to the most estranged members of the community. Here is a commitment to promoting a form of integral, open-ended evangelization, which is committed to the pursuit of justice and "sees itself in a circular and open manner." In summary, Hispanics want to participate fully as members of the U.S. Church—but without renouncing their own culture and particular way of expressing their faith.

In the end, the experience of the Third *Encuentro* challenges Hispanics as well as all the members of "the majority Church": it calls for "a continual conversion," signifying a Church that is on an ongoing journey.

4. "Prophetic Church." Elaborating on the former point, the text cites the faithful's prophetic role in proclaiming the faith and denouncing wrongs—specifically the arms race, consumerism, commercialized eroticism, pornography, and so on as well as injustices inherent in certain social and political systems. The task calls for the promotion and formation of a leadership that is capable of influencing society. Leadership of that caliber can stir up the ferment of the kingdom, and stand up to protect and uphold the family, the poor, youth, and women; and defend the rights of the unborn, the undocumented, migrant farm workers, and all who are marginalized.

La Mistica

This section is comprised of four meditations on the values and sentiments of the journey of the Hispanic people. The first three were composed by the bishops of the Ad-hoc Committee for

Hispanic Affairs, during the meeting in Tucson, Arizona, January 21–22, 1986. The music was composed by Bishop Jose J. Madera of Fresno, California. The final prayer was composed by clergy and laity during a theological-pastoral reflection held in Seattle, Washington, October 1–4, 1985.

The first two elements are interconnected litanies and the last two are prayers. The first three insist more on the dimension of giving thanks, while the fourth reaffirms the pride found in being Hispanic. The first three clearly have a positive thrust, although they also touch on the painful side of the Hispanic reality; the last is more confrontational, even as it steers clear of embracing extremism or unacceptable forms of liberation theology.

3.2 PROCEEDINGS OF THE THIRD *ENCUENTRO*

Description of the Agenda

On Thursday, August 15, 1985, activities begin quite early, although, officially, registration would begin at 3:00 p.m. in Monroe Hall. This process goes on well beyond 7:30 p.m., as planned, due to flight delays and other hiccups that are part and parcel of this kind of operation. Nevertheless, a little past 5:30 p.m., supper is served in the various dining areas.

A little after 8:00 p.m. in the Sanctuary of the Immaculate Conception—opening with a very long procession—the liturgy formally marking the start of the *Encuentro* begins. Archbishop Roberto F. Sanchez of Santa Fe presides. In addition to the hymns and readings, there are words of welcome by Archbishop James Hickey of Washington, DC, the local ordinary. The official convocation is pronounced by Bishop James W. Malone, of Youngstown, Ohio, president of the NCCB/USCC.

The following day, Friday, August 16, Mass is said in the crypt of the Sanctuary at 7:00 a.m., followed by breakfast in the University Center and the northern dining hall. At 8:45 a.m., in the gymnasium, the program begins with Morning Prayer and the greetings and blessings of Pope John Paul II, which are delivered by Archbishop Pio Laghi, Apostolic Nuncio.

Next, Sister Consuelo Tovar, Director of the Executive Committee of the National Promotional Team, provides the necessary practical directions, reminding all of the system of working in groups and subgroups, indicating where the various meetings will be held, and so on. The first day is dedicated to the "prophetic lines."

At 11:30 a.m., there is another Mass, also in the crypt of the Sanctuary; those who had attended the morning liturgy are invited to take the first turn for lunch in the northern dining hall; at 12:15 p.m., following the Mass, a second round of lunch begins.

At 2:15 p.m., in five different locations, so-called "mini-plenary" sessions are given early reports and produce an initial synthesis of deliberations; there is an opportunity to exchange ideas, make suggestions, and so on. In the same locations, at 4:15 p.m., the afternoon prayer is presented, and starting at 5:30 p.m., dinner is served in the various dining halls.

Just after 7:15 p.m., the General Assembly begins in the gymnasium; there is the formal presentation of the synthesis of the deliberations on the "prophetic lines" and related issues. The assembly votes using colored markers. The Editorial Committee commits to working the approved statements into a final draft and sending it on to the Secretarial Committee. After 8:30 p.m., there is joyful fellowship in the gymnasium and on the adjoining field called the "Hill of Saint Thomas."

The program the following day is similar, but in the morning, subgroups work on the prophetic "commitments," which deliberations are subsequently worked into a synthesis. In the afternoon, during the mini-plenary sessions, the five syntheses of the five priorities are presented and turned into a draft of the definitive synthesis of the commitments. Then, at 3:30 p.m., planning sessions are held to discuss the follow up to the Third *Encuentro*, after which participants return to working in two subgroups. At 5:15 p.m., there are more mini-plenary sessions, which lead to a provisional draft of the ultimately definitive synthesis dealing with the follow-up action steps.

At 6:45 p.m., solemn evening prayer is said in the sanctuary, followed by supper served on the "Hill of Saint Thomas." The long day concludes with a dance held in the gymnasium.

On Sunday, August 18, from 7:00 a.m. on, breakfast is served in the two dining halls and at 9:00 a.m., the subgroups begin deliberating the evaluation of the Third *Encuentro*, followed by the preparation of the "creed." The General Assembly begins at 10:15 a.m. in the gymnasium; its task is to read and approve the three drafts ("prophetic lines," commitments and follow up), and to present them formally to Monsignor Daniel Hoye, General Secretary of the U.S. bishops' conference.

At the conclusion of the assembly, lunch is served in two shifts. The *Encuentro's* closing Mass begins at 1:30 p.m. in the sanctuary.

Complementary Materials

Each participant is given a substantial "kit," in which two items stand out: the report and the song book. Additional items cover the celebration of the Fifth Centenary of the Evangelization of the Americas and other material is practical in nature, such as a schedule of meetings and a map of the university grounds.

The report affirms that more than twelve hundred persons participated. The number of "observers" is not included, as was the case at the Second *Encuentro*. Bishops in attendance are given a red ribbon and special guests wear a light blue ribbon.

There are four categories of meetings: the General Assemblies, or Plenary Sessions, are held on a few occasions in the gymnasium. The "mini-plenary" sessions are held in the five "halls," each with a capacity of 225 persons. The twenty-five groups meet in classrooms with a capacity of forty or forty-five persons, and the seventy-five subgroups, comprised of twelve to fifteen participants each, can easily organize their meetings.

At each "level," a facilitator oversees the process; thus, there are, for example, five facilitators in the "halls"; the facilitator team also includes a coordinator. In each of the twenty-five groups, there is a facilitator and a reporter, whose functions are interchangeable. The facilitators wear white labels with black letters and a green ribbon. Each of the twenty-five groups have to choose three coordinators from the respective subgroups. There are also a number of observers and additional staff, and so on, wearing white labels with red letters.

In addition, there are the norms and guidelines concerning parking, the bus schedules, the colors assigned to those who participated in each of the five halls (Red: Maloney Hall; Green: Caldwell Hall; Salmon: Theological College; Yellow: Ward Hall; and Blue: Gowan Hall; Roman numerals indicate each of the five halls, and the letters A, B, and C designate the subgroups).

Liturgical norms are also in force, although they are quite unusual; a solemn Eucharist is not planned. Each day, participants are offered two Masses, and depending on their choice, are requested to bring along the appropriate text. The official language of all the proceedings is Spanish, but simultaneous translation into English is offered in both Caldwell Hall and Maloney Hall for the "mini-plenary sessions," and in the gymnasium for the plenary sessions. Each participant has three colored cards: green to show agreement, red to indicate opposition, and yellow to propose an amendment or voice an objection.

As to the songbook, it contains twenty-four songs, and there are some complaints that they are "too liberal." Two are in English and two are explicitly religious, although with a bent toward liberation theology: "Prophesy" and "Nicaraguan Creed." There are various folk songs, including "I Am Called Cumbia," "My Old San Juan," "Guantanamera," and "Boricano Lament."

3.3 CONCLUSIONS OF THE THIRD *ENCUENTRO*: "COMMITMENTS"

The conclusions of the Third *Encuentro*, following the formula of the Working Document, are grouped into five thematic sections, with each of them following a similar sequence. First, there is a relatively brief introduction; next, a substantive description titled "Looking at Our Reality"; and finally, there are "commitments," which are numbered, beginning with the nine "prophetic pastoral lines."

Evangelization

1. The introduction affirms that evangelization is the essential mission of the Church, that it consists of proclaiming the Word of God, and aims at the conversion of those who accept the kingdom announced by Jesus. Today, the introduction proposes, evangelization must start with considering the individual as being incarnate in a particular place and time. An inculturated approach to evangelization is essential in ministering to all peoples, especially to Hispanics in the United States. The temptation of cultural assimilation is always present, and once succumbed to, it is an assault against the person and the Gospel, the text charges.

2. "Looking at our reality" makes three major points: first, there is the description of a "cold" Church with a feeble missionary dimension and one with which Hispanic people find it hard to identify and in which they are given little responsibility. That is to say, they lack pastoral attention, since their reality is not taken into account; there is no pastoral "continuity"; there are no channels of participation, and so on. In summary, Hispanics "have not felt accepted, attended to or heard in the Church."

   The second charge concerns the lack of all kinds of resources for Hispanic ministry, for which familiar excuses are cited. Third, the text touches on additional flaws in pastoral care for Hispanic faithful. No attention is given to tragedies in the family; also there is a lack of appreciation of the role of women, insufficient pastoral attention targeting youth, a lack of Spanish-language media, and neglect and ignorance with regard to migrant farm workers.

3. There are eight commitments made: the first is to create and support "small ecclesial communities," which are briefly described. The second is to collaborate in the elaboration of an overall pastoral plan. The third is to promote the creation of pastoral centers for leadership training. The fourth is to seek greater authority and resources for offices serving the Hispanic apostolate. The fifth is to develop a more personal style of evangelization, a style oriented

toward the small communities. The sixth is to raise awareness about the state of the media, calling attention to its
false set of values. The seventh is to develop and produce
radio and television programs that reflect Hispanic values
and aim to reach listeners and viewers with integral evangelization. Finally, the eighth is a commitment to become
authentic agents of evangelization, promoting positive values while eradicating abuses and all forms of exploitation.

Integral Education

1. The introduction opens with a proclamation of the principle that education is an inalienable right of all people—as
guaranteed by the United Nations and proclaimed by the
social doctrine of the Church, as expressed especially at
Vatican II, Medellín and Puebla. Proper education covers
many areas of teaching, says the text, upholding integral
education as an ideal: it is a comprehensive, wholistic formation that leads to maturity in the faith. Plus, given the
marginalization of so many Hispanics, integral education is
of great importance in the process of bringing about spiritual, social, and political liberation. Jesus—as the Way, the
Truth, and the Life—illuminates education, says the text,
ensuring that integral education is a form of evangelization
ensuring that everyone might see, judge, and act with the
mind-set of Christ.
2. "Looking at our reality" makes three major points. The first
points at the lack of educational formation; that is to say, it
notes the lack of educational resources that respect
Hispanic culture. Those who are exiled, refugees, prisoners,
the marginalized, immigrants, and the undocumented
urgently need an integral education, the text insists. The
economic condition of the bulk of Hispanics is a limiting
factor. But basic education is necessary to transform society,
the text argues, noting that marginalization is constant and
that there is also a grave lack of political education.

Next, the text speaks of what it calls the lack of commitment on the part of the Church, charging that it's not aware

of its obligations toward Hispanics. There is a call for more Hispanic clergy as a defense against assimilation. As it stands, says the text, many non-Hispanic parish priests simply do not know what to do with Hispanics; and Hispanic youth urgently need to be catechized.

Additional urgent needs mentioned are: family education, leadership training, training centers for laypeople, and better professional training for those working in communication media.

3. Five commitments are made. The first is to create a program of integral education that features spiritual, socioeconomic, political, and multicultural elements, and operates according to a clear set of priorities. The second is for the Hispanic community, clergy and lay, to collaborate in raising awareness throughout the community of the importance and vitality of the Hispanic language, culture, history, and religiosity. The third is to establish bilingual and bicultural pastoral centers and mobile teams at all levels. The fourth is to acquire and produce Hispanic radio and television programming, especially content targeting the most marginalized members of the community. And the fifth is to add a Hispanic dimension to the programs in both Catholic and public education systems, to lobby for programs and materials that are bilingual, to make advanced education more accessible to Hispanic students, to ensure better student orientation and assistance, to provide religious education to Hispanics; to defend human rights, and to offer special educational programs tailored to the needs of migrant farm workers.

Social Justice

1. The introduction reminds readers that social justice is at the core of the Judeo-Christian tradition, that it emanates from the teachings of Jesus, and that it has been a rich pursuit in the Church's history—in both action and writings. The topic, insists the text, remains significant, as countries deal with foreign debt, underdevelopment, oppressive systems,

and so on. It is noted that Hispanics have already dealt with this subject in the First and Second *Encuentros*, and so on.

2. "Our socioeconomic reality" emphasizes three major points. The first refers to the injustices in society: social differences between rich and poor; the difference between the United States and the underdeveloped Latin nations; the arms race; urgent, unaddressed needs of the undocumented, who often suffer abuse and live in fear; the exploitation of farm workers; inadequate education and health; abuses by the police; and the failure of the media to raise the awareness of North Americans about Hispanics, their culture, their needs, and so on.

The second point refers to what are called injustices within the Church, linked, in particular, to an alleged disconnect between preaching and practice. The Church is urged to do more in the realm of immigration, contribute more to the fight against discrimination of Hispanics, and so on. There are still many parishes in which Hispanics live as strangers and face rejection, charges the text.

The third point takes note of the part of the United States in the injustices suffered in Latin America, due to American economic and political interests (such as those in Central America). The United States plays a role in the proliferation of arms, and so on, the text charges.

3. The commitments proclaimed are seven. The first is to denounce injustices and struggle for human rights—especially the right to work without discrimination; the right to a just salary, living quarters, and social services; the right to refuge for the persecuted; and the right to life from the time of conception. The second calls for support of the bishops in their efforts to come to the aid of immigrants and the undocumented, and to promote just laws that do not discriminate. The third (No. 25) is to denounce violence and injustice through the media. The fourth is to work hard to increase the awareness among Hispanics of the most important challenges facing their community; to improve their social formation, legal defense, literacy training, civic training, medical care, and so on. The fifth is to work hard

in order that the Church become an example of social justice. The sixth is to bring about the renewal of the traditional parish so that it becomes multicultural. Finally, the seventh is for Hispanics to develop sharp critical thinking when confronted with oppression, the arms race, and what the text describes as imperialist interventionism.

Youth

1. The introduction affirms that young people are the future of the Church and its youth community, but that many feel marginalized and forgotten. The Third *Encuentro* has made them a priority.
2. The "reality of the Hispanic youth" is characterized by several key aspects: First, youth are largely estranged from the Church, yet they constitute 54 percent of the Hispanic community. Almost all keep their distance from the Church and the faith, as they get involved with drugs, obtain abortions, and so on. The dominant U.S. Anglo culture seeks to uproot them from their native culture, says the text, and as a result, so many youth are ashamed to be Hispanic; their values are confused; and they find themselves in a cultural, moral, and spiritual vacuum.

    The second point addresses the poverty of Hispanic youth. There is an expression of frustration about the lack of financial support given youth; many must seek employment rather than staying in school; their parents are often absent; and many experience abuse as minors within the family.

    The third point is that young Hispanics are hungry for training and formation, but the Church lacks programs to respond to this desire, leaving the door open for other denominations. By way of at least a partial remedy, the text urges that the Hispanic cultural feasts must be observed in such a way that respects their original religious meaning (for example, the *quinceañeras*). The text charges that there is a great lack of youth leadership and outreach to all those who are estranged from their faith; parents often discourage vocations; and there is hardly any Church personnel trained specifically to work with Hispanic youth.

The fourth point addresses the difficulties in the communication between parents and children. There is an urgent call for a national coordination of responses to this specific pastoral responsibility in the context of an overall, national pastoral plan. The text holds up Hispanic youth as a crucial cultural bridge—they are able to take the best from both cultures.

The fifth acknowledges "prophetic" youth who are eager to proclaim Gospel values and the prayer for peace, as they promote brotherly love and good will, while protecting the family and the culture. These youth are urged to denounce materialism, all forms of injustice, oppression, hunger, poverty, violence, the arms race, the "melting pot" theory, abortion, drugs, and alcohol. They are also urged to struggle for peace; a simpler lifestyle; and to express solidarity with the poor without regard for nationality, race, language, and socioeconomic level. The text does express joy and enthusiasm about the predominant Hispanic liturgical style, and expresses confidence that Hispanics can change the world by remaining faithful to their original, authentic way of life.

3. The commitments are nine: The first is to create a national coordinating office for Hispanic youth ministry. The second is to implement a Hispanic Youth Pastoral Plan within the context of an overall pastoral plan; the plan provides for a national coordinator and integral training. The third is a call for Hispanic Catholics to become missionaries serving their own youth. The fourth spotlights appreciation of the importance of bilingual and bicultural assistance. The fifth is a commitment to change educational systems. The sixth aims for the creation of programs promoting youth leadership. The seventh seeks funds and scholarships. The eighth is to promote family unity. And the ninth is for Hispanic youth—and their families—to provide examples of practical, lived-out Christianity.

Leadership Formation

1. The introduction reminds readers that the mission of the Church depends on the faithful's active commitment—adding that it is, in fact, worrisome that there is a need for leadership training.

2. The "reality-on-the-ground" is considered in four ways: The first refers to the lack of Hispanic participation in the Church as well as in the political realm. The second refers to the shortage of committed leaders, along with the lack of recognition of those leaders who are successful, and the lack of publicity and the deficiencies on the educational front. (Most leaders do not have the qualities to be effective, due to a lack of formation, not knowing how to organize people, or lacking sensitivity to the many problems at hand.) The third mentions the lack of training for lay ministers in religious disciplines and in community methodology—deficiencies that are most serious when it comes to pastoral care for marginal groups. The fourth refers to the need for greater awareness in the Hispanic community—as 90 percent of Hispanics do not participate fully in the Church; especially notable is the people's lack of participation in the Church's evangelizing mission. The text points to the great need for true leaders who can be examples for others.

3. The commitments are six: The first is to recruit and support leaders who are truly from the people—who know them and live with them. The second is to work to make sure that Hispanics can participate at all levels of decision-making in the Church. The third is to create centers of training—with mobile teams—to take responsibility for the continuing formation of leaders. The fourth is to promote vocations to the priesthood, diaconate, and so on, and giving them a formation that is steeped in Hispanic culture. The fifth is to encourage bishops, priests, and so on to spend more time with Hispanics, to live among them. Finally, the sixth commitment is, to cultivate awareness—with the help of grassroots organizations—of the needs of Hispanics among civic leaders.

3.4 EVALUATION OF THE THIRD *ENCUENTRO*

Projected Continuity

The Third *Encuentro* carefully put in place ways to prolong its effects and enshrine its image; key to success are the two dozen commitments that participants approved. They are grouped into five sections:

1. The first section is labeled "General Guidelines" and consists of seven commitments: The first is to maintain or set up an EPD (Diocesan Promoter Team) with four key responsibilities: to promote and implement the Third *Encuentro*; coordinate the production and distribution of a bulletin; organize local meetings; and maintain and develop contacts made at the *Encuentro*, using the means of social communication. The second is to propose and implement diocesan pastoral plans. The third is to support the regional offices, enabling them to execute five key tasks: provide advice and counsel for the diocesan plans, defend the conclusions of the Third *Encuentro*, convoke biennial regional *Encuentro*s, inform the Hispanic community and the community at-large about the results of the Third *Encuentro*, and assure its evaluation. The fourth is to establish concrete goals in relation to the Third *Encuentro* and evaluate them periodically. The fifth is to begin the implementation immediately. The sixth is to use the Pope's video message. And the seventh is to form Basic Ecclesial Communities to carry out the commitments of the Third *Encuentro*.

2. The second section is titled "Delegates" and it features three commitments: the first is to meet with the EPD no later than within a month after the Third *Encuentro*. The second is for the delegates to report on their experiences to all levels of the Hispanic community. The third is to organize workshops to publicize the work of the Third *Encuentro*, doing so with the support of the diocesan office that oversees pastoral care for Hispanics.

3. The third section is headed "Diocese" and lists five commitments: the first is to ensure that those bishops already committed to the task seek to engage fellow bishops who are not—this way the entire U.S. Church will implement the Third *Encuentro*. The second is to motivate students and professors at the college and university level. The third is to include material produced at the Third *Encuentro* in the programs of renewal (RENEW), retreats, Cursillos, and so on. The fourth is to propose the establishment of a "Third *Encuentro* Sunday" in each parish. And the fifth is to develop a missionary program targeting Hispanics who are estranged from the Church, to encourage the formation of Basic Ecclesial Communities, and to promote dialogue with other ethnic groups in the Church.

4. The fourth section is dedicated to the "National Secretariat" and contains six commitments: the first is to publish the conclusions of the Third *Encuentro*. The second is to promote a national campaign to promote this publication. The third is to establish one Sunday during the year that will feature a "fiesta of the prophetic people." The fourth (No. 63) is to encourage the various movements, and so on to revise their plans and programs in accordance with the "prophetic lines" of the Third *Encuentro*. The fifth is to evaluate the Third *Encuentro* and all developments in its wake within three years. And the sixth is to organize another national *Encuentro*.

5. The fifth section is directed to the "bishops" and presents three commitments: the first is to encourage the bishops to meet with the *Encuentro* delegates in their dioceses in order to support and plan pastoral care of Hispanic Catholics. The second is that the bishops meet with their parish priests, deacons, and other pastoral agents to implement the commitments of the Third *Encuentro*. And the third is that bishops convoke meetings to evaluate the Third *Encuentro*, which would be the starting point for organizing the Fourth *Encuentro*; the Fourth *Encuentro*, the text says, should be held in 1992, coinciding with that year's commemoration of the Fifth Centenary of the Evangelization of the New World.

Report of Archbishop Sanchez
(November 1985)

On November 11, 1985, Archbishop Roberto F. Sanchez of Santa Fe, New Mexico, presents a report on the Third *Encuentro* at the Plenary Assembly of U.S. bishops in Washington, DC. He begins by underscoring two areas: the evaluation of what happened in August, and the preparation of integrating the findings of the Third *Encuentro* in the National Plan for Hispanic Ministry that was already announced in the U.S. bishops' pastoral Letter on Hispanic Catholics.

Concerning the execution of the Third *Encuentro*, he thanks Father William Byron, president of Catholic University, for allowing the use of the school's campus for the various meetings and that of the neighboring Sanctuary of the Immaculate Conception for the Masses. He reports on the participation of 2,100, including delegates from 123 dioceses, 56 bishops and Major Superiors, who, combined, represent millions of Catholics. He praises the "fiesta" spirit of the liturgies and expresses appreciation for the presence of the Holy Father by way of video message as well as the presence of the Pro-Nuncio. He also thanks Archbishop Hickey of Washington, DC, and Bishop Maloney, president of the bishops' conference, for their participation. The archbishop concludes that attendees were moved by the proceedings, enjoying a new experience in Christ. He also makes note of the participation of representatives from El Salvador, Nicaragua, Guatemala, Mexico, and other developing nations, who clearly motivated attendees and gave them a sense of the international implications and significance of the Third *Encuentro*.

The archbishop argues that the presence of the laity was a beautiful experience, noting in particular what he describes as the magnificent participation of women, youth, and migrant farm workers. The prelate speaks of the *Encuentro* as a powerful experience of the Church as community, characterized by collaboration and teamwork. He also praises the *Encuentro*'s missionary dimension, geared especially toward those who are estranged from the Church.

Comparing the Third with the Second *Encuentro*, held seven years earlier, the Archbishop credits the Third *Encuentro*'s particular emphasis on unity—a dimension that was mentioned repeatedly in the conclusions, titled "We the Hispanics." In addition, the Third *Encuentro*, says the prelate, shows a high degree of maturity, as reflected in the "commitments" and in the prior pastoral lines mapped out before the *Encuentro*, as well as in the preparatory theological reflections.

He thanks Monsignor Hoye, general secretary of the bishops' conference, as well as the entire team that represented the NCCB/USCC, led by Pablo Sedillo and Father Vicente Lopez. The archbishop calls on the bishops' conference to formulate a National Plan for Hispanic Ministry targeting the diocesan, regional, and national level, and he adds a broad overview of the Plan's content.

Meeting in Los Angeles (December 3–5, 1985)

This is a meeting of the committee mandated to ensure the continuity of the process initiated by the Third *Encuentro*. The general objective is to develop a method that would lead to the formulation of a National Plan for Hispanic ministry—which is understood as an overall pastoral plan. The plan would be designed to be inculturated in accordance with the very identity of the Hispanic people; the plan would aim to create a way of being Church that is particularly responsive to Hispanic needs as well as to those of other minority groups. Such a Church would honor a preferential option of solidarity with the poor and marginalized, favor the family as the priority target of pastoral action, observe a preferential option to favor youth, and would appreciate and promote the role of women.

To further the afterlife of the Third *Encuentro* and promote its fruits, the meeting aims to connect with the Basic Ecclesial Communities as an incarnation of the parish; pursue common ground with other ethnic groups; make use of facilities, learning tools, and resources already available; and collaborate with the Catholic school system.

The meeting also produces a theological-pastoral reflection, earmarked to lead to the organization of workshops at the grassroots level and the creation of institutes of pastoral reflection at the diocesan, regional, and national levels. Meeting participants also designed a program for formation and training that focuses on making significant progress in four key areas: social awareness based on Church documents and civil legislation, permanent analysis of the "reality on the ground," ministerial missionary formation, and pastoral planning. In addition, the meeting seeks to determine the allotment of resources; ensure the creation of pastoral centers and their mobile teams; coordinate the Youth Pastorate, and so on. The meeting also discusses the establishment of a "National Hispanic Foundation"; the creation of an informative National Bulletin; and the development and production of programs for print, radio, and television. Lastly, the meeting lays out a complete schedule of activities culminating in November 1987 with the approval of the National Plan for Hispanic Ministry.

Evaluation by David Scott Blanchard (June 1, 1986)

Researcher David Scott Blanchard, in 1985, proposes writing a book titled "The Third *Encuentro*: Theology of an Ecclesial Event." The work would feature a preface by Pablo Sedillo and an introduction by Blanchard himself, in which he would present the history of the Third *Encuentro* as an event interpreted historically, pedagogically, ecclesiologically, and canonically, while adding a substantial bibliography and making an explicit link between the *Encuentro* and the liturgy. A subsequent piece by Sedillo—headlined "The Third *Encuentro* in Its Historical and Cultural Context"—would underscore the influence of Latin America with regard to Basic Ecclesial Communities, Medellín and Puebla, as well as liberation theology. Further on, John Rivera and Vicente Lopez would write about the pedagogy of the Third *Encuentro*, stressing its postconciliar dimension; reflecting on the development of the *Encuentro* and the pedagogy of the process it applied to the Church.

Blanchard would again take up theological issues and prepare an ecclesiology of the Third *Encuentro*, holding it up as a model of the prophetic Church, the Church of the marginalized, youth, and women; a missionary Church, servant of justice and of human rights. With all this in mind, a method to develop such a

Church would be designed, drawing on, in part, the results of a survey.

Arturo Carrillón would prepare an entry on canon law in service of the *Encuentro*; he would demonstrate how in the *Encuentro* various aspects of canon law are in force, and how the *Encuentro* was a reflection of Vatican II and the code of canon law.

Father Virgilio Elizondo, echoing the thrust of his work "Galilean Journey," would describe the *Encuentro* as a biography and a journey for the Hispanic people. This would be an analysis from the perspective of both the local and the national level, including the diocesan and regional levels.

Juan Sosa and his team from SEPI would study the Third *Encuentro* as "Eucharist," taking a liturgical angle, pointing out the symbolic value and the importance of the various ceremonies held during the *Encuentro*.

Finally, Bishop Wilton Gregory, Auxiliary of Chicago, an African-American, would attempt to "translate" the religious experience of the process of the Third *Encuentro* in terms meaningful to black Catholics; and Archbishop Roberto F. Sanchez, Archbishop of Santa Fe and President of the Ad-hoc Committee for Hispanic Affairs, would present a theological reflection on the Third *Encuentro*.

Little came of his ambitious project. However, participants at the Third *Encuentro* were polled using a bilingual questionnaire, and David Scott Blanchard on June 1, 1986, presents a document with 153 statistical findings.

There were seventy-six questions in the polling document, and they were grouped into eight sections:

1. The first nine questions were generic; they confirmed age, sex, linguistic ability, citizenship, ethnic background, region, position in the church, employment in the Church, and activity in the Church.
2. Questions 10 to 14 sought to evaluate the Hispanic representation in terms of years of study, occupation, family situation, and membership(s) in civic and/or community organizations.
3. Questions 15 to 20 were designed to identify the role of the

responder within the Third *Encuentro*: assigned tasks, attendance in the First and/or Second *Encuentros*, participation
in the Consultation; in the diocesan *Encuentro*; and in the
regional *Encuentro*.

4. Questions 21 to 29 sought to specify a particular role or
   activity in the General Assemblies, in the groups of 250 persons; in those of 45, and in those of 15; in the preparations
   for the *Encuentro*; or membership in a Basic Ecclesial
   Community or another community; in the EPD; or in one
   of the committees.

5. Questions 30 to 40, which required a rating on a scale from
   1 to 4, measured opinions about preparations at the local,
   diocesan, regional, and national level. They also probed
   how useful the videos had been as well as the training sessions and the reflection guides, and how effective had been
   the EPDs and the groups of fifteen. The final question read:
   Did you feel adequately prepared for the Third *Encuentro*?

6. Questions 41 to 63 sought to measure the degree of participation of the responder and how much opportunity he or
   she found for expression; the experience of their participation in subgroups, groups, and mini-assemblies; whether
   coordinators and group leaders were impartial; and
   whether the respondent's opinion was respected. This set of
   questions also sought to measure the impact of the
   Encuentro on the life of the responder and the local community; did the experience boost the respondent's sense of
   responsibility for the Hispanic community at large; did it
   have an impact on his or her experience of God; was the
   sense of community strengthened; did the community
   mature; was there growth in the respondent's self-respect as
   an Hispanic? This section also measured the importance of
   the three *Encuentros* in the respondent's view; the impact
   they had on the young, on the family, their tackling of the
   problem of poverty, their approach to women's problems,
   their impact on evangelization efforts, their appreciation of
   Hispanic culture, and so on. The final question in this section was: What was your experience of Christ and of the
   Church in the Third *Encuentro*?

7. Questions 64 to 69 referred to the implementation of a pastoral plan based on the Third *Encuentro*; and also to the quality of communication with those who did not participate in the *Encuentro*, especially the non-Hispanics, and so on.
8. Questions 70 to 76 evaluated the logistical facilities of the meeting halls, meals, shelter, transportation facility, ease of registration, and so on. The final question: How would you evaluate your experience of the Third *Encuentro* in general?

Blanchard's final document consists of an introductory letter addressed to Pablo Sedillo; an introduction that describes the work done, featuring a citation from liberation theologian Jon Sobrino. Then follow six main parts: the first features an evaluation of the process; in the second, the author presents the results of the poll; in the third, he presents the Third *Encuentro* within the context of a Christian anthropology and the history of salvation—he defines it as something classically religious; in the fourth, he touches on crucial areas, such as the situation of Hispanic youth; the communication to non-Hispanics of the entire process involved in the Third *Encuentro*; and the pedagogy, ecclesiology, and so on of the *Encuentro* itself.

Undoubtedly, most important is the fifth part of the report, which is dedicated to 153 statistical tables, grouped in various sections:

1. In the first section, he reports that 62.3 percent of those polled about the Third *Encuentro* were between forty-one and sixty-five years of age; 26.2 percent between twenty-six and forty; 8.7 percent between eighteen and twenty-five; and 2.8 percent over sixty-five; 53.3 percent were men (232 of responders) and 46.7 percent were women; 91 percent said they were bilingual; 6.9 percent spoke only Spanish; and 2.1 percent spoke only English; 77.7 percent were citizens of the United States; 24.5 percent were Mexican-American; 16.4 percent were Mexican; 15.2 percent were Puerto Rican; 9 percent were Cuban; 6.5 percent were from South America; 5.1 percent were from Central America; 3.9 percent were from Spain; and 19.4 percent from elsewhere. In the data, the

Northeast was represented with 28.3 percent of respondents; followed by the Midwest with 18.8 percent; the Southeast with 15.8 percent; the Southwest with 12.3 percent; the Far West with 8.1 percent; the Northwest with 6 percent; the Mountain states with 5.6 percent; and the North Central region with 5.1 percent. Bishops represented 5.6 percent of those surveyed; priests accounted for 18.1 percent; religious workers, 15.7 percent; deacons, 4.7 percent; seminarians, 0.7 percent; Major Superiors, 0.5 percent; and the rest, 54.7 percent, were laypersons.

2. In the second section, among other facts, the report states that 79.9 percent of the delegates were surveyed; as were 9 percent of the special guests, 8.8 percent of the staff, and only 2.3 percent of the volunteers. It was noted that 65.3 percent of those surveyed were not members of Basic Ecclesial Communities.

3. The third section reports that the local preparation was considered good (40.8 percent) or even excellent (38 percent); the diocesan preparation was rated excellent (41.6 percent) or good (38.8 percent); the regional preparation was considered good (44.9 percent) or excellent (36.7 percent); and the overall preparation of the Third *Encuentro* was also considered good (46.4 percent) or excellent (36.9 percent); the guides were rated as good (51.3 percent) or excellent (27.7 percent), and so on.

4. In the fourth section, those polled reported that they had a good opportunity to express themselves (40.4 percent), some even rated the opportunity as excellent (37.8 percent). The participation in the subgroups was evaluated by 49.5 percent as good and by 35.9 percent as excellent. With regard to the groups, 49 percent rated them as good and 27.4 percent as excellent. Mini-assemblies: 44.9 percent thought they were good and 24.1 percent said they were excellent. The entire process was considered good (46.4 percent) or excellent (36.2 percent). The experience of God was rated as excellent (48.9 percent) or good (35.6 percent). The three *Encuentros* were considered excellent (51.7 percent) for the North American Church or good (30 percent); however, the

ratings go down a bit when it comes to the Third *Encuentro*'s effectiveness in dealing with youth problems, with 42.7 percent considering it was good and 35.6 percent rating it as excellent. The analysis of the family was considered good (45 percent) or excellent (27.7 percent). The analysis on poverty in the Hispanic community: 40.9 percent said it was good and 26.4 percent rated it as excellent. The analysis of the treatment of women's issues was considered good (36.7 percent), followed by acceptable (30.1 percent) and excellent (21.2 percent). Regarding the *Encuentro*'s handling of cultural issues, the responses of good and excellent were tied at 40.7 percent each. The experience of Christ and of the Church in the Third *Encuentro* is evaluated as excellent (56.5 percent) or good (32.7 percent).

5. The fifth section reports on respondents' evaluation of the communication of the *Encuentro* process to those who did not participate; 50.7 percent said it was good, followed by regular (25.4 percent); non-Hispanics considered that the communication was good (38.1 percent), followed by regular (34.1 percent). This same tendency is seen in the results of questions measuring the perception of the possibility that the Third *Encuentro* would or should implement a diocesan pastoral plan; 38.5 percent believed that it is a good opportunity, while 27.8 percent rated it average (No. 44). In the parish, 32.5 percent considered it good and 30.3 percent regular, while 27.1 percent gave it a low rating to the likelihood of a diocesan pastoral plan.

6. The sixth section reports that the Northeast region had the highest participation in the three *Encuentros*, followed by the Midwest; for the Second *Encuentro*, the Northeast accounted for 29.3 percent of participants; the Midwest, for 21.7 percent; for the Third *Encuentro*, those figures were 28.3 percent and 18.8 percent, respectively.

7. The seventh through tenth sections present results by region, which, arguably, are not particularly interesting or relevant.

8. The eleventh section presents striking sociological data concerning the employment status of those surveyed: 75.6

percent in the First *Encuentro* reported being employed; that figure stood at 87.7 percent in the Second, and 83.3 percent in the Third. Also, 14.6 percent in the First *Encuentro* were unemployed; 11.1 percent, in the Second; and 8.4 percent, in the Third.

9. The diocesan section specifies the ethnic composition of attendees at the three *Encuentros*, with Mexican-Americans always coming in at first place: 24.5 percent in the First, 35.9 percent in the Second, and 24.5 percent in the Third. Cubans accounted for 14.3 percent in the First, 10.9 percent in the Second, and 9 percent in the Third. Puerto Ricans accounted for 10.2 percent in the First, climbed to 12 percent in the Second, and 13.2 percent in the Third.

10. The thirteenth section shows that the level of participation of men compared to that of women was fairly balanced: 53.1 percent men and 46.9 percent women took part in the Third *Encuentro*; 53.3 percent men and 46.7 percent women, in the Second. Similar figures apply to diocesan *Encuentros* as well as to the regional *Encuentros*. There is only a slight change in the figures with regard to the preparation of the *Encuentros*: 52.4 percent men and 47.6 percent women. The same proportion applies to the Third *Encuentro* with regard to preparations undertaken at the parish level (No. 115).

The sixth and final part of Blanchard's work presents the models of the questionnaire used, both in English and in Spanish.

3.5 LOOKING BACK

Strengths and Weaknesses

The Third *Encuentro* was the product of a process that climaxed with the creation of the National Pastoral Plan for Hispanic Ministry, and with which it is in complete harmony. (For my reflection [anno 2014] on the dynamics and logistics involved in developing a Pastoral Plan for Hispanics, please see Appendix A.)

To evaluate from the present day, the Third *Encuentro* is equivalent to evaluating to what degree the plan has been applied.

Certainly, the "building" or structure created by the Third *Encuentro* is significant, and should be a source of pride for the U.S. bishops' conference, for the Committee for Hispanic Affairs, the corresponding Secretariat, and for the Hispanic Pastorate overall. However, the application or achievement of commitments made at the Third *Encuentro* has been relatively minimal; and with the passing of time, its influence has diminished still further, turning off its lights and reducing its inner dynamism, to speak in poetic terms.

This is disappointing and surprising, because the Third *Encuentro*, and above all, the plan that ensued are the product of a difficult and rare constellation of ecclesial factors: the support and direction of the hierarchy combined with the expression of the popular will of the people of God who were thoroughly consulted. There may be questions on specific points, concerning expressions that may be extreme in one direction or another, and about a focus on matters of only marginal importance. But these imperfections, if there are such, are but few and tangential—they do not take away from the overall greatness and complexity of the enterprise. This is especially true in considering the Third *Encuentro* from a methodological point of view. This methodology is of the greatest importance, even if, at times, it constituted a kind of pastoral straitjacket.

No one with any ecclesiastical sense questions the importance of pastoral planning. It is an urgent need. Institutions in the Hispanic world, such as the Latin American Episcopal Conference (CELAM), are deeply committed to such planning. The Latin American Episcopal Conference has already designed, with unquestionable success, a series of four-year comprehensive plans; in fact, pastoral planning has become synonymous with ecclesiastical wisdom; moreover, the formula created by CELAM allows for adaptations and is highly practical. Each four-year plan is revised in accordance with yearly assessments. New pastoral plans and formulas are organically linked to those that preceded them, while they are also forward-looking. That process has not yet been realized in the case of the Third *Encuentro* and the subsequent National Pastoral Plan; there has been no continuity, no process of evolution, adaptations, and changes. As a result, the rich planning produced by the Third *Encuentro* and contained in the National Pastoral Plan have ossified and lost their life-giving power. All the documents involved risk becoming so many bibliographical references.

There is a need, therefore, to review the Third *Encuentro* and the Pastoral Plan, to closely revisit its deliberations, evaluate the results—even at the distance of so many years—and do some reengineering. The goals should be to make the plan operative within a period of no longer than three to five years, with the process including periodic evaluations along the way. There is no possibility of creating pastoral plans that can stay in force indefinitely, however admirable they may be.

There is much to recover and learn from the Third *Encuentro* and the plan; even after all this time, there still is a clear view of the process, whose merits are beyond doubt. But there now is an urgent need to incorporate, for example, relevant material drawn from the encyclicals of Pope John Paul II, including *Evangelium Vitae, Veritatis Splendor*, and *Ut Unum Sint* as well as those dealing with the Church's social teaching, *Laborem Exercens, Sollicitudo Rei Socialis*, and *Centesimus Annus*. Then there is the postsynodal document *Christifidelis Laici*, the letter *Tertio Millenio Adveniente*, as well as many other ecclesiastical documents, including those produced by CELAM at Santo Domingo, the pastoral letters of the U.S. bishops' conference, and the documents produced during the Synod of the Americas.

Summing up, those responsible for Hispanic ministry must make a serious effort to revisit the Third *Encuentro* and the subsequent Pastoral Plan. Such an effort would create a new dynamism as the *Encuentro* deliberations and documents, along with the plan, are adapted and rejuvenated. Failing this, the Hispanic community and the Church at large could lose the richness of their foresight, which would be an affront of the Spirit. It would undo years of hard work, prayer, and commitment. To move forward, it is necessary to know something more of the Pastoral Plan. Let us see.

An Inheritance: The National Pastoral Plan for Hispanic Ministry

The Third *Encuentro* is inextricably linked to this document that was published by the National Conference of Catholic Bishops in November 1987, following a process of more than two years of reflection. This document is the U.S. Church's most valuable official contribution to Hispanic ministry and—even though as a human work it has its imperfections—it features an impressive methodological systematization.

The plan has a preface, nine parts that are unequal in length, the sixth of which is the most important, and the document concludes with some notes. The preface is vital because it lays out certain ecclesiastical criteria that have guided the writing of the document. The preface states that, first, this Pastoral Plan engages the entire U.S. Church. It addresses the pastoral needs of Hispanic Catholics, but it also challenges all Catholics as members of the same Body of Christ (see 1 Cor 12:12–13). The preface insists that this plan be carefully studied, because it is the result of years of work in which thousands of persons have participated, including all those who took part in the Third *Encuentro*. In fact, the plan develops a strategy based on the conclusions of that *Encuentro*.

Second, the U.S. bishops state that they are adopting the objectives of this plan, endorsing the specific means it contains to reach the intended pastoral targets. Acknowledging the need for local adaptations, the bishops call on dioceses and parishes to put this plan into action. The bishops express a clear sense of urgency, pointing to the enormous challenge posed—and opportunity offered—by the presence of a growing number of Hispanics in the United States. The bishops declare not only that they accept this presence as part of their pastoral responsibility—as they are conscious of the mission with which Christ commissioned them (Matt 28:18–20)—but they do so with joy and gratitude. The bishops present this plan in a "spirit of faith."

The introduction delineates the integration of all the parts of the document. The "framework of Hispanic reality" is explained in terms of history, culture, and social reality. In the second part, there is a diagnosis of the biggest challenges facing Hispanic Catholics.

With due respect, the third and fourth parts are less than satisfying: the third is dedicated to the "doctrinal framework," and the fourth to "spirituality"; the fifth part develops a methodology to attain the "general objective" of the plan, featuring a well-designed organizational chart, which methodologically integrates the whole plan.

As noted, the sixth part is the most important. Titled "Specific Dimensions," it tackles four vital subjects in great depth. The first subject refers to Hispanic ministry at large, stressing four key activities: pastoral integration, coordination, advisory provisions, and pastoral communication. The second subject tackles evangelization and focuses on two activities: one referring to the Basic Ecclesial Communities; the other, to parish renewal. The third subject discusses missionary initiatives with six categories of beneficiaries: migrant farm workers, leadership, military personnel, families, women, and youth. The final section of the sixth part discusses training, broken down in five activities: raising awareness, research, vocations, training, and the production of formation materials.

The seventh part refers to the evaluation process; the eighth reflects on spirituality and *mistica*; and the ninth contains four appendices: a bibliography, the index of references, an organizational diagram, and a glossary titled "Terminology." Footnotes conclude the document.

Today, more than thirty-five years after the publication of this National Pastoral Plan, the reader must answer some difficult questions: What has come of so much intellectual work? How many of these pastoral strategies remain relegated to being mere bibliographical references? How can the plan's recommendations be brought back to life and put into practice—even when they need some adjustments?

There is no reason to be pessimistic; this plan, as is true for so many other documents, needs a firm commitment to be put into practice. There is an obvious comparison: even more than fifty-five years after Vatican II, many of its dispositions and orientations have not yet been implemented—but one can say with certainty that the Council has changed the course of Church history.

The National Pastoral Plan is clearly the fruit of the Third *Encuentro*; and although the Hispanic community cannot rejoice over its execution, the plan continues to serve, continues to illuminate, and continues to challenge the entire U.S. Church to make a commitment to the Hispanic community. Satisfaction and pride can be found in the NCCB/USCC's publication of this plan—along with two other crucial documents: the pastoral letter "Hispanic Presence" and the "Prophetic Voices" of the Third *Encuentro*—in a 1995 bilingual edition. It features a foreword prologue by Bishop Roberto O. Gonzalez, coadjutor of Corpus Christi, Texas, and President of the Episcopal Commission for Hispanic Affairs. This publication is a sign of life, a guarantee that Hispanic ministry is continuing on its vital path, secure in its oversight by its legitimate pastors—the U.S. bishops.

This publication has opened a new, more mature perspective that is grounding the work at hand. The journey has been very long, but the Third *Encuentro*, in union with the National Pastoral Plan, has earned its place in the life of the U.S. Church.

Perception of What Is Needed

To finalize this perspective on the Third *Encuentro* and the Pastoral Plan, here follow a few reflections on actions needed today, so many years later.

The first reflection is ecclesiological, representing the hierarchical viewpoint of the U.S. Church. It relates to the preface of the plan, there where it affirms: "We, the bishops of the United States...." Therein lies the key. A new reading of the Third *Encuentro* must be done from this perspective, one that obliges the U.S. bishops' conference to take charge, and which obliges Hispanic ministry work to be an integral part of the overall pastoral mission of the North American Church. In fact, this take on the *Encuentro* implies a bond that joins all the churches of the Americas in a common effort.

The second reflection is pastoral in a dual sense: it involves social pastoral responsibility as well as cultural pastoral responsibility. The Third *Encuentro*, considering North American society and culture, points out a specific role for Hispanic Catholics—a role that allows them to integrate seamlessly into the life of the society and the Church, and without losing their cultural identity. Indeed, the Third *Encuentro* and the Pastoral Plan, complementing the work of CELAM in Santo Domingo, could be the basis for a new Christian culture in the United States, a culture in line with the country's venerable tradition of welcoming strangers; they also form the foundation for carrying out in an authentic way the "human promotion" of Hispanics in the United States and, indirectly, Hispanics in their countries of origin. Hispanic Catholics can make fundamental contributions to fundamental Christian culture precisely by being true to who they are as members of society and as members of the Church.

The third reflection is prophetic, perhaps not in the sense presented in the Third *Encuentro*—which was marked by the controversy inherent in liberation theology—but in the sense of Hispanic faithful contributing to building of a new and more just and humane U.S. society. The messages of John Paul II during his visit to the United States in October 1995 can help shore up the commitments made: In *all* of the Americas, the twenty-first century will be the Hispanic century!

CONCLUSION

THE VIEW FROM 2014—
TIME FOR ANOTHER
NATIONAL *ENCUENTRO?*

There is today an office for Hispanic/Latino Affairs at the U.S. Conference of Catholic Bishops, and it is housed under the umbrella of "Cultural Diversity in the Church." Unfortunately, the stand-alone and potent Secretariat for the Hispanic Affairs is no more, having fallen victim to cost-cutting and the restructuring of the National Conference of Catholic Bishops/U.S. Catholic Conference, which has become the U.S. Conference of Catholic Bishops. Still, the Church has continued to pay significant pastoral attention to Hispanics.

To an extent, the numbers speak for themselves: the number of parishes with Hispanic/Latino ministry is now close to 4,500, well over a third of all parishes; and for the first time in its history, the U.S. Church has two active Hispanic archbishops—Archbishop Jose Gómez of Los Angeles, the largest diocese in the country; and Archbishop Gustavo García-Siller, who heads the Archdiocese of San Antonio. There are twelve Hispanic ordinaries and another fifteen Hispanic auxiliary bishops. In the not too distant future, Hispanics will form the majority among the U.S. Catholic population—already, Hispanic Catholics account for more than 35 percent of all Catholics.

There certainly is strength in numbers. Hispanic Catholics in the United States form part of what Pope Benedict XVI has called "the vastness of human experience" and the "vastness of the word of God." Their voices deserve to be heard; indeed, they must be heard. But is their voice really heard throughout the Church?

Arguably, forming a subsection under the Cultural Diversity section at the Conference—alongside Native Americans, Asian/ Pacific Islanders, African Americans and Migrants, Refugees and Travelers, each with their own as yet unexploited gifts to the Universal Church, and to the U.S. Church, in particular— Hispanics are still relegated to the margins of the mainstream. The conference's organizational model still presumes, more or less, the old melting-pot vision, with newcomers cared for separately until they are ready to join the mainstream.

Of course, the immigrant model of the past is no longer relevant—a new culture is emerging. Rather than the traditional melting pot, experts such as author-philosopher Ronald Austin now talk of cultures that are converging, finding common ground as each pursues identity and purpose. Here, the Latino Catholic has a huge contribution to make: grounded in his or her faith, the Hispanic Catholic brings to his or her adopted land a deep sense of beauty and sanctity, authentic Catholic culture in the form of art and devotion of the saints. According to Austin, "the revelation of God's presence in beauty and the saints" is particularly important in the United States and throughout the West when the secular tide runs so very high (see Appendix B).

Hispanics must be given their due and be embraced without reservation by their Anglo brothers and sisters, lay and clergy, bishops, priests, and religious—and without relegation, however well intended and perhaps efficient, to the multicultural sidelines. On the one hand, the U.S. Church must do everything it can to encourage and enable Latino Catholics to immerse themselves in their heritage of faith in order to better serve all their neighbors in the process. On the other hand, the Anglo-Catholic community must fully embrace the Hispanic faithful as full-fledged members of the "One Body" that is the Universal Church and the U.S. Church, in particular. Their ethnic label must be dropped—if such is conceivable—and, ideally, the U.S. bishops would stop treating them as special-needs Catholics who, whether they like it or not, as such are subject to the Church's version of affirmative action.

Such was the cry of the three *Encuentros*, leaving aside the time-bound radical demands for women deacons and married priests or the insistence that Basic Ecclesial Communities are the *sine qua non* of evangelization: Hispanic Catholics want to be recognized for who they are in themselves and as how they see themselves; they want to be fully integrated into the life and structures of the Church, at all levels—again, without being designated as requiring special treatment of any kind—and to be in full communion with the Church and at liberty to fully participate in the Church's life.

Such was the consistent plea of the *Encuentros* for integration rather than assimilation—which would mean, precisely, repressing the very essence that makes them Hispanics for the sake of fitting in with the Anglo majority. As Saint Paul insists, "the body is not a single part, but many" (Cor 12:12–30), each part distinct but belonging with the others and indispensable for the functioning of the whole: "For in one Spirit we were baptized into one body, whether Jews or Greeks, slaves or free persons, and we were all given to drink of the one Spirit."

On his 2008 visit to the United States, Pope Benedict XVI put it thus: "Two hundred years later, the Church in America can rightfully praise the accomplishment of past generations in bringing together widely differing immigrant groups within the unity of the Catholic faith and in a common commitment to the spread of the Gospel. At the same time, conscious of its rich diversity, the Catholic community in this country has come to appreciate ever more fully the importance of each individual and group offering its own particular gifts to the whole."

Such was the insistence of the *Encuentros* that the Church care particularly for the poor, for migrant workers, for women, for people on the margin of society—alcoholics and drug addicts, the undocumented, those suffering abuse or sexual exploitation. The now familiar concept of the Church's preferential option for the poor was a groundbreaking reorientation for the Church in the 1970s and 1980s. This instinct of the *Encuentros* found confirmation in Pope John Paul II's 1999 apostolic exhortation summing up the work of the Synod of the Americas:

The Church in America must incarnate in her pastoral initiatives the solidarity of the universal Church towards the poor and the outcast of every kind. Her attitude needs to be one of assistance, promotion, liberation and fraternal open-

187

ness. The goal of the Church is to ensure that no one is marginalized. The memory of the dark chapters of America's history, involving the practice of slavery and other situations of social discrimination, must awaken a sincere desire for conversion leading to reconciliation and communion.

Concern for those most in need springs from a decision to love the poor in a special manner. This is a love which is not exclusive and thus cannot be interpreted as a sign of partiality or sectarianism; in loving the poor the Christian imitates the attitude of the Lord, who during his earthly life devoted himself with special compassion to all those in spiritual and material need.

The Church's work on behalf of the poor in every part of America is important; yet efforts are still needed to make this line of pastoral activity increasingly directed to an encounter with Christ who, though rich, made himself poor for our sakes, that he might enrich us by his poverty (cf. 2 Cor 8:9). There is a need to intensify and broaden what is already being done in this area, with the goal of reaching as many of the poor as possible. Sacred Scripture reminds us that God hears the cry of the poor (cf. Ps 34:7) and the Church must heed the cry of those most in need. Hearing their voice, "she must live with the poor and share their distress. By her lifestyle her priorities, her words and her actions, she must testify that she is in communion and solidarity with them."

Such also was the anguish expressed by the *Encuentros* about the U.S. Church's neglect or failure to appreciate the importance of popular religiosity (as also argued forcefully by Ron Austin; Cf. Appendix B). In fundamental agreement with the concerns expressed at the *Encuentros*, the *lineamenta* of the Synod of the Americas tackled the issue as follows:

Some signs which indicate the importance of popular religious culture are: the increasing participation of people in pilgrimages to shrines (especially Marian shrines), the tradition in families of baptizing children, the giving of alms for the souls in Purgatory and celebrating Masses for the deceased, patronal feasts with their characteristic processions and the celebration of Holy Mass (generally attended by large numbers of people), devotion to the saints, not only those of the universal Church but also those of the American continent, etc....

These and many other expressions of popular piety offer excellent opportunities for the faithful to encounter the living Jesus Christ. In fact, the ecclesial community, in coming together for the celebration of the Word and Sacrament in memory of the saints, remembers in a particular way those who faithfully imitated in their lives the Savior of the world, and that same community enters into communion with those who are part of the heavenly Church. It is for this reason that popular piety—purified and duly catechized—may come to be a decisive element in the new evangelization. This is a point on which most of the answers to the *Lineamenta* agree.

As confirmed by the answers to the preparatory document, within popular piety—but not limited exclusively to this category—a privileged place is occupied by devotion to the Virgin Mary, a clear sign of the Catholic identity of the People of God. The Catholics of America are a Marian people. This is borne out by the many titles by which she is invoked by believers, as also by the innumerable Marian shrines throughout the American hemisphere. Among her many titles, the most noteworthy is that of Our Lady of Guadalupe, which owes its origins to the appearance of the Virgin to Juan Diego on American soil, on the hill of Tepeyac (Mexico), in 1531. This Marian event has always been considered as a sign of the protection of the Mother of God for the men and women of the American continent, based on the words addressed by the Virgin to Juan Diego and conserved in the traditions of the faithful: "Am I not here, who am your mother? Are you not under my shadow and protection? Why do you fear, if you are in my mantle? If you are in my arms?"

Such was the *Encuentros'* proclamation—repeated again and again—that a truly integral education and formation of believers is indispensable for the success of the new evangelization. In his apostolic exhortation (*Christifidelis laici*, 1988), summing up the deliberations of the Synod on the Laity, John Paul II wrote as follows:

> In discovering and living their proper vocation and mission, the lay faithful must be formed according to the *union* which exists from their being *members of the Church and citizens of human society.*
>
> There cannot be two parallel lives in their existence: on the one hand, the so-called "spiritual" life, with its values and demands; and on the other, the so-called "secular" life, that is, life in a family, at work, in social relationships, in the responsibilities of public life and in culture. The branch, engrafted to the vine which is Christ, bears its fruit in every sphere of existence and activity. In fact, every area of the lay faithful's lives, as different as they are, enters into the plan of God, who desires that these very areas be the "places in time" where the love of Christ is revealed and realized for both the glory of the Father and service of others. Every activity, every situation, every precise responsibility—as, for example, skill and solidarity in work, love and dedication in the family and the education of children, service to society and public life and the promotion of truth in the area of culture—are the occasions ordained by Providence for a "continuous exercise of faith, hope and charity...."
>
> Where are the lay faithful formed? What are the means of their formation? Who are the *persons and the communities* called upon to assume the task of a totally integrated formation of the lay faithful?
>
> Just as the work of human education is intimately connected with fatherhood and motherhood, so Christian formation finds its origin and its strength in God the Father who loves and educates his children. Yes, *God is the first and great teacher of his People,* as it states in the striking passage of the Song of Moses: "He found him in a desert land / and in the howling waste of the wilderness; / he encircled him, he cared for him, he kept him as the apple of his eye. / Like an

eagle that stirs up its nest, that flutters over its young, spreading out its wings, catching them, bearing them on its pinions, / the Lord alone did lead him, and there was no foreign God with him" (Deut 32:10–12; cf. 8:5).

God's work in forming his people is revealed and fulfilled in Jesus Christ the Teacher, and reaches to the depths of every individual's heart as a result of the living presence of the Spirit. *Mother Church* is called to take part in the divine work of formation, both through a sharing of her very life, and through her various pronouncements and actions. It is thus that the *lay faithful are formed by the Church and in the Church* in a mutual communion and collaboration of all her members: clergy, religious and lay faithful. Thus the whole ecclesial community, in its diverse members, receives the fruitfulness of the Spirit and actively cooperates towards that end.

The *Encuentros'* almost drumbeat insistence on the engagement of, and care for, Hispanic youth found an echo in the words of Pope John Paul II as he looked ahead at the third millennium:

The future of the world and the Church belongs to the *younger generation*, to those who, born in this century, will reach maturity in the next, the first century of the new millennium. *Christ expects great things from young people*, as he did from the young man who asked him: "What good deed must I do, to have eternal life?" (Mt 19:16)....Young people, in every situation, in every region of the world, do not cease to put questions to Christ: *they meet him and they keep searching for him in order to question him further*. If they succeed in following the road which he points out to them, they will have the joy of making their own contribution to his presence in the next century and in the centuries to come, until the end of time: "Jesus is the same yesterday, today and forever." (*Tertio Millennio Adveniente*, 1994)

The *Encuentros'* insistent call for the formation of Basic Ecclesial Communities—modeled on those in Latin America, the cornerstone of the Church as envisioned by liberation theology—went unheeded in the end. But the instinct to focus on the importance of living and breathing communities of faithful was on the mark:

> This re-evangelization is directed not only to individual persons but also to entire portions of populations in the variety of their situations, surroundings and cultures. Its purpose is the *formation of mature ecclesial communities*, in which the faith might radiate and fulfill the basic meaning of adherence to the person of Christ and his Gospel, of an encounter and sacramental communion with him, and of an existence lived in charity and in service.
>
> The lay faithful have their part to fulfill in the formation of these ecclesial communities, not only through an active and responsible participation in the life of the community, in other words, through a testimony that only they can give, but also through a missionary zeal and activity towards the many people who still do not believe and who no longer live the faith received at Baptism. (*Christifidelis Laici*)

The Spirit has been stirring in the Hispanic Catholic community in the United States with particular vigor ever since Vatican II. As noted, the *Encuentros* were precisely the U.S. Hispanic community's response to the Council's call for renewal and for its insistence that the laity live out the fullness of their vocation. It certainly is fitting to revisit their accomplishments—as well as to consider the long way to go still ahead—at a time when the Church recently observed the fiftieth anniversary of Vatican II.

The legacy of the *Encuentros*—also spurred on by CELAM's groundbreaking meetings at Medellín and Puebla, their respective progressive and conservative thrusts both taking their cue from the Council as well—endures and continues to make demands on all U.S. Catholics, Hispanics and non-Hispanics alike. The Hispanic gifts to the U.S. Church are fully alive, even if their deeper, yet unstoppable, movements lie hidden.

Just as the legacy of Vatican II is still unfolding even after fifty years, so the often difficult, but ultimately hopeful and glorious story of the Hispanic faithful in the United States continues. The three *Encuentros* deserve renewed, intensive study. I should mention that there has, in fact, been a Fourth Encounter, though not, technically speaking, an Hispanic *Encuentro*, even though the event was organized by the Hispanic community; the Encounter 2000—that opened the Jubilee Year of 2000—had as its theme "Many Faces in God's House: A Catholic Vision for the Third Millennium" and was open to all ethnic communities in the U.S. Church, including, of course, the Anglo community.

More significantly, this particular Encounter lacked the comprehensive consultation process that characterized each of the first three *Encuentros*, and which engaged the hundreds of thousands Hispanics "from the bottom up," all the way to the top leadership of the Hispanic community and the Church at large.

It is my hope that this book will be a spur to action and that it may, God willing, make a modest contribution toward the eventual convocation of a Fifth National *Encuentro*: and meanwhile play a vital part in "the pastoral-theological reflection process of *Encuentro* in Hispanic ministry" called for by the U.S. bishops to take place 2013–2016.

Painful developments during the last few decades in the life of the U.S. Church have demonstrated, above all, the depth of U.S. Hispanics' faith. There is the trauma of the priestly sex abuse scandals and the attendant grave damage to the image of the Catholic Church; there have been waves of parish and school closings—disproportionately and dramatically impacting the lives of poor, urban Hispanics—and, all along, there has been the aggressive proselytizing of Protestant denominations.

Still, the bulk of the Hispanic Catholic community—supported by extraordinary leaders—has stood firm, loving their Church even more in the process, practicing their faith with ever more zeal, and being committed to make ever-greater contributions to the Catholic community in the United States. Significantly, the *Encuentros* clearly rejected the admittedly radical proposals to pursue a Hispanic rite, or to form a national Hispanic Church with its own, separate jurisdiction.

Such is the calling of Hispanics in the United States—to live in the heart of the local Church. Pope John Paul II put it thus: "The Church has endured for 2,000 years. Like the *mustard seed* in the Gospel, she has grown and become a great tree, able to cover the whole of humanity with her branches (cf. Mt 13:31–32)." The Second Vatican Council, in its Dogmatic Constitution on the Church, thus, addresses the question of *membership in the Church and the call of all people to belong to the People of God*: "All are called to be part of this Catholic unity of the new People of God....And there belong to it or are related to it in various ways, the Catholic faithful as well as all who believe in Christ, and indeed the whole of mankind, which by the grace of God is called to salvation." Pope Paul VI, in the Encyclical *Ecclesiam Suam* illustrates how all mankind is involved in the plan of God, and emphasizes the various *"circles of the dialogue of salvation"* (*Tertio Milennio Adveniente*).

A Fifth *Encuentro* would, for one, take stock of the Hispanic community's dramatic progress, without glossing over the darker side of recent history (including the personal failures of some of the key figures at the first three *Encuentros*). One remarkable phenomenon of recent years that would give dramatic shape to a new *Encuentro* is the present and continuing influx of a large number of Colombian, Dominican, Mexican, and Central American priests. In the 1960s and 1970s, most of the Hispanic priests working in the United States were Spanish-born missionaries. This makes for an entirely different dynamic in Hispanic ministry.

Another trend is the dramatic change in the identity of Hispanic newcomers to the United States. There are still those coming north, fleeing political upheaval and economic hardship, though the number of migrant workers has dropped off sharply, in part due to the still enduring economic crisis. But in recent years, the United States has also begun to receive massive numbers of young, educated, middle-class immigrants as well as a growing number of entrepreneurs—all looking for a new home where they can enjoy the full protection of the rule of law. This new generation of immigrants, too, would color the deliberations of a new *Encuentro*.

Above all, a new *Encuentro* would celebrate, and urge on to still further progress, a U.S. Hispanic community that has moved to the very heart of the U.S. Church, changing its very face.

APPENDICES

Appendix A

THE PASTORAL PLAN FOR HISPANICS—WHAT IS A PASTORAL PLAN?

Mario Paredes

Planning is essential to any activity. Every activity has a certain objective, certain policies of action, a way of implementing and coordinating tasks and personnel. The objective, the policies, and their implementation and coordination form the plan.

The pastoral endeavor[1] germinates Christ (by the pastoral endeavor we mean the collective, official apostolate of the Church). It has as its objective to construct the kingdom of God. Its efficacy derives from the supernatural order and from grace, but it is nevertheless a human activity, subject to all that may condition collective labor. The pastoral endeavor, then, has its objective, its policies or criteria of action, and a model for coordinating people in line with its objective. Planning is, therefore, necessary for the pastoral endeavor. Every parochial or diocesan pastoral endeavor has some plan, even if it is not in writing or formulated and even if it is very simple. To lack any plan is to live in anarchy and to produce no results.

There are times when it is necessary to explicate the plan for the pastoral endeavor taking place, to do so fundamentally, to articulate it, to take cognizance of the Christian theological and ecclesial principles that direct it. The desirability of formulating a pastoral plan can have various grounds. The endeavor may be inefficacious because of scattered and uncoordinated activity or confusion about its objectives and criteria. New and complex challenges may be confronting the pastoral endeavor wherein the planning of times past proves inadequate. It requires updating and new coordination between objectives and pastoral policies (this is what happens in diocesan pastoral synods). Some aspect of the pastoral endeavor may acquire great importance or exhibit a special nature, like the arrival of new groups of people. In such a case, the endeavor may demand objectives and policies of a special sort that have to be presented and offered in the form of a plan (this is the case with the pastoral endeavor among Hispanics).

A pastoral plan for a group of people with special characteristics like Hispanics does not oppose or run parallel to a diocese's plan. Rather, it is an examination and application of the diocesan plan with particular nuances and practices. Normally, specialized pastoral endeavors in the Church integrate themselves with the total endeavor. Many dioceses have a diocesan pastoral plan within which there are plans pertaining to rural people, youth, intellectuals, and so forth. The diocesan pastoral plan and the specialized plans enrich one another in the same way they mutually enrich the Church's unity and pluralism.

The National Pastoral Plan for Hispanics indicates the above at its outset. It insists that it be taken as flexible and open to local adaptation. While directed toward Hispanics, it also wants to challenge and enrich the rest of the Church and the broader pastoral plans of the various dioceses. Some examples of this are its emphases on lay ministries and on lay participation, on an evangelizing critique of society from the vantage point of the poor, and on a greater commitment to questions of justice and human dignity.

WHY A PASTORAL PLAN FOR HISPANICS?

For some time now, the elaboration of a Hispanic Pastoral Plan has been practically inevitable as well as necessary, ever since the time Hispanic presence in the United States became a more and more decisive reality for the Church. Not only do Hispanics comprise a notable percentage of all Catholics in the United States, but also their number is huge in comparison to the other Catholic minorities. Hispanics have also acquired a significant recent pastoral past in this country. The United States episcopate's pastoral letter on Hispanic ministry and three national *Encuentros* have set the course for and are the immediate cause of the Pastoral Plan.

At the very beginning, the Pastoral Plan sets forth its major objectives:

1. To continually encourage the integration and participation of Hispanics in the Church of the United States.
2. To help Hispanic communities with a style of being Church and of ministry that is in tune with their needs and their own forms of Catholicism, even while integrating them within the Church in the United States and guarding boundaries of legitimate Catholic pluralism.
3. To formulate into a plan of action the great objectives and ideas set forth by the bishops in their pastoral letter on Hispanic ministry.
4. To lay out a positive pastoral response to activity by the sects. The pastoral plan will aid in the renewal of parishes, will provide an impulse for Hispanic ministry, and above all, create in everyone a missionary attitude.
5. To assist Hispanic communities in the realization of a better "unified pastoral endeavor,"[2] and thereby, to aid the whole Church.

A PASTORAL PLAN FOR A "UNIFIED PASTORAL ENDEAVOR"

The text of the Pastoral Plan for Hispanics declares that its objective is tied to a "united pastoral endeavor" in the diocesan churches, so that: a) all their ministries, institutions, and activities will be coordinated toward a common objective; b) their ministries will thrive at the diocesan level, thanks to co-responsibility, collaboration, and coordination; c) all valid pastoral initiatives already existing in the diocese will be taken advantage of; and that d), those that the Holy Spirit may incite in the future will integrate themselves with them. The Pastoral Plan and a "unified pastoral endeavor" go together.

"Unified pastoral endeavor" is a concept at one with what is most essential to the diocesan apostolate. Although they may not use so formal a phrase, synods, meetings for coordination, and the like, do in fact search for a better "unified pastoral endeavor."

WHAT IS CALLED A "UNIFIED PASTORAL ENDEAVOR" IN THE CHURCH?

A *unified pastoral endeavor* can be defined as "an enduring force for putting into motion before the world in need of salvation all the Church's sons and daughters, with all their institutions and resources, under the authority of the bishop with his mission of coordinating and directing them, thus himself being enabled to exercise in fullness his special task."

The idea of "unified pastoral endeavor" was explicitly put forward in the Church shortly before the Second Vatican Council. Discourses of Pope Pius XII in 1955 already refer to it as "a reasonable coordination of ministries within a sufficiently ample frame" and as "discernment of the problems evangelization of a territory presents and of the means to resolve them."

As we can see, the idea of a "unified pastoral endeavor" is theologically identified with the pastoral endeavor, in general, and with the objectives of a pastoral plan.

THE HISPANIC PASTORAL PLAN'S METHOD

The Hispanic Pastoral Plan supposes two things:

1. A mystique and spirituality of communion, of a mission, and of a sense of Church.
2. A method.

(A comment on method: the Hispanic Pastoral Plan's method is not original. It is employed widely throughout the Church, for example, in the Roman and in other diocesan synods and in conferences of bishops, like those at Medellín and Puebla.)

THE HISPANIC PASTORAL PLAN'S GENERAL OBJECTIVE

The general objective of the Hispanic Pastoral Plan finds itself formulated in the plan itself:

Vivir y promover, seguir una pastoral de conjunto un modelo (o estilo)—to live and to promote, to follow a *pastoral de conjunto,* a pastoral focus and approach to action arising from shared reflection among the agents of evangelization, which is very particular model or style of being Church.

Que es fermento del Reino de Dios en la sociedad—which is the ferment of the kingdom of God in Society.

Here, in the Pastoral Plan's general objective, we have nothing more than a restatement of the way the Church, rooting itself in Vatican II, understands its historic renewal today. It is impossible for this objective to oppose any other diocesan or national plan into which the Hispanic apostolate may be integrated. Rather it reinforces such plans.

Given that every Catholic community must search for a "unified pastoral endeavor," any such initiative must possess a communitarian, evangelizing, and missionary style; has to be open to everyone, that is, to the diversity of cultures; has to exemplify justice and promote it; and must integrally educate its leaders.

What is original about the Hispanic Pastoral Plan's general objective? Original to the Hispanic Pastoral Plan's general objective are what the plan calls "specific dimensions," the particular pastoral nuances suggested by the Hispanic reality. Peculiar to the Pastoral Plan are its urgency, its special importance for Hispanics, and how the "specific dimensions of the general objective" are presented and developed in a manner adapted to them.

THE SPECIFIC DIMENSIONS OF THE PASTORAL PLAN

The Pastoral Plan offers four specific dimensions for fulfilling its objective: a "unified pastoral endeavor," evangelization, missionary options, and formation. Exposition of these dimensions takes up an important part of the Pastoral Plan. Not only does the plan have to explain their individual objectives, but also it has to go into the programs and projects that pertain to their implementation. The specifics of each interests us here:

1. "Unified pastoral endeavor."

We have already recalled the Catholic criteria for this "unified pastoral endeavor." The Pastoral Plan underscores greater communion among all those doing evangelization in the Church in the United States—serving both Hispanics and non-Hispanics—greater integration of Hispanics within the Church in the United States and more teamwork.

It also underscores better communication within the Church at all levels, in all its groups, movements, parishes, and so on. This dimension of this "unified pastoral endeavor" looks not only for better coordination in the Hispanic pastoral endeavor, but also at the full integration of Hispanic Catholics within the Church in the United States at every level.

2. Evangelization.

The Pastoral Plan wants to make evangelization at the parish level more powerful and, at the same time, search for an answer to the challenge of the sects. Noteworthy are:

a. the emphasis on the value of the parish as the base for the Church's pastoral action in general and, therefore, for action on behalf of Hispanics.
b. the importance given to developing small communities within parishes that are integrated within them and will aid Hispanics in having a true experience of Church, fraternity, their own evangelization and the evangelization of others.

The small communities just mentioned often already exist. They are the groups, movements, and associations that function within a parish. Beyond them, however, the Pastoral Plan recommends: "the creation, encouragement, recognition" of ecclesial communities without "specialization," that is, unlike prayer groups, the Legion of Mary, and so on. Rather, these communities are to represent the parish on a smaller scale, with their experience of Church and of evangelization. In this way, the parish and ecclesial communities mutually enrich one another, but only if the small community is firmly united with the parish and with the rest of its groups.

(Note: Small communities in the parish are of universal value, not simply for Hispanics. Numerous Church statements affirm this, including those of popes. Given Hispanic culture, the confusion brought to the lives of Hispanics caused by migration and the pressures of the sects, small communities have special value for Hispanics.)

3. Missionary options.

The third specific dimension of the Pastoral Plan, missionary options, points out certain categories of Hispanics to be given greater attention in evangelization. Stronger missionary options are owed Hispanics who find themselves in specially delicate or "missionary" situations.

The categories are as follows:

a. the most poor (here again the Pastoral Plan is at one with the overall pastoral endeavor of the Church).
b. those placed most at the edges of the Church's spheres of action (likewise, this is coherent with the thinking of the Church).
c. the Hispanic family (there is no need to underline its importance and the dangers to which it finds itself exposed).
d. Hispanic youth (youth make up the majority of Hispanics in the United States; they are the future of Hispanic lead-

ership and of Hispanic Catholicism in this country; the "missionary option for youth" is a standard pastoral option in today's Church).

e. women (on account of their frequent neglect, despite their great influence in the handing on of the faith).

(Note: In the Hispanic world, the "women's question" does not have the characteristics exemplified by the feminist movements in the United States. Matters of ordination, power, and competition are not in play nor does the subject produce an aggressive climate.)

4. Formation.

The specific objective of Hispanic formation, especially of Hispanics working at evangelization and of Hispanic leaders, is the Pastoral Plan's lifeblood. (Embraced by the objective are the search for and development of Hispanic vocations to the priesthood and religious life.) The plan looks toward the evolution of programs and formative materials for all the many levels of integral Christian formation among Hispanics.

EVALUATION AND SPIRITUALITY

The Pastoral Plan first closes with a reflection on the importance of periodic evaluation at every level and of the whole plan after a certain period of time. Responsible persons and methods of evaluation are indicated.

The most important thing to note here is that every pastoral plan is limited as to the time of its application, whether in its totality or in its parts. Depending on the matter at hand, pastoral plans last from three to five years. Afterward, they need revision, re-adaptation, and new formulation (in fact, the episcopates of the various countries that draw up pastoral plans go through the process with that kind of regular frequency). Experience alone can show where a pastoral plan is unrealistic, lacks means, is confronted with changed situations, or requires greater integration within the diocesan pastoral endeavor, and so on.

Finally, the Hispanic Pastoral Plan ends by reflecting on spirituality as the source of every apostolate and as the plan's moving force. This reflection is very beautiful and brief. It includes elements proper to Hispanic spirituality, Hispanic devotions, and popular religiosity. The text is to be read as it is.

Notes

1. In Spanish, one says *la pastoral*. The term embraces everything involved in pastoral efforts, theory, and practice. That is the import of the phrase used in these pages, "the pastoral endeavor."

2. *Pastoral de conjunto* has become a technical term in Spanish for unified, coordinated pastoral endeavor, again embracing both theory and practice. It is to this concept that "unified pastoral endeavor" refers here.

Appendix B

Excerpt from *Peregrino: A Pilgrim Journey into Catholic Mexico,* by Ron Austin (Grand Rapids, Michigan: Eerdmans, 2010).

Hispanics have come to North America bearing gifts, not in the least those pertaining to the realm of la mistica, *an aspect of the Hispanic faith experience studied extensively at the Third* Encuentro. *With regard to this dimension and others, Austin's reflections on Mexican Catholicism can, to a large extent, be said to apply to Hispanic Catholicism as a whole. (Of the 65 million Hispanic Catholics in the United States, 30 million are of Mexican origin.)*

Mexican identity is itself radically new, the first new race, so to speak, to emerge from the New World. Our American identity is, while also new, more conceptual and based on a commitment to certain political ideals. How these two forms of identity relate to our Catholic faith might provoke some useful questions about the nature of a more fundamental and shared identity.

Religious belief among Mexican Catholics, as we shall see, is not so much based on abstract theories as it is on concrete relationships. Ideally this should be true of all Christians. Catholics should be, as the song says, "known by our love" but as we must admit this is not always the case. The form the Catholic faith takes among common people, many still relatively uneducated, may provide some food for thought about the nature of religious commitment.

This change of perspective might also connect concepts of ritual, beauty and memory in ways perhaps unfamiliar to our American perceptions....The historic encounter that is now taking place between the two cultures, American and Mexican, has many dimensions and has provoked at times fear and controversy. But what is its larger meaning for us as Catholics? There is a "mystery of vocation" that confronts a people as well as individuals. An understanding of that vocation requires spiritual discernment.

The Catholic faith and beliefs of Mexicans is that of the universal Church but what are the distinct cultural expressions of that faith that Mexicans offer? I would suggest that the most valuable are those which do not separate Mexicans from others but reconnect us all to those aspects of Catholic tradition that are sometimes neglected or forgotten. When our distinctions lead us to a greater understanding of the nature of that which unifies us, we are truly "Catholic."...

A loss of the sense of the tragic constitutes one of the most serious losses in contemporary consciousness. The tragic is not merely a deeper degree of sadness or pain, but contains a great potential for revelation. This is another way of saying that we've lost our ability to respond to the fullness of life that includes the redemptive nature of suffering. In current times, no Christian concept has been more rigidly resisted or resented than this. Yet there remains in Mexican culture a residual Catholic attitude toward suffering. It stems, of course, from the perception of the suffering of Christ as the prelude to new life....

[The US Church has ready access to] the rich inheritance of the Mexican Catholic culture. The vivid images and even the music may offer for many of us the best means of understanding this tradition, but let's briefly explore some of its distinct characteristics.

Mexican spirituality reveals itself by outward signs

To understand the theology of Mexican Catholicism one must focus on concrete manifestations rather than texts. Devotional prayers, processions, images and objects are more prominent than concepts. In part this relates to the indigenous heritage. Osvaldo Pardo and other contemporary scholars have recognized the fundamentally aesthetic character of Nahua religion as did the earliest observers such as Fathers Sahagun and Duran.

Mexican spirituality is ritualistic

While ritual can be abused and emptied of content, the power of repetition and gesture, evident in all the world religions, has been weakened by a modern emphasis of the "personal" aspect of faith and salvation. The ability to affirm one's own religious experience is strengthened by these shared litanies and formalities.

Mexican spirituality is iconic

The images are an important medium of worship yet inevitably are at times objects of worship themselves. The Church patiently guides worshippers toward inner as well as outer manifestations while providing the most influential and beloved of all the icons: the Virgin of Guadalupe.

Mexican spirituality is primordial

While this aspect of Mexican spirituality is also drawn primarily from its indigenous sources it doesn't mean that it is merely syncretistic or "primitive." The pre-Hispanic spiritual "seeds" provide an important sense of continuity, but they also reclaim basic elements of religion that our self-conscious present-day view often neglects, such as ritual dance, decoration and sacred dress. Anthropology, as Pope Benedict has noted, thus provides one of the most fruitful conjunctions with religious thought. Religion has always retained a strong element of instinctive behavior and cannot be reduced to a system of concepts or customs. This is the danger of the modern reductive interpretations. Our biblical religion is, in this sense, not just two thousand years old but more than ten thousand. Mexican Catholic culture reveals, more than most, its deepest roots.

The Mexican Catholic lives in a sacred world

Mexican Catholicism lives in and outside of church. There is, for many, a continuous sense of the Presence of God even in the most mundane aspects of life. There is, therefore, often a thin line between this awareness and the celebration of ordinary events. The sacred and the profane are often thoroughly intertwined.

Mexican spirituality is experiential and relational

Mexicans shape and test their faith through the experience of family and work. Prayer is highly personal. It is said that Mexicans "talk to God and His Mother" and they do so directly and intimately. The saints, esteemed as "family members," are often part of the conversation. Kinship plays a uniquely strong role, particularly the practice of *compadrazago* or "God-parenting."

Mexican spirituality is marked by a strong feminine temperament

There are, of course, masculine and feminine aspects of all cultures in terms of "spirit" or psychological disposition. A masculine character is more evident in the European orientation toward power and a goal-directed linearity. The Mexican Catholic temperament, on the other hand, is more nurturing and consoling than objectively critical. The centrality of the figure of the Virgin of Guadalupe, and other Marian devotions is evidence of this inclination. God is found in intimate "feelings"—*sentimientos*—but this does not mean a lack of intelligence or critical acumen. It stems from a "maternal" emphasis on the healing power of love.

Mexican spirituality is popular and egalitarian

The Mexican *fiestas*, especially the feast days of the saints, offer a highly communal form of spirituality as well as hospitality to others. The many popular devotions, some of which we will address further, cross lines of class and education that parish life alone might not. In no other aspect of Mexican life will one find a more genuine equality than in church.

The foundation of Mexican spirituality resides in the lives of the saints

The devotion to the Saints is an essential aspect of Mexican spirituality in that it provides concrete models rather than systems of abstract "values" or postulates of morality.

Mexican spirituality draws heavily on beauty

Beauty in this regard includes not only the celebrated and ornate places of worship but poetry, song, dance and bold architecture. Far from mere decoration, Beauty is a manifestation of the Divine. It is one of the most valuable gifts that Mexicans offer us.

Mexican spirituality is a journey in time

Sometimes this is also a literal passage as migrants. This story of a migrant or pilgrim people resonates with all the stories and metaphors of the Bible. Journeys transform people and over time can provide a new identity. Spaniards and the various indigenous peoples in time became "Mexican" through extensive journeys that finally converged. There are inner as well as outer explorations that have produced their lasting imagery, songs, and mythic as well as historical accounts of Mexican origins and trials. None of us, Mexicans or Americans, knows the end of our present pilgrimage.

The key to Mexican popular religion is undoubtedly the shared suffering of a long and painful history, but this is a participation in the suffering of Christ that extends beyond historical circumstances. Injustices must be redressed, but the meaning of suffering is that of the Cross, and the healing to be found only in the Resurrected Christ. The crucified and risen Christ is no more a Mexican or an American than he was simply a first-century Jew. He is all of us, and more. Only when suffering, including poverty and rejection, are perceived as a commonality, including a shared struggle, does the *fiesta* become prophetic and point to a life beyond death.

Appendix C

Excerpt from "Pastoral Planning for the Spanish-speaking in the United States of America"—An Address to the First National *Encuentro* by Father Virgilio Elizondo (Source: Antonio M. Stevens Arroyo, ed., *Prophets Denied Honor—An Anthology of the Hispanic Church in the United States* (Maryknoll, New York: Orbis Books, 1980).

Recognizing our uniqueness, there is a growing determination to preserve, perpetuate, and share with our fellow citizens the substance of our culture and our language. It is true that, for practical reasons, we accept certain forms of acculturation and the language of this country; but, at the same time, we retain the essence of that which constitutes us as a bilingual and bicultural minority. We are not ashamed of what we are. On the contrary, we are proud of the heritage we have received from our parents and ancestors. We are proud to be descendants of our great Indian and European forebears. We are proud of the fact that we are truly a "new people" and as such we will serve as a prophetic people to our fellow North American citizens who, for the most part, are mostly transplanted Europeans and not truly a new people in the New World, as the *mestizo* indeed is! This growing consciousness is helping us to discover our self-identity. Rather than forgetting our past, there is a growing desire to preserve it and share with the rest of America the best of our cultural traditions and language. This phenomenon is of utmost importance when we are considering the integration of our people and our active participation in the social, religious, economic, and political structures of our country.

Appendix D

Excerpt from: "The Church: Diocesan and National"—an address by Monsignor Patricio Flores (now Archbishop Emeritus of San Antonio, Texas) to the First National *Encuentro*.

The church cannot ignore the presence of 15 million Spanish-speaking persons in the United States. They cannot be put into the same institution without taking into account their own particular background. The Mexican Americans who were here before the coming of the English-speaking, as well as the Spanish-speaking who have migrated here recently, have brought and have their own mentality, their language, their culture, their religion, and their own needs. All these elements are part of a beautiful spiritual heritage which will last in the Spanish-speaking outside of their Motherland. This heritage, so rich in values, should be highly esteemed.

The church cannot insist that in order to be first-class citizens and Christians we must "AMERICANIZE OURSELVES"... the mere statement disorients us. If we were born on this continent we are already "Americans." What do we have to be or do in order to "Americanize" ourselves? The true Americans are our brothers and sisters, the Indians on the reservations: "To Americanize ourselves" means to absorb a little of or all [of] the different European cultures. This would be alright because it would enrich our own culture even more. But if to "Americanize ourselves" means to learn English well, we are really saying that if we learn English well, all will be well, we will be well accepted, etc. I don't know if the bishops and priests believe that—I don't! For one thing, the black North Americans spoke only English; they didn't speak Spanish at all, and I ask: "Were they treated as first-class citizens and Christians?" And for another, I think that I learned English well, and even when I had three years of college in the seminary some Catholics would still not employ me—simply because I am brown, my name is Flores, and I am a descendant of Mexicans.

I cannot convince myself that "to be Americanized" means to speak English well and that speaking it well will mean total acceptance.

If the Catholic Church in North America has these attitudes but does not want to lose the Spanish-speaking, then, while the American hierarchy is taking care of 75 percent of the faithful, it should allow other structures for the other 25 percent.

Appendix E

"Editorial: The Second Encounter" (Source: *Cara a Cara*, 4, September–October 1977).

The Second National Encounter of the *Hispanos* is now part of the history of Spanish-speaking Catholics in the United States. The Encounter represents both the accomplishments and the failures of the Spanish-speaking people in the United States. It illustrates how far we have advanced but it also indicates that we still have a long way to go. Through this national interchange, the Hispanic peoples declared: We are present and have certain specific needs. We have made many valuable contributions both to the church and to the nation and we will continue this participation. To the Church, they said: We are the largest ethnic group in the Church. We are tired of receiving second-rate service. Ministries must now be tailored to fit our particular reality. They must be saturated with our culture and heritage and carried out by priests, deacons, sisters, bishops and laity from our own communities. Evangelization must also be rooted in our culture and emerge from our present reality. We, the Spanish-speaking Catholics in the United States, reaffirm our solidarity with our brothers and sisters in our native lands. Their suffering is not alien to us but rather a part of our existence.

During the Second National Encounter, an embryo of unity was formed among the Spanish-speaking. However, if this unity is based only in cultural terms, it will be extremely fragile. In order to strengthen and expand this unity, the various Hispanic communities here in the United States must realize that they are also closely related to their social and economic situations. These ties are rarely considered, as evidenced by the lack of solidarity between those *Hispanos* who have escaped the migrant stream and those who are still migrants. Although Spanish-speaking people often state that they do not want to assimilate into the United States society, their alternative has not yet become clearly defined.

The recommendations made in the areas of political responsibility, human rights and integral education indicate that the United States Hispanic Community is still weak in its social and political analysis. This weakness presents a challenge to the Hispanic leaders, especially to the Regional and National Offices which were created as instruments of growth and liberation for the Spanish-speaking people. In a world where justice is an essential dimension of life, the ability to analyze the political and social structures is imperative for a true Christian.

The Second National Encounter reflected the failure of society to allow the poor to speak. Parliamentary procedure, which was used throughout the Encounter, is extremely technical. Without previous experience or extensive study, it is quite difficult to understand. Even many of the facilitators were unclear as to the proper procedure. This methodology limited the participation of many of the delegates. We *Hispanos* must become extremely conscious of the need to develop methodologies which are consistent with our reality and which also allow the most ample participation of our people.

The Encounter was another step on the long road of the history of the Spanish-speaking people in the United States. We must now prepare ourselves for what lies ahead—moments of struggle, of defeat and of accomplishment. We must always keep in mind that we are a people with a history and a destiny.

BIBLIOGRAPHY

A. BOOKS AND BOOKLETS

Blanchard, David Scott. "An Evaluation. III Encuentro Nacional Hispano de Pastoral," N.C.C.B./U.S.C.C., Washington, DC, 1986 (Ed. Informal).

Bosque, Sch.P., Rev. James. "Dios en su Historia (I Sacramentos de Iniciación) Programa de Evangelización. Misión Compartida," C.C. P.H.N., NY, S.F. (24 pp.).

Centro Catolico de Pastoral para Hispanos del Nordeste. "A Report: The Hispanic Community the Church and the Northeast Center for Hispanics," C.C.P.H.N., NY, Ed. Bilingüe, 1982 (146 pp.).

Centro de Planificacion Nacional Para el Secretariado de Asuntos Hispanos. "Recordar las Hazañas de Señor. Guía de Reflexión Teológico-Pastoral Sobre el III Encuentro." N.C.C.B/ U.S.C.C., Washington, DC, Ed. Bilingüe S.F. (40 pp.).

Del Riego, Rev. Rutilio J. "Identificación Survey: Hispanic Priests in the United States," N.C.P.C.H., NY, 1981.

Diaz Vilar, SJ, J. Juan. "El Dios de Nuestros Padres," N.C.P.C.H., NY, I Ed.: 81; II Ed.: 82; III ed.: 85 (218 pp.) (Prólogo de S.E.R. Mons. Rene Valero, Obispo Auxiliar de Brooklyn).

————. "Un Encuentro en el Camino: Tres Desafíos a las Comunidades Hispanas: Unidad-Pluralidad; Participación: Laicos y Jóvenes; Evangelizacion." N.C.P.C.H., NY 1985 (96 pp.).

————. "Somos una Sola Iglesia. 10 Temas de Reflexión Sobre la Carta Pastoral de los Obispos de los Estados Unidos:

Presencia Hispana: Esperanza y Compromiso," C.C.P.H.N., NY, Ed. Bilingüe 1984 (64 pp.).

Division for the Spanish Speaking "I Encuentro Nacional Hispano de Pastoral," N.C.C.B./U.S.C.C., S.N., Washington, DC, Ed. Bilingue, 1974.

Elizondo, Rev. Virgilio, y otros (Rev. Frank Ponce; S.E.R. Mons. Patricio Flores y S.E.R. Mons. Roberto F. Sanchez). "Los Católicos Hispanos en los Estados Unidos," C.C.P.H.N., NY, Ed. Bilingüe con autorización de N.C.C.B./U.S.C.C., I Ed.: 10,80; II Ed.: 05,81; (76 pp.). (Prólogo de Mario Paredes).

Fitzpatrick, SJ, Rev. Joseph P., and Rev. Roberto O. Gonzalez, OFM. "Hispanic Americans and the Church in the Northeast. Response to a Survey," N.P.C.H., NY, S.F.

————. "Hispano-Americanos y la Iglesia en el Nordeste. Respuesta a una Encuesta," C.P.H.N., NY, 1977.

Galilea, Rev. Segundo. "Anunciar el Evangelio Todos los Días. Para la Homilía y la Meditación Cotidiana," N.C.P.C.H., NY, 1984 (224 pp.).

————. "El Dios de los Pobres," C.P.H.N./N.P.C.H., NY, 1980 (64 pp.) (Prólogo de Mons. Agustin Ruiz de la Orden).

————. "El Futuro de Nuestro Pasado. Ensayo Sobre los Misticos Españoles Desde America Latina," N.C.P.C.H., NY, 1983 (64 pp.) (Prólogo de S.E.R. Mons. Ricardo Ramirez, C.S.B; Obispo de Las Cruces).

————. "La Misión de los Evangelios," N.C.P.C.H., NY, 1982 (64 pp.) Prólogo de S.E.R. Mons. Theodore E. McCarrick, Obispo de Metuchen).

————. "Religiosidad Popular y Pastoral Hispano-Americana," C.C.P.H.N., NY, 1981 (64 pp.) (Prologo de S.E.R. Mons. Roberto F. Sanchez, Arzobispo de Santa Fe).

————. "El Seguimiento de Cristo," N.C.P.C.H., NY, 1985 (64 pp.) (Prólogo de Mario Paredes).

Gonzalez, OFM, Rev. Roberto O., y Michael La Valle. "The Hispanic Catholic in the United States. A Socio-cultural and Religious Profile," N.C.P.C.H., NY, 1985 (230 pp.) (Prólogo de S.E.R. MONS. John Cardenal O'Connor, Arzobispo de Nueva York).

N.C.C.B./U.S.C.C. "Hispanic Ministry: Three Mayor Documents: The Hispanic Presence: Challenge and Commitment; Prophetic Voices: the Document on the Process of the III Encuentro Nacional Hispano de Pastoral; National Pastoral Plan for Hispanic Ministry," N.C.C.B./U.S.C.C., No. 197.0, Washington, DC, Ed. Bilingue, 1995 (99 pp.=Prólogo de S.E.R. Mons. Roberto O. Gonzalez, OFM, Obispo Coadjutor de Corpus Christi).

————. "The Hispanic Presence: Challenge and Commitment," N.C.C.B./U.S.C.C. No. 891-6, Washington, DC, Ed. bilingue, 1983 (73 pp.).

————. "Una Llamada a la Accion. Documentos de Trabajo," Reimpresion del C.R.P.H.N.E., NY, 1977.

————. "Prophetic Voices: The Document on the Process of the III Encuentro Nacional Hispano de Pastoral," N.C.C.B./U.S.C.C. No.983-1, Washington, DC, Ed. bilingue, 1986 (50 pp.).

Paredes, Mario J. "La Pastoral Hispana a Partir del Tercer Encuentro" en la Revista Hispanic American Pastoral Studies/Estudios Pastorales Hispanoamericanos," Vol. 2ª, No.1, Diciembre 1987 en la p.76'84 (La versión inglesa en la pp. 67–75). Editada por C.C.H.N., NY.

Riofrio, Rev. Carlos. "Dios en Nuestro Caminar. Mision Compartida." C.C.P.H.N., NY, 1985 (12 pp.).

Sandoval, Moises. "Hispanic Challenges to the Church," N.C.C.B./U.S.C.C., Washington, DC, 1979 (92 pp.) (Ed. informal).

Secretariat for Hispanic Affairs. "Hispanics and Catholics in the United States: Some Preliminary Demographic Observations and Comparisons between 1970 and 1980. Figures" N.C.C.B./U.S.C.C., Washington, DC, 1982 (35 pp.) (Ed. informal).

————. "Pueblo de Dios en Marcha. Proceedings of the II Encuentro Nacional Hispano de Pastoral," N.C.C.B./U.S.C.C., Washington, DC, Ed. Bilingüe, 1978 (95 pp.).

————. "Pueblo Hispano. Voz profetica. Documento de Trabajo," N.C.C.B./U.S.C.C., Washington, DC, Ed. Bilingüe, 1985 (126 pp.) (Ed. Informal).

———. "III Encuentro Nacional Hispano de Pastoral," N.C.C.B./U.S.C.C., S.N., Washington, DC, Ed. Bilingüe, 1985.

B. DOCUMENTS

Ad-Hoc Committee for Hispanic Affairs. "Pastoral Planning Process," (Materiales Previos al III Encuentro), S.F. (2 pp. mas 2 sobre la reflexion teologica).

Ad-Hoc Committee for the Spanish-Speaking. "Conclusiones of the Primer Encuentro Hispano de Pastoral," 1972 (17 pp.).

———. "Conclusiones Regionales" (Materiales Previos al II Encuentro), S.F. (37 pp.).

———. "Documento de Trabajo: Resumen de las Conclusions de las Diversas Regions" (Materiales previos al II Encuentro) S.F. (29 pp.).

———. (Guias para la Preparacion del II Encuentro Hispano Nacional de Pastoral); Orientation Guide (8 pp.); 1 Evangelization (20 pp.); Ministries (8pp.); 3 Human Rights (8 pp.); 4-Integral Education (8 pp.); 5-Political Responsibility (8 pp.); 6-Unity in pluralism (8 pp.), S.F.

———. (Materiales preparatorios al Il Encuentro) S.T. 1977 (8pp.).

———. "Programa del II Encuentro Nacional Hispano de Pastoral" 1077 (16 pp.).

———. "Report of the N.C.C.B. Ad-hoc Committee for the Spanish-speaking on the Conclusions of the Primer Encuentro Hispano de Pastoral," 1973 (11 pp.).

Blanchard, David S. "Research proposal. Washington Theological Union" (Propuesta Complete Previa al Trabajo de Investigación) S.F. (18 pp.).

Conferencia Catolica. "Primer Encuentro Hispano de Pastoral" (Materiales previos al II Encuentro) Ed. Bilingüe, 1972 (17 pp.).

Division for the Spanish Speaking. "Primer Encuentro Hispano de Pastoral" (Materiaels previos al I Encuentro), 1972 (21 pp.).

Instituto Pastoral del Sureste. "Fines y Pasos del III Encuentro para la Formación de los Equipos Promotores Diocesanos," S.F. (5 pp.).

N.C.C.B./US.C.C. "Report to General Meeting of Bishops by Archbishop Sanchez. November 11, 1985" (8 pp.).

N.C.P.C.H. "The Implementation of the II Encuentro in the Northeast: An Evaluation," 1984 (30 pp.).

Obispos Hispanos. "Somos Hispanos" (Mensaje con Occasion del II Encuentro) 1977 (6 pp.).

Ponce, Rev. Frank. "Religion and the State of Hispanic North America" (10 pp.).

Sanchez, Mons. Roberto F. "Evangelizacion" (Palabras en el II Encuentro) 1977, (10 pp).

Secretariat for Hispanic Affairs. "Guias para los Encuentros Diocesanos y Regionales, Pasos no 1 y 9," Ed. bilingüe, S.F. (55 pp.).

———. "Guias para la Rreflexión Eologico-pastoral" (Materiales del III Encuentro) S.F. (11 pp.).

———. "Manual Guía para la Formación de los Equipos Promotores Diocesanos" (Materiales previos al III Encuentro) S.F. (25 pp.).

———. (Materiales preparatorios al III Encuentro, siendo el primero la agenda) S.T. 1985 (14 pp.).

———. "Media Info. Packet" (Materiales para al Reunion de Rosemont, Illinois, abril de 1984). Ed. Vilingue (12 pp.).

———. "Notas de los Papelones de la Reunión de Lo Angeles, 3 al 5 de diciembre, 1985" (4 pp. mas 2 sobre elementos de planificación).

———. "III Encuentro: A Proposal by the National Advisory Committee to the Secretariat for Hispanic Affairs," 1982 (4 pp.).

———. "Third National Hispanic Encuentro," S.F. (6 pp.).

C. ABREVIATIONS USED IN THE BIBLIOGRAPHY

C.C.H.N.	Centro Católico Hispano del Nordeste
C.C.P.H.N.	Centro Católico de Pastoral para Hispanos del Nordeste
C.H.C.N.	Centro Hispano Católico del Nordeste
C.P.H.N.	Centro de Pastoral Hispana parra el Nordeste
C.R.P.H.NE	Centro Regional de Pastoral hispana parra el Nord Este
Ed. o ed.	Edición o edición
Mons.	Monseñor
N.C.C.B./U.S.C.C.	National Conference of Catholic Bishops/ United States Catholic Conference
N.C.P.C.H.	Northeast Catholic Pastoral Center for Hispanics
N.H.C.C.	Northeast Hispanic Catholic Center
N.P.C.H.	Northeast Pastoral Center for Hispanics
OFM	Orden Franciscana Menor (Sigla de los Franciscanos)
pp.	paginas
Sch.P.	(Sigla de los Escolapios)
S.E.R.	Su Excelencia Reverendísima (Tratamiento del Obispo)
S.F.	Sin fecha
SJ	Societatis Jesus/Compañía de Jesus (Sigla de los Jesuitas)
S.N.	Sin número
S.T.	Sin título

On "Strangers No Longer"

Perspectives on the Historic U.S.-Mexican
Catholic Bishops' Pastoral Letter on Migration

Edited by Todd Scribner and J. Kevin Appleby

A collection of essays by Americans and Mexicans who offer
their own perspectives on the difficult and controversial subject
of migration.

978-0-8091-4828-8   Paperback

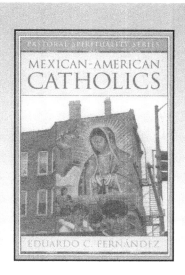

Mexican-American Catholics

Eduardo C. Fernández

Presents the history of Christianity in Mexico via Spain, the conditions of Mexican Catholics in America, the challenges facing Mexican-American Catholics, and suggestions on how to meet them.

978-0-8091-4266-8   Paperback

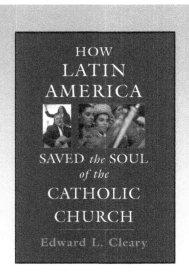

How Latin America Saved the Soul of the Catholic Church

Edward L. Cleary

Tells the remarkable story of the transformation of the Latin American church on every level, from professional theologians to the individual in the remotest Latin American village.

978-0-8091-4629-1   Paperback

The Challenge of Priestless Parishes

Learning from Latin America

Edward L. Cleary, editor

This book traces the origins of priestless regions of the Catholic Church in five Latin American countries and demonstrates that the situation was far more common than previously described.

978-0-8091-4869-1   Paperback

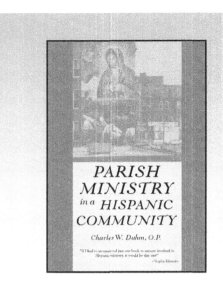

Parish Ministry in a Hispanic Community

Charles W. Dahm, OP

This unique book helps the reader understand the diverse aspects of Hispanic faith and culture while presenting a coherent practical and theoretical model of pastoral ministry applicable to Hispanic parishes across the United States.

0-8091-4272-4   Paperback

Bishop of the Barrio

The Life of Bishop Alphonse Gallegos, OAR

John Oldfield, OAR,
with a foreword by Bishop Francis A. Quinn
and an afterword from Cardinal Roger Mahony

Traces the life of this saintly man who worked with farmworkers throughout California.

0-8091-4430-1   Paperback

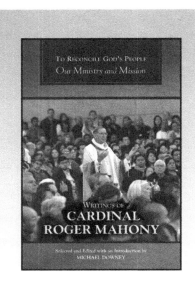

To Reconcile God's People

Our Ministry and Mission

Writings of Cardinal Roger Mahony, Selected and Edited with an Introduction by Michael Downey

A collection of writings of Cardinal Roger Mahony that covers a range of topics. What they have in common is a concern for ministry to meet the needs of the local church in Los Angeles. He focuses on priestly ministry and identity, and broadens to include attention to the ministry of lay persons, deacons, women, and bishops.

978-0-8091-4669-7   Paperback

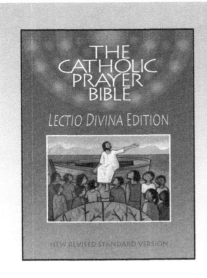
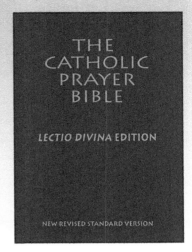

The Catholic Prayer Bible (NRSV)

Lectio Divina Edition

Paulist Press

An ideal Bible for anyone who desires to reflect on the individual stories and chapters of just one, or even all, of the biblical books, while being led to prayer through meditation on that biblical passage.

978-0-8091-0587-8   Hardcover

978-0-8091-4663-5   Paperback

978-0-8091-4766-3   Deluxe Edition